DUBUQUE'S FORGOTTEN CEMETERY

Iowa and the Midwest Experience

SERIES EDITOR William B. Friedricks,
Iowa History Center at Simpson College

DUBUQUE'S FORGOTTEN CEMETERY

Excavating a Nineteenth-Century Burial Ground in a Twenty-First-Century City

ROBIN M. LILLIE AND
JENNIFER E. MACK

University of Iowa Press, Iowa City

UNIVERSITY OF IOWA PRESS, IOWA CITY 52242
Copyright © 2015 by the University of Iowa Press
www.uiowapress.org
Printed in the United States of America

DESIGN BY TERESA W. WINGFIELD

The University of Iowa Press is a member of Green Press Initiative
and is committed to preserving natural resources.

Printed on acid-free paper

ISBN: 978-1-60938-321-3 (pbk)
ISBN: 978-1-60938-322-0 (ebk)

Library of Congress Cataloging-in-Publication Data
is on file at the Library of Congress

To my family, both the living and the dead. JEM

To Jack, Kate, and Ian—have a party. I won't mind. RML

I urge on my brethren to consider whether it is not better now, and during our time, to place our dead in a permanent resting place, than to leave them to the tender mercies of our successors, who perhaps may not be as careful of them.

—DUBUQUE MAYOR WILLIAM KNIGHT, 1870

Contents

ONE

The Story Unravels

1

TWO

Lead in the Bluffs, 1833–1880

16

THREE

Slumbering on the Bluff

39

FOUR

Abandoned to Desecration, 1880–2013

51

FIVE

The Untold Story

65

SIX

The Things They Took with Them

80

SEVEN

Humanizing the People of Third Street

101

EIGHT

The Kindhearted Gunsmith's Family

112

NINE

The Brick Maker's Unfortunate Family

127

TEN

Conjured from Paper and Stone

142

ELEVEN

Forgetting and Remembering the Dead

157

TWELVE

Mediating for the Dead

171

THIRTEEN

Continuity of Care

181

FOURTEEN

The Tender Mercies of Our Successors

187

Acknowledgments   *191*

APPENDIX: People Buried at the Third Street Cemetery   *195*

Notes   *219*

Recommended Reading   *223*

Index   *225*

DUBUQUE'S FORGOTTEN CEMETERY

ONE

The Story Unravels

IN JULY 2007 the Dubuque Police Department contacted the University of Iowa Office of the State Archaeologist (OSA) Burials Program to report that a man walking his dog had found human bones scattered around the site of a planned condominium complex on a bluff overlooking the Mississippi River. The new development was unpopular with many locals, but history suggested that the bones were probably not evidence of foul play—at least, not the kind of foul play the police are responsible for. The property where the bones were exposed had once been the site of the Third Street Cemetery, Dubuque's first Catholic graveyard, associated with St. Raphael's Cathedral, which still stands on Bluff Street at the edge of downtown.

Immediately west of the cathedral, the land rises steeply to a height of 180 feet and then levels out, creating a plateau where the early settlers buried their dead. The cemetery property continues to slope uphill toward its western perimeter, where about half a dozen private residences border the site. A small condominium building stands downslope on an artificial terrace created on the northern edge of the graveyard, which is bounded by its namesake, Third Street. In 2007 the southern half of the bluff lay bare, the expansive, four-story St. Dominic Villa having been razed by the land developer A. J. Spiegel. The lawn of the St. Dominic Villa, built in the late 1940s by the Sinsinawa Dominican sisters, extended well into the former cemetery. The bones had been disturbed in this lawn area and scattered across the bluff by heavy machinery.

It seemed likely to everyone that the bones found in 2007 were remnants of those resting in this long-abandoned burial ground. OSA Burials Program personnel already knew of the potential for historic graves on the bluff top. In 1994 construction of a retaining wall on residential property on the northeastern portion of the bluff exposed four graves from the old Catholic cemetery. The Burials Program staff had been consulted about the disturbance to human remains on that occasion, as well. The understanding of the city planners, local residents, and the Burials Program staff was that very few of the dead would have been left at the cemetery. Everyone believed that the graves had been moved in the late 1800s.

WHAT DO WE DO WHEN the bones of people who died from the ordinary causes of disease, accidents, and old age appear where we do not expect them to be? Who mediates when the living disturb the dead and, as a consequence, the dead disrupt the plans of the living? Because old cemeteries frequently stand in the way of contemporary building plans, communities across the United States must address these questions. Most states and the federal government have laws governing the excavation of the deceased, and discoveries like the one in Dubuque require archaeologists, skeletal biologists, and historians to act as detectives. But beyond the legal requirements, what do landowners, descendants, current residents, and the involved specialists owe the dead?

When the Dubuque police called the Office of the State Archaeologist, a team of excavators and analysts took on the job of answering these ethical questions, as well as the practical ones of whether the bones were human, where they came from, and how many more might be found on the building site. Author Robin Lillie, skeletal biologist for the OSA Burials Program, oversaw the project from the beginning of excavation to publication of the report. Jennifer Mack, a historical archaeologist, joined the project in 2008 and helped complete the osteological and grave goods analysis; she also conducted all the historical background research. Throughout the story of the Third Street Cemetery, we are the narrators. But ours is the combined voice of the dozens of people who contributed to our knowledge and understanding.

Because we were called in unexpectedly and because we initially had to work quickly in advance of the developer's bulldozers, we did not have any specific research objectives, and we were unable to track down potential descendants prior to fieldwork. Our plan from the very beginning, though, included analysis and prompt reburial of all the remains. Through the processes of excavation, careful examination of the skeletal remains and other grave materials, and background research, we developed questions to guide our investigation. Who was buried in the cemetery, and where did they come from? What were the demographics of the cemetery, and how do they compare to the profile of the living community? How did these people die? What can we learn about the health and mortality of early Dubuque from their remains? How did burial practices change over time? And how were these people forgotten? This book offers some answers to these questions.

DISCOVERY AND EXCAVATION

Iowa laws protect all burials. Those less than 150 years old fall under the jurisdiction of the Iowa Department of Public Health. Protection of those 150 years old or older is the legal responsibility of the state archaeologist. The Third Street Cemetery's period of active use (ca. 1833–80) falls on both sides of the 150-year cutoff. The landowner applied for and obtained permission for burial removal from both agencies, along with a disinterment permit issued through the Dubuque County courts. The Burials Program director then provided the landowner choices about how he could proceed. One option was to monitor tree-stump removal for evidence of burials tangled in tree roots, followed by use of heavy equipment to carefully excavate within the footprint of the proposed condominiums prior to the beginning of construction. Any burials found would be mapped, archaeologically excavated, studied, and reburied. A second option was to allow construction to go ahead, with archaeologists monitoring the site for burials that might be uncovered in the process. This could potentially cause delays in the construction activities, since the excavation of each encountered grave would interrupt the ongoing work on the condominiums. The third option was for slab foundations, which would not disturb the graves below them; streets and parking lots on the surface; and archaeological monitoring during any trenching for utilities.

The landowner chose option one, with the OSA stipulating that mechanical stripping be done in carefully controlled layers. Given the money he had already invested in purchase of the land and architectural plans for a high-rise condominium building, he wanted to be sure that no burials would remain to disrupt progress once construction began. He agreed to pay the Burials Program to conduct archaeological excavation of any burials found within the area to be impacted by his construction plans. These costs included the crew's wages, their lodging and meals, utilities to the house used as a storage area and on-site lab, portable toilets, plywood, plastic sheeting, the wages and expenses of the backhoe operator on-site from time to time (the landowner's employee), and flood mitigation (pumping of water from burials), among other expenses.

WHEN WE STARTED WORK in August 2007, we assumed that we would find only a few forgotten graves and we would be able to excavate and remove them in a matter of less than a month. However, due to the lack of headstones, markers of any kind, or even indentations in the soil, we could not predict exactly where the dead might be. The archives of the Archdiocese of Dubuque held no map showing the locations of individual plots. A heavy-machine operator used a backhoe to carefully scrape the ground in thin layers until grave shafts or other evidence suggestive of a grave, such as changes in soil color or coffin wood or nails, became visible. Each potential resting place was assigned a number. Archaeological field technicians then used shovels and trowels to expose the burials, with the more intricate excavation executed with bamboo picks. We used a GPS unit to record the location of each burial. Figure 1 displays each grave as a single dot.

We started off the excavation by monitoring tree-stump removal on the western and northern sides of the project area. Burial 1, found on the first day of monitoring, contained the disturbed bones of a child entangled in tree roots. Investigation of the location of an overturned headstone revealed a second burial. Once the tree stumps were removed, we began careful, shallow stripping in rows running from east to west. Though this project began as a "salvage" excavation, in which quick removal was the main objective, it soon became clear the work would not be completed at the speed the developer would have liked.

Nearly all the burials that we found during the 2007 season were just below the sod, an indication that a substantial amount of soil had been removed from the area before our work began. We also found that the

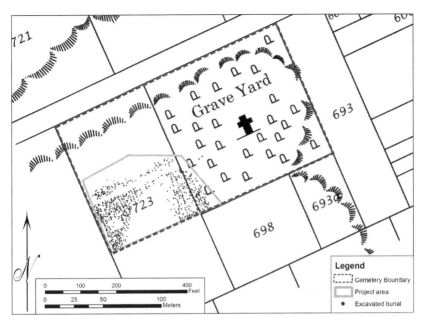

FIGURE 1. Map of Dubuque, Iowa, showing the full extent of the Third Street Cemetery, the boundaries of the archaeological project area, and the locations of excavated burials (base map redrawn by Tyler Perkins from the original 1837 plat map of Dubuque, Iowa, Julius Hutawa, lithographer).

central, flat portion of the project area contained no graves at all, although burials rimmed this void, and most of these were disturbed or damaged to some degree. Several years would pass before we learned the whole story of what caused the "empty zone" and burial disturbances. The field season ended in late November with nearly ninety potential graves identified and most of them excavated. Over the course of those four months, our crew of two expanded to include several trained and even more untrained volunteers. The excavation was turning into a much bigger job than we first thought.

All archaeological indications pointed to the existence of many more burials than had yet been found, so for the 2008 field season a crew of ten archaeological field technicians joined the project. Between May and late November, we excavated 520 more graves. Our efforts were made more difficult by the floods of that year, the worst in recent history. The rains made field excavation treacherous, with slick mud. Half-excavated burials filled with water, and one low-lying area became a pond inhabited over several weeks by ducks and frogs.

During the project, we maintained a minimum three-foot buffer along the perimeter of the project area to avoid disturbing the property fence and to leave intact any burials that extended beyond the property boundaries. As work commenced on the western portion of the site, we encountered very closely spaced graves, as well as the first instance of stacked coffins. It became challenging to excavate one burial without disturbing another that might be immediately adjacent to it in any direction. We came across stacked burials more frequently, finding up to three coffins placed in almost the exact location but at different depths. Other burials were slightly offset from each other, as if a grave digger had accidentally encountered an older coffin and then just placed the newer one on top of the older one. Because the shafts were not dug to a standard depth, a second, third, or even fourth round of backhoe stripping was necessary in some areas in order for us to find all the burials.

Then another kind of disaster delayed our work. Due to the economic downturn of 2008, the landowner canceled archaeological work for the 2009 season. He was frustrated and resentful at the discovery of so many graves on the property he had recently acquired. During his visits to the archaeological site, he repeatedly grumbled that someone was responsible for not telling him about all these burials. Someone had to know they were there! And someone had to pay. Ultimately, he brought suit against the Sinsinawa Dominican sisters who had sold the property to him, which led to hard feelings in the largely Catholic community of Dubuque. (For the landowner's response to the discovery of human remains and the lawsuit, see chapter 12.)

Lawyers deposed dozens of people for this lawsuit, including the director of the OSA Burials Program and the project manager. There is no public record of the resolution of the case. The confidentiality provision of the 2012 settlement agreement allows the parties to say only that they "have mutually agreed to resolve and dismiss the litigation." The lawyers for both sides conceded to our request to review the deposition records once the suit was settled. While it is unfortunate that the situation led to wrangling and vast legal expenses for both parties, the depositions proved to be a goldmine of information not recorded anywhere else. Together with our historical research, they helped us to figure out why the cemetery had been forgotten.

Fieldwork started up again in August 2010 with a crew of ten field technicians and continued until late November, with 253 burials excavated. Our investigations concentrated on the eastern portion of the site, where burials were deeper than any previously encountered due to the spreading of fill soil over that area in the past. One burial was found at a depth of twelve feet below the modern surface. It was during this field season that we tentatively delineated the southern boundary of the site (see figure 1).

The final field season ran from June to mid-August 2011, with an additional ninety-three burials excavated despite two major floods. A July 2011 flood turned out to be much more devastating to the excavations than the longer flood period of 2008. We had dug a trench along the eastern portion of the site that was up to twelve feet deep. Although we had already removed most of the burials from this area, two were left unexcavated when a storm inundated much of Dubuque, causing streets and basements to fill with water. Within twelve hours, ten to fifteen inches of rain fell, most of it overnight. The following day, the crew was greeted by a lake on the eastern portion of the property, with water several feet deep and extending for approximately two hundred feet north–south. Partially excavated burials in a second area, along the northern edge of the project area, were completely filled with water. A gas-powered pump drained much of the northern area, and we used buckets to remove water from the burials. Nothing could be done about the lake on the eastern side.

During 2011 we encountered a deep former ravine in the southwestern corner of the project area that had been filled in with unstable soil and topped with "dirty fill" in the historic past. We found no burials in the ravine, which appeared to form the natural southern boundary of the cemetery. As we found out later when we examined historical maps of the cemetery property, this ravine was congruent with the official southern property line (see chapter 2).

Our fieldwork proceeded at a fast pace compared to the academic excavations featured in documentaries and television shows. The valiant crew worked through rain, cold, snow, blistering heat, and mud (figure 2) in order to complete work in a timely fashion. The romanticism of fieldwork dissipates quickly when you spend days and months away from friends

FIGURE 2. Part of the archaeological crew after a particularly muddy day onsite. *From left*: Nicole Geske, Matt Cretzmeyer, Joe DeAngelis, Liz Macken, and Sarah Harrah.

and family. Microwave meals and subpar motel accommodations quickly get old. Fortunately, the camaraderie developed by the crew made these discomforts more bearable.

WORKING WITH THE COMMUNITY

Because our project area was located in the middle of Dubuque, immediately adjacent to several houses, many local people were aware of our presence and purpose. They responded to our work in a variety of ways. From the first days of the project, neighbors took an interest in the excavation going on practically in their backyards. Several residents of nearby houses came up to the fence to talk to us or even walked onto the site. However, Burials Program policies prevented us from having extensive interactions with curious locals. Continuity of care is vital to our professional practice: our actions must be an extension of the respectful handling provided by loved ones in preparation for funeral rites. The lengthy interval since death does not negate the individual's right to be treated with dignity. We could not allow neighbors or the media to observe our work, out of respect for the dead and their descendants. Nevertheless, since the property gates were sometimes open to provide access to the condominium sales model, it was easy enough for people to stroll in from the street.

During the archaeological excavations, local residents and a few site visitors talked with us about their memories of the Third Street Cemetery. Two elderly gentlemen reported having played along the bluff among the headstones in the 1930s or 1940s. They also described a wall of blocks that was likely the abandoned foundation of a never-completed seminary just south of the cemetery. We received only one direct inquiry from a gentleman asking if we had found his relatives—he knew he had ancestors buried in the Third Street Cemetery. Unfortunately, there were no standing headstones or cemetery maps to follow, and most of the materials buried with the dead had disintegrated, so we were not able to identify any specific individuals during the archaeological phase of the work. It was only much later, owing to thorough historical research and some luck with coffin hardware preservation, that we succeeded in positively identifying a few people (see chapters 8 and 9).

The local media sent photographers and reporters to the site, though we could not permit them on the grounds, instead directing them to contact the Burials Program office with questions about the project. Stories appeared in the *Dubuque Telegraph Herald* each field season, but always with several inaccuracies. One article, which included an intentionally provocative photograph of two crew members smiling, drew negative commentary on the newspaper's website. The women in the picture were, in fact, laughing at the photographer, who was lurking along the fence line with a telephoto lens. Based on this misleading image, the commenters expressed concern that the excavations failed to include proper respect for the dead, and a few were angry that the dead were being disturbed at all.

Neighbors whose back porches overlooked the excavations watched through the fence with curiosity as we worked, though we did our best to shield the human remains from public view. Many people who made inquiries were thoughtful and showed interest in the project. Others expressed a prurient interest, the excavation of the dead a heady subject for the average person. Television programs glamorizing forensic scientists and forensic anthropologists only seem to fill people's heads with misinformation about what archaeologists and human osteologists (specialists in the study of human bone) do and how they do it. Fortunately, the sincere interest, care, and compassion of our field crew helped dispel any sense of disrespect for the dead. We received little negative feedback, though many people expressed a strong dislike for the land developer. His plan to build a high-rise condominium complex on the property, blocking the beautiful view of the Mississippi River, was not popular in the neighborhood nor with many others in Dubuque, and this colored the public reaction to the removal of burials from the land. A few people were annoyed with our policy of excluding sightseers from the project area and our inability to share our excavation information with them. A Third Street Cemetery neighbor who expressed open hostility toward one of the authors complained about the general noise and nuisance of the project, which he felt contributed to the decline of the neighborhood. However, neither he nor any of the other nearby residents offered any opinion about the sanctity of a burial ground or the ethics of disturbing the dead. This kind of reaction left us wondering whether it is possible for archaeologists to balance the requirements of their jobs with the strong feelings of local residents.

Because the Third Street excavations were not expected to involve more than a few burials or take more than a couple of weeks, we prepared for the study and reburial of the remains, but we made no arrangements for community involvement. We had no time to do more background research prior to fieldwork in 2007, since efficient removal of the dead was the objective. Based on our experience in Dubuque, we now strongly believe a neighborhood meeting to explain the nature and purpose of our excavations could have done much to alleviate any anger or mistrust on the part of the nearby residents, as well as help them understand why they were not allowed to be on the site. Most of our in-depth exchanges with locals occurred after the excavation was completed and the veil of secrecy lifted. The information that was later provided to us by Dubuque genealogists and historians could have helped our understanding of the cemetery before excavations got under way.

When our archaeological investigations concluded at the request of the landowner in 2011, the excavation of the Third Street Cemetery was the largest project ever undertaken by the Burials Program. Over the four field seasons, and including the four burials removed in 1994, the crew excavated 939 graves. Thirty-one of them contained the remains of more than one individual, while some disturbed—and undisturbed—burials contained no preserved remains whatsoever. The number of complete and incomplete skeletons totaled 889, with an additional 15 people represented by bones scattered across the surface of the site. And these burials were not the only ones still present in the old Third Street Cemetery. Because our agreement with the developer was limited to the land he owned, we excavated only one-fourth of the total cemetery grounds. And although the outlines of grave shafts were visible in the cut face made by the backhoe and manual excavations along the northern perimeter of his property, this area went unexcavated because his development plans reportedly would not impact these graves.

What did we learn from the archaeological excavations? Thorough study of the materials and skeletons continued for years as we attempted to bring the lives of these forgotten people to light. There was also much to be gleaned about the settler community from the excavation itself. Certain patterns of burial layout became apparent during the second field season in 2008.

All of the dead were laid out with the head pointed slightly south of due west and the feet toward the river and St. Raphael's Cathedral. Traditionally, Catholic cemetery burials orient with the head to the west. The position of the body within the coffin was consistent: the person was placed on his or her back with the legs extended. Normally, arms rested along the sides of the body, with the hands either along the sides, on the tops of the thigh bones, on the hips, or clasped over the pelvis. Some people had their elbows bent, arms crossed at the waist or slightly higher.

The nineteenth-century sextons of the Third Street Cemetery worked somewhat haphazardly, digging graves close together, but not in what can be described as orderly rows. Along the western portion of the site, near the fence line, there was almost no space between burials. Clearly, crowding was an issue in this cemetery, at least in the portion we excavated. Perhaps plots were resold over time as markers decayed or disappeared. In the intact portion of the cemetery within the project area, burial density ranged from twenty-nine to fifty-one graves per 100 square meters (1,076 square feet). Assuming this same density and extrapolating, this means that the empty zone at the center of our excavation once contained an additional 375 to 665 burials. One of the key questions we wanted to answer was, Where did all these burials go?

We noted several different types of previous disturbances during the excavation. Historic trash dumps littered the western side of the property behind some of the older houses backing onto the project area. Backhoe and hand excavations yielded displaced headstones and headstone fragments, especially on the eastern side of the property, where they had been deposited in groups or singly in the fill soil. One large monument, "erected by Mrs. Kennedy," came from an area that we thought was a burial because of a large rectangular stain in the soil the size of a grave shaft. This proved to be a mechanically excavated hole, with the monument pushed into it. Three other displaced headstones were discovered on the surface; one that lay in the alley behind the houses on the western side disappeared before we could collect it. Only Burial 28 still had a remnant of a burial marker in its original position, a wooden stake found immediately next to the head of the grave. Several headstones were moved to a dedicated section of Mt. Olivet Cemetery in the 1940s, and it is likely others were removed over time after the Third Street Cemetery was abandoned.

We discovered evidence of larger-scale disturbance in the form of earth-moving. The empty zone, where we found no burials, made up a significant portion of the project area, 14,000 square feet, or approximately one-fourth of the total area excavated. Geophysical investigations confirmed that this part of the old cemetery had been cut and leveled at some time after the property was abandoned. The eastern portion of the site was built up with a "dirty fill" layer up to eight feet thick containing brick, metal, large rocks, limestone blocks, charcoal, and dark soil not native to the area.

Some graves contained bones from more than one person, evidence of disturbance in the historic past. In six cases, we came across displaced bones from earlier burials that had been deposited in the grave shaft on top of or next to the more recently interred coffin. In one case, three older burials were removed to make room for the new interment; then the remains of the disturbed burials were placed in the space between the new coffin and the outer wooden crate, which served as a vault (see chapter 7). Each of the six burials that disturbed earlier graves had fairly elaborate coffins, though this fact may reflect increasing coffin embellishment of the later nineteenth century and overcrowding rather than the status of the individuals occupying these newer graves (more about this subject in chapter 2). We also found evidence of intentional removal of the dead (disinterment), probably performed when family members decided to rebury their loved ones in other cemeteries. We encountered seventy-six disinterments, and, in several cases, haphazard removal techniques meant that a few skeletal elements, grave goods, and coffin hardware were left behind. In one burial excavated in 2011, we found human remains without a skull, although an indentation where the skull had been resting was still evident in the soil; this may have resulted from earlier vandalism or an unusual case of selective disinterment.

Excavating the burials was just the start of our investigation. Cleaning and analysis of the human skeletal remains, coffin hardware, and grave goods took place at the OSA lab in Iowa City. We completed the analysis in the summer of 2012 and the technical report in 2013.[1] At almost a thousand pages, this report is so voluminous that only three paper copies were produced, and we suspect few people will ever read the entire document. In this more reader-friendly book, we present a summary of what we found and what it can tell us about the people laid to rest in the Third Street Cemetery.

In the next few chapters, we will draw on historical newspaper accounts and county records to illuminate the history of nineteenth-century Dubuque and the Third Street Cemetery. In the later part of its active use, the cemetery was caught up in political controversy motivated by personal grudges and simple greed. Changing attitudes in the later nineteenth century, including the "beautification of death" and the rural cemetery movement, led many to advocate closing the cemetery and removing its occupants to other graveyards. At the time, new ideas about sanitation resulted in the "removal" of many American cemeteries to locations outside urban centers.

The life story of the Third Street Cemetery, following its "closure" in the late 1800s, is one of abandonment and loss of memory. The graves were disturbed on numerous occasions, and people complained that the grounds were neglected. Ultimately, most residents of Dubuque came to believe that all the burials had been moved. Much of what people "knew" about the Third Street Cemetery became wrapped up in myths about mass graves and the legend of a reclusive old miner. The excavations at the cemetery proved some of the local stories to be just that—stories.

One of the most important results of our archaeological investigations was the establishment of the actual cemetery boundaries, which encompass a greater amount of land than was represented on later maps. We also learned a great deal about the health of Dubuque's nineteenth-century residents. Most illnesses that struck down Dubuque citizens lasted for short periods of time and left no evidence on the bones. But evidence of childhood disease or malnutrition often marked the remains and painted a picture of a rough early life for many of the Third Street dead. The Third Street Cemetery project was unique, involving the largest European American (Euroamerican) Catholic cemetery excavated to date and providing a glimpse of a cross section of society, from the wealthiest to the poorest, not usually observed in such excavations. The analysis of the burial materials, including coffin hardware, grave goods, and the skeletal remains, provides interesting data not only about the lives of the Third Street Cemetery residents but about the lives of American settlers in the Midwest.

WHY DO WE FORGET the dead? We address some of the major reasons and also discuss the efforts of those who do not want them to fall from memory. Changes in land use, development, and urban expansion will continue to impact both large and small cemeteries across the nation, and in many cases archaeologists will be called in to excavate and remove the dead. Our story starts with a man walking his dog and ends with reburial of the human remains with Catholic rites. But it doesn't really end there. More condominiums will be constructed, airports and roads will need expanding, a new subdivision will be built. With a humanistic, compassionate approach to the excavation, study, and reburial of the dead, we can allay some of the controversy that often surrounds these cemetery relocations. We hope that by making more information about cemetery removals available outside of technical reports and the occasional website, we can show people how much can be learned about the history of an area, its people, and the current community through such excavations. This is our way, and perhaps our obligation, to keep the memory of the Third Street people alive.

TWO

Lead in the Bluffs, 1833–1880

HISTORIES OF DUBUQUE frequently begin with a biographical sketch of a gentleman who had absolutely nothing to do with the founding of the city in northeastern Iowa. Though Julien Dubuque's name was appropriated for both the county and the county seat, he never actually set foot in the town, since it did not exist until decades after his death. The mining operation he established a few miles downriver from what would eventually be the city's center was only a temporary settlement. After his death in 1810, American and European settlers were not officially permitted in the territory for another twenty-three years.

Josiah Conzett, a Swiss immigrant who resided in Dubuque until the 1890s and wrote his memoirs at the turn of the twentieth century, describes his impressions of the town as it appeared when he and his family first arrived, crossing the Mississippi River by horse ferry on a frigid morning in March 1846 (we have retained his original spelling and punctuation):

> It was A rough Frontier Village off about 3500 Inhabitants. . . . The Sorunding Bluff were then Hony combed with Minneral Holes and about half the Town was engaged in Mining for Lead — the Country all over from Catfish Creek to Perue Bottom was Rich with Mineral and up to 1850 was the Chief attraction and Source of Weath and the Hope off the Poor Man that draw him these Mining Claims. . . . There were Then Lots off Indians in the Vicinity, and it was no unusual Sight to see them and thier Squaws on Main St. and thier Boys Shooting at Pennies with thier Bows and arrows. These were also The great Steam Boat days—Seldom was any out of Sight on the River.[1]

Lead mining was indeed the hope of the poor man and the chief attraction of the region for centuries. Thousands of years ago, Archaic period people collected the lustrous ore crystals and traded them as far away as Louisiana. In the eighteenth and nineteenth centuries, Native Americans, particularly the Meskwaki, mined the ore in the vicinity to satisfy the European hunger for lead and their own desire for manufactured goods. And in the 1830s and 1840s, the pioneers who arrived from the eastern United States, from Canada, and from across the Atlantic Ocean chose this particular spot in hopes of profiting from the mines.

In the eighteenth and early nineteenth centuries, the area that would become Dubuque County was the turf of the Sauk, Meskwaki, Ioway, and Winnebago groups. When the Europeans arrived, the territory was claimed first by the French, then the Spanish, then the French again, until the land was turned over to the United States as part of the Louisiana Purchase in 1803. The territory was officially opened to American settlers on June 1, 1833, less than a year after the end of the Black Hawk War and the signing of a treaty that officially removed all Native American groups from the area. Of course, eager miners had been making unlawful incursions into Indian Territory long before the formal opening. U.S. troops expelled these trespassers from the Dubuque mines in 1830 and again in 1832. Some of the ejected adventurers moved their belongings no farther than the islands in the Mississippi, directly across from the mines, and bided their time until they could legally reoccupy their claims. Early histories of Dubuque describe these persevering entrepreneurs in heroic terms, and the tales perhaps convey something of the community's standard of an admirable character. The archetypal Dubuquer was hardworking and persistent, with a flexible attitude toward the law.

For the first three and a half years, from its initial settlement to its official incorporation, Dubuque flourished like any boomtown. In the first year, the register for the General Land Office reported granting over a thousand mining permits for the Dubuque District. Asiatic cholera struck the community in the summer of 1833, taking around fifty lives in the county, with most fatalities occurring in the more densely populated new town. The City Cemetery, which would eventually become Jackson Park, was created to bury the dead. Local historians believe the Third Street Cemetery was also founded during this epidemic so that Catholics who died from the disease could be buried on appropriately consecrated ground. No documentation exists that proves or disproves this theory, however, and it is not part of the popular version of the cemetery history.

Ask any Dubuque resident to tell you what he or she knows about the Third Street Cemetery, and you will likely get an answer something like this: *The cemetery was founded in 1839. Most of the people buried there were poor immigrants. The grounds filled up quickly because of the cholera epidemics. So many people were dying that they had to be buried in mass graves. Families who were not Catholic buried their dead in the cemetery without permission, anxious to be rid of the bodies. The cemetery was closed in 1856 (or 1867 or the 1870s) because it was overflowing (or because the bishop felt it had been desecrated by the burial of non-Catholics). The bishop ordered all the graves moved to Mt. Olivet Cemetery. The graves were moved in the 1870s (or the Mt. Olivet Cemetery Association moved them at the turn of the century). There were just a few graves left in the 1940s, and those were moved when the archdiocese sold the property. The graves that were still on the bluff in 2007 were probably the mass graves or the unrecorded non-Catholic burials.*

These accounts, inaccurate in almost every detail, were repeated not just by average residents but by employees of the archdiocese and members of the local media. The stories also appeared in articles on websites like *Wikipedia* and *Encyclopedia Dubuque*. However, the existing evidence—gathered from the excavation data, analysis of the skeletal remains, and examination of historical documents—disproves most of the common wisdom. This chapter explores what the written (and archaeological) record tells us about the cemetery and its role in Dubuque's history.

THE EARLY DAYS OF THE THIRD STREET CEMETERY

Because of the lack of documents from the 1830s, the precise details of the founding of the cemetery remain clouded. What little we know comes from an unsigned, undated copy of a petition apparently sent to the U.S. Congress by a group of concerned citizens during a dispute over ownership of the cemetery property in the 1870s. In this document, the petitioners state that an early pioneer named Patrick Quigley first preempted the Third Street Cemetery land in 1833. "Preemption" was a legal term for squatters' rights; those who made preemption claims on lots through settlement and cultivation had the privilege of purchasing the lots at the minimum price from the government after the public lands were surveyed and put up for sale. However, Mr. Quigley never purchased the property. Instead, he transferred his rights to the cemetery lot to John Dowling of Galena, Illinois. In 1834 Mr. Dowling transferred the rights to Rev. Samuel Mazzuchelli, the priest who headed the Catholic Church in Dubuque at the time. When Bishop Mathias Loras took control of the diocese—in 1839, not in 1834, as the petition mistakenly claims—all of Mazzuchelli's property, rights, and claims were conveyed to the new bishop. Transfers of preemption rights were not legally recognized under the Preemption Act of 1834, but since the petition to Congress included no supporting documents for these transfers, the point is moot. The petition also declares that it was Father Mazzuchelli who decided to set the land aside for use as a Catholic cemetery.

Despite the devastating cholera outbreak of 1833, the lure of mineral wealth continued to attract settlers. By the spring of 1834, the town's population was estimated at three hundred. Several saloons, as well as the first hotel, opened their doors that year. Construction of the first churches, the Methodist chapel and the Catholic St. Raphael's Cathedral, began in 1835. By 1836 the population had reached approximately twelve hundred, and the town boasted about fifty shops, three churches, two or three schools, and a bank. An early eyewitness account written in 1859 offers somewhat contradictory details about the character of the community: "The population almost without exception was of the roughest sort, being composed mostly of miners, whose amusements consisted in gambling and drunken frolics on the most villainous whiskey. . . . The standard of morality was infinitely low, the taking of a life or any other species of crime was regarded less a wrong than a pastime. Acts of extreme lawlessness, however, were rare for there was a regular system of organization among the miners by which was administered a set of laws with inflexible impartiality."[2]

A historian writing in 1880 was even less generous, describing the justice meted out by the early settlers as "in many instances so devoid of equity as to partake somewhat of criminality."[3] The entertaining Wild West picture painted by these editorializing historians renders only a small part of the larger mural of Dubuque history. Most of those who eventually settled in Dubuque were intent on establishing a better life for their families. Many were ambitious, perhaps, but not murderously so.

In July 1836 an act of Congress ordered the first survey of the town of Dubuque, Julien Township, Iowa. The official plat map that resulted from this survey clearly shows the Third Street Cemetery marked as "Grave Yard" (figure 3). This map proves the cemetery was in use prior to 1839, the year archdiocese records show it was consecrated by Bishop Loras. The Catholic Diocese of Dubuque, established in 1837, encompassed all of the land now identified as Iowa and Minnesota and was administered from the town of Dubuque. Though Catholics made up only a quarter of the town's population at the time, the bishop founded a small seminary, which would later become Loras College.

In the early years, the centrality of mining in the local economy was visible in the skewed population of the town, where men made up the vast majority. The 1836 census of Dubuque County lists 1,964 adult males and 610 adult females. As a result of the shortage of women, those who lived in the community reportedly made excellent wages for housework. Presumably, some of these early pioneer women made excellent wages as prostitutes as well, but the histories are mute on that subject.

The 1840s brought statehood to Iowa and a greater influx of settlers. By 1850 the population within the city limits had risen to 3,108. The city

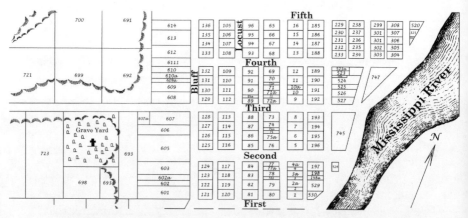

FIGURE 3. Portion of the 1837 plat map of Dubuque, Iowa, showing the Third Street Cemetery as "Grave Yard" (redrawn by Tyler Perkins from the original 1837 plat map of Dubuque, Iowa, Julius Hutawa, lithographer).

was divided into three wards for the purpose of electing city aldermen. The wards corresponded roughly to the existing three-part social division. Many of the Irish settled in "Little Dublin" on the southern end of the city in the First Ward, which is depicted in histories mainly as a shantytown of unskilled workers. To the north, in the Third Ward, lived the craftsmen and shopkeepers of "Germany." Between these two communities sat the middle ground known as "Babel," the Second Ward, where the lavish homes of some of the wealthy families of Dubuque adorned the bluffs. The 1856 Iowa state census nativity table indicates that almost half of the population of Julien Township (which included the city of Dubuque) was foreign born, with the majority of these immigrants coming from Ireland and Germany, the two main sources of migrants to the United States in this period. Furthermore, the American-born children of these immigrants tended to retain their ethnic identity. Yet despite the emphasis on division so often found in histories, early settler Lucius Langworthy described the community of Dubuque as unique, claiming, "The German liberalism, the New England Puritanism, and Celtic nationalism mixed and mingled in all the elements of society."[4]

Lead-mining outputs peaked in 1845, and a gradual decline followed due to falling lead prices and the fact that the easily accessible ore had already been mined. As the industry's supremacy waned, the community's entrepreneurs diversified, opening breweries, iron foundries, brick factories, rope works, steam sawmills, and a soap and candle factory. Though the majority of its citizens were listed merely as "laborers," Dubuque also boasted 155 merchants, 38 lawyers, 22 physicians, and 5 dentists in 1856. The 118 professions listed for the town included nonessential workers like the 8 musicians, 8 actors, 7 confectioners, and 2 sculptors. Dubuque's location on the river also contributed to the continued economic growth. Steamboats connected the city to New Orleans, St. Louis, and St. Paul and all the stops in between. Understanding the importance of adding east–west transportation capabilities, the enterprising city government helped fund the laying of westward rails throughout the 1850s, though the railway bridge across the Mississippi that would connect Dubuque's trains directly to the eastern lines was not begun until 1867.

Dubuque prospered and continued to expand through the 1860s and 1870s. The meatpacking and lumbering industries, as well as the Cooper Wagon Works, flourished, though the mining business was by no means dead. The city introduced its first full-time, paid police force and its first streetcars in the 1860s. The Civil War brought out deep divisions in the community, especially since some of the early settlers had migrated from southern states. Young men from Dubuque fought on both sides of the conflict, though it appears the majority volunteered to join the Union forces. Exactly how many soldiers from Dubuque perished in battle is unknown, but we found documentation for at least nineteen Civil War casualties and veterans buried in the Third Street Cemetery.

The population of the city increased from 13,000 in 1860 to 18,434 in 1870 and 22,254 in 1880. Residents had access to a wider variety of goods and entertainment than one might expect in an Iowa town during this time period. Baseball games, fairs, musical performances, balls, charity dinners, plays, operas, lectures on science and history, and visits from circuses and traveling menageries were all advertised and reviewed daily on page 4 of the *Dubuque Herald*. In addition to the dozens of patent medicines advertised in the papers, local purveyors offered pianos, oysters, exotic fruits, and the latest fashions. For those who could afford luxuries, life in Dubuque must have been almost on a par with larger urban centers like Chicago and St. Louis.

Another industry that grew steadily during this period was the funeral business, and not just because more people meant more deaths. Ideas about proper burial and remembrance changed significantly during the nineteenth century as the "beautification of death" movement spread westward from its late eighteenth-century beginnings on the East Coast, bringing to the Midwest greater public expressions of sentimentality toward death and dying. Previously, American funeral customs focused on the community's shared sense of loss rather than dwelling on the deceased, who had the good fortune to pass on to the glorious afterlife. The imagery associated with death was predominantly religious or cautionary in nature, and angels, skeletons, death's heads, scythes, and hourglasses frequently adorned the grave markers of the seventeenth and eighteenth centuries. In the nineteenth century, the soul of the deceased became the focus of funeral rituals, and only the immediate family took up mourning formally and publicly. The literature of the time portrayed death as a part of nature and as God's will; thus melancholy beauty became the dominant theme in funerary art. Classical motifs like columns and urns joined flowers, willows, and lambs on coffin decorations, tombstones, and other memorials to the dead.

The new outlook on death and mourning led to more ostentation in funeral accoutrements. Whereas formerly most people were buried wearing simple shrouds, now they often went to the grave in fine clothing that either belonged to the deceased during life or was specially purchased for the funeral. Embellished burial containers became popular thanks to advances in mass production capabilities, improvements in transportation, and the capitalist spirit. While most of the coffins buried at Third Street in the 1830s and 1840s were simple containers made as a sideline business by local carpenters and cabinetmakers, a half dozen undertakers were available to provide decorated custom-ordered and ready-made coffins in the 1860s and 1870s. According to newspaper advertisements, these undertakers provided a variety of services in addition to coffin sales, though Dubuque did not have a true funeral home until Hoffmann Mortuary opened around 1882. In 1877 the Dubuque Furniture and Burial Case Company began large-scale manufacture of coffins for wholesale and retail.

Accompanying these other changes was a trend toward placing cemeteries in rural areas instead of in the middle of towns. Increasingly, people preferred to bury the dead in a peaceful place of natural beauty where the living could quietly contemplate mortality. The shift away from overcrowded, poorly maintained urban churchyards also appealed to new sensibilities about sanitation that were gaining credence at the time. The spread of these ideas about death and burial resulted in the Third Street Cemetery appearing in the local newspapers over and over again from 1865 to the early twentieth century. Articles and editorials chronicle the community's increasing dissatisfaction with the unkempt property, a tangled wilderness of weeds with rooting hogs and roaming cattle; the heated battle over ownership of the land and mineral rights; and the ever-changing plans for the abandoned grounds and the interred dead.

THE BURIAL REGISTER

Unfortunately, the first three decades of the cemetery's use are not as well documented as the later period. Besides the petition sent to Congress, the main source of information concerning the early years of the Third Street Cemetery is the burial register of St. Raphael's Cathedral, which covers the period from August 1839 to July 1856. According to a county history compiled under the Work Projects Administration, records from the years prior to the creation of the Dubuque diocese were stored in Galena, Illinois, and destroyed at some point by a church fire. Another possibility is that missionary priest Samuel Mazzuchelli, who ministered to Dubuque before the arrival of Bishop Loras in 1839, sent all of his records back to his Dominican home base in Sinsinawa, Wisconsin. The register covering the years 1856–1900 has been missing for decades and may have been discarded in accordance with Archbishop John Hennessy's wishes that all of his papers, both official and personal, be destroyed upon his death in 1900.

The extant burial register is obviously incomplete, recording only three deaths for the last five months of 1839. Five deaths are shown in 1855, with nothing recorded after May. The 1856 record covers only April to July. Its other limitations are less obvious at first glance. According to the Archdiocese of Dubuque, the register contains the names of individuals who received the burial rites of the Catholic Church but not necessarily all who were buried in the cathedral's cemetery. Additionally, the book may include funerals performed outside the city of Dubuque, since the cathedral was home base for missionary priests. Therefore, some of the 697 individuals named in the register might have been buried in cemeteries other than Third Street. The book also includes entries for twenty-eight unnamed individuals, most of whom were listed as having been buried without rites or without the permission of the church. One such entry from 1849 simply states, "2 children have been buried by the parents without giving notice of it to the clergy." Another similar entry gives family information: "A child which was born dead on this day of Catherine Geren and John Geren was buried in unconsecrated ground in the Catholic graveyard." We presume that these burials took place at the Third Street Cemetery, since unofficiated burials in far-flung parishes were unlikely to have been reported.

Though incomplete, the burial register offers many insights into the Catholic community of Dubuque during the early years of the diocese. The entries rarely give information about the nativity of the deceased, but the recorded names indicate parishioners of Irish, German, and French heritage. A set of entries from the spring of 1842 includes Mary Ryan, Louis Latourelle, William Dugan, Merance Desnoyers, and Christine Louise Beutzen. The French-speaking community resulted from population migration along the Mississippi and from Canada. The Irish and Germans, however, came in response to efforts by Bishop Loras, who wrote letters throughout his episcopacy to eastern Irish-American newspapers and German-language Catholic periodicals, inviting immigrants to come to Dubuque. Four individuals in the register are listed as "colored" at a time when "blacks" and "mulattos" constituted about 8 percent of the city's population. A single individual—Fabella Caliceur—is recorded in the register as "a half breed woman," which implies that she was part Native American. Census records from Dubuque do not list Native Americans as living in the county, though their presence is recorded in contemporary newspaper articles and Dubuque memoirs.

Few of the funeral entries list cause of death, and the officiating priests more often recorded details of violent and accidental deaths than deaths due to natural causes. Patrick Murray was stabbed to death; Michael McHagan fell in a mine; and Michael Dugan fell off a horse. Clusters of deaths indicate outbreaks of disease. In July 1850 six deaths were attributed to cholera, and many of the twelve other deaths that month may also have been cholera-related, particularly those of a husband and wife who died within a two-day period. Another interesting cluster of deaths occurs between June 6 and June 8, 1852. Ten people died during this period, eight of whom were men between the ages of twenty and fifty. The state or country of birth was recorded for each of these men, which suggests they were not considered local. Four were Irish, two were French Canadian, one was German, and one was from Kentucky. Unfortunately, Dubuque newspapers from this time period have not survived, and we found no records elsewhere reporting an incident such as a mine collapse, a steamboat accident, or an outbreak of cholera on a ship. City records do, however, mention the opening of a temporary cholera quarantine hospital on June 1.

If a map showing the layout of individual and family lots within the cemetery ever existed, it has not survived. A few lot sales were recorded in the burial register, as well as in the personal daybook of Bishop Loras, so we have some idea of the costs. Lots purchased in the public grounds ranged from $1.00 to $3.00, while private, numbered lots sold for $3.00

to $12.00. The lots sound quite cheap, until one considers that a common laborer earned as little as $0.60 a day in 1845, while a clerk made about $45.00 a month. The highest numbered lot sale recorded was Lot 282, sold to Francis Mangold in 1847.

From its consecration in 1839 until 1856, the Third Street Cemetery—which was sometimes called the Cathedral Cemetery, St. Raphael's Cemetery, or the Old Catholic Grave Yard—remained the official and only cemetery of the Catholic Church in Dubuque. According to the archdiocese archivist, a second Catholic graveyard, Key West Cemetery, opened to the south of Dubuque in 1856. Around the same time as the founding of Key West, the burial ground on Third Street began to expand onto an adjacent lot owned by an early pioneer and lead miner named Thomas Kelly. This well-known character of Dubuque had claimed all of the property to the south and west of the cemetery in the early days, and the entire landform was (and still is) known as Kelly's Bluff. The archdiocese archives hold no records regarding the first burials occurring on Kelly's Outlot 723, though correspondence from July 1856 may refer obliquely to its use.

Another significant event occurred in the Catholic community around this time. The German-speaking members of the congregation split off from St. Raphael's Cathedral, establishing their own church, Holy Trinity, in 1849 and their own burial ground, St. Mary's Cemetery, in 1861. After the opening of the German cemetery (now known as Mt. Calvary) north of town and Key West Cemetery south of town, Catholics had three cemeteries to choose from. It is impossible to ascertain what percentage of the parish was interred at Third Street after that, but it probably included many of the Irish, who lived in the vicinity of the cathedral cemetery, as well as families who had already purchased plots.

In April 1865 an article about the Third Street Cemetery appeared in the *Dubuque Democratic Herald*. In addition to announcing an upcoming meeting of lot owners, the author commented on the neglected state of the cemetery, left to the "ravages of brute beasts." A vista of thriving weeds, broken-down lot enclosures, fallen monuments, and wandering livestock reportedly greeted visitors to the burial ground. Perhaps new ideas of what a cemetery should look like transformed local perception of the unkempt property; it was no longer just a typical churchyard but an eyesore and an embarrassment. Moreover, the bluff-top location that was once somewhat isolated from town now lay within the sightline of several neighbors. Seven months after this article appeared, a group of concerned parishioners formed a fence-building committee and began soliciting subscriptions to pay for the fence. They finally collected the pledged money in April 1866 and had the fence built sometime that year. During the initial meeting, one attendee suggested that the committee needed to establish how much ground actually belonged to the cemetery. Apparently, they were concerned with usage rather than legal ownership. The bishop had not yet formally acquired the portion of Outlot 723 onto which the cemetery had expanded, yet that land was encompassed, along with the original cemetery lot, by the new fence.

The committee members had little time to sit back and enjoy their success. Just a few months after the fence was completed, it was damaged in an incident that further embarrassed the church. Richard "D. J." Hennessy, the brother of then-bishop John Hennessy, and Dennis Hartney, a "man of all work" in the bishop's household, were charged with destroying the steps leading to the entrance of the Third Street Cemetery and demolishing part of the fence. The episode apparently began when the two tried to prevent a funeral procession from climbing the steps and entering the grounds. The surviving news articles give no further explanation for this odd behavior. Entries in the burial register imply that burial without consulting (or paying) the clergy was a perennial problem. Hennessy and Hartney may have been trying to collect payment for a plot initially, but the confrontation escalated to the point that one of them took an axe to the steps and the fence.

The next week, on March 3, 1867, Bishop Hennessy announced from the pulpit that the Third Street Cemetery was to be closed, and henceforth no interments would be permitted therein. No reason was given at the time for the closing, but later newspaper items state that the cemetery was nearly full. However, on May 15 of the same year, miner Thomas Kelly died of lead poisoning. Upon his death, his many landholdings, including the cemetery expansion in Outlot 723, passed to his brothers and sister.

FIGURE 4. Plat map of Dubuque, Iowa, showing (in gray) bluff-top lots acquired for the Diocese of Dubuque by 1867 (base map redrawn by Tyler Perkins from the *Original Town of Dubuque* map, Joseph C. Jennings, 1852).

His brother Patrick sold his interest in the Kelly's Bluff properties to his unmarried sister, Elizabeth, for $1,400. In turn, Elizabeth Kelly sold the same property to Bishop John Hennessy for the sum of one dollar. The reason for this generosity is not documented, but Thomas Kelly's obituary states that he had not paid taxes on any of his properties for many years. A massive back-tax obligation would render the lots worthless to heirs. A receipt held at the Archdiocese of Dubuque archives suggests that the bishop and Miss Kelly made private arrangements to exchange the bluff-top land for payment of back taxes on several of the inherited properties, including those she still owned.

With this substantial land acquisition (figure 4), the expansion in Out-lot 723 officially became part of the cemetery property. In February 1868, almost a year after the cemetery was closed, Bishop Hennessy announced that all persons who already owned lots in the cemetery would be permitted to inter their dead but that no more lots would be sold. Lot sales did in fact continue, but these may have been transfers between owners rather than official purchases from the parish.

DEATH AND TAXES

The acquisition of Kelly's land proved problematic for the bishop.[5] The city council was planning to grade and improve the rough track that was Third Street at the expense of owners of the abutting properties, and several aldermen attempted to collect from Bishop Hennessy the fees assessed for his land on Kelly's Bluff. Hennessy refused to pay for the 675 feet of frontage belonging to the cemetery. His petition for exemption included a map showing the original cemetery lot and Outlot 723 (figure 5). This plat is the *only* known map that shows the northern two-thirds of Outlot 723 as part of the cemetery. On all previous and subsequent city maps the cemetery label appears only on the original lot.

The legal quarrel over the street improvement fees dragged on for four years. Meanwhile, the cemetery itself fell into jeopardy. On January 13, 1870, while the bishop was in Rome, Mayor William Knight announced to the city council that he had leased the mineral rights to the original cemetery lot to Michael White and Patrick McEvoy and asked the council to pass a resolution confirming the lease. How did he justify his illegal

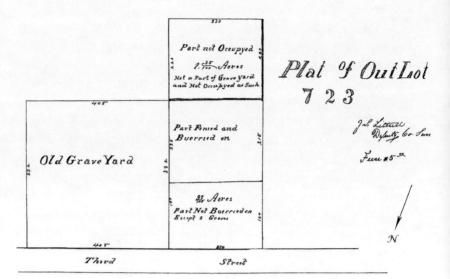

FIGURE 5. Reproduction of Bishop Hennessy's tax exemption petition map (ca. 1868) showing the northern and central portions of Outlot 723 as part of the cemetery.

actions? He claimed that the tract of land had never been officially purchased from the U.S. government. Nevertheless, the bishops of the diocese, without any legal right, had sold lots in the cemetery and exercised complete control over it for many years. And yet when asked to pay his share of the Third Street improvements, Bishop Hennessy had denied ownership of the land. Mayor Knight claimed that the city's rights to the property were grounded on the use of taxpayer money for the street improvements and on the abandonment of the property by the only power controlling it. The mining lease, he stated, was intended to safeguard the city's claim until the government granted an official patent to the city of Dubuque. He promised that the mining work would not disturb the graves. He also complained about "the spectacle of a graveyard in our midst, abandoned to desecration," and insisted that the bodies should be removed to a more suitable location. Finally, he proposed that once the tract was emptied of bodies, it would be an ideal location for a public park.

The mayor's announcement kicked off a flurry of activity on the editorial pages of the local newspapers. For two months, the mayor wrangled back and forth with cemetery supporters, and many accused him of corruption. One allegation claimed that Mayor Knight had a personal vendetta against Bishop Hennessy; another that the move intentionally coincided with the bishop's absence; and a third that James Rowan, city councilman, and Thomas Finn, member of the board of supervisors, were the actual lessees of the mineral rights, using the names of White and McEvoy as a cover for the fact that they had essentially granted themselves use of the property. Cemetery supporters also pointed out that the city had no right to profit from the mining leases if, as the mayor claimed, the land still belonged to the U.S. government. They further claimed that, despite the mayor's promise, the miners had damaged the cemetery fence and were digging within fifteen or twenty feet of the bottoms of the graves. Not content to fight the battle with words, a group of concerned lot owners incorporated the St. Raphael's Cemetery Association of the Catholics of Dubuque for the purpose of improving, controlling, and managing the Catholic cemetery. Besides organizing their own petition, this group mobilized support from the Early Settlers' Association.

Mayor Knight fired back at his detractors. He claimed that Reverend Donnellan of St. Raphael's had given Rowan and Finn his approval for the mining and that the priest even suggested that the profits could be used to pay the city for the street improvements. Knight also presented testimony from witnesses who were present when Bishop Hennessy told the previous mayor, Solomon Turck, that it was improper to have a cemetery in the heart of the city and that he would like the city council to exercise authority over the cemetery to compel its abandonment. Knight acknowledged that lot owners had the greatest legal claim on the cemetery but insisted that, as a Catholic himself with relatives buried on the bluff, he would prefer to have the land safe in the city's hands and the bodies moved elsewhere. Addressing the city council and the residents of Dubuque, the mayor said, "I urge on my brethren to consider whether it is not better now, and during our time, to place our dead in a permanent resting place, than to leave them to the tender mercies of our successors, who perhaps may not be as careful of them."[6] He had no idea how accurately he was predicting the future.

Father Donnellan denied that he ever gave approval to the mining plan and emphasized that he had no authority to grant permission anyway. Rowan and Finn accused the priest of evasion if not outright dishonesty.

Rowan asserted that other miners who were working under the bishop's authority on a different lot were also coming close to encroaching on the cemetery, but the vicar-general, Reverend Brazil, denied this claim. Meanwhile, the new cemetery association petitioned the city to desist attempting to acquire legal title to the original cemetery lot. Only the original lot was under attack, since Hennessy had obtained clear title to the cemetery addition from the Kelly family.

The editorials about the Third Street Cemetery stopped abruptly in March. In April rumors swirled that the House of Representatives had passed a bill giving the city of Dubuque title to the graveyard. This tale turned out to be false, as the bill referred to a different lot altogether. So what actually happened? Did public outcry end the mining, or did the digging continue until all the lead was gone? A petition was sent to Congress requesting that title to the land be granted to Bishop Hennessy, but when was it sent? Surviving copies of the petition are undated and unsigned, but the document must have been prepared prior to the 1893 elevation of the diocese, since Hennessy is referred to as the bishop rather than the archbishop. It seems likely that the petition was drafted by members of the St. Raphael's Cemetery Association.

The historical sources are mute on the resolution of the controversy, but it is clear that the cemetery was not closed at this time. Many subsequent obituaries dated from 1870 to 1880 give the Third Street Cemetery as the place of interment. The property was as neglected as ever, with hogs and cattle roaming the grounds, although the cemetery association raised money to repair the fence and to build a sexton's residence on the property. In December 1876 Dennis Hartney accepted the post of sexton. According to the newspaper, "Mr. Hartney is a reliable, careful man and under his care the cemetery grounds will be protected as they should be."[7] This Mr. Hartney is the same gentleman who helped the bishop's brother destroy the cemetery steps with an axe in 1867!

The city began keeping official death records in 1880. The entry for Mary Naugle, an infant who died of convulsions on July 31, 1880, gives Third Street as the place of interment. She is the last person known to have been buried on the bluff, though the cemetery was still not officially closed. Little documentation of disinterments exists. Forty-eight people were moved by their families to Key West and New Mellary cemeteries between 1878 and 1879. An 1897 article mentions that "many bodies" had been moved from Third Street to Key West "in recent years." Unfortunately, that cemetery, which changed its name to Mt. Olivet in 1901, did not keep burial records prior to the twentieth century, so we have no way to investigate the reported removals. Even if lot sale records existed, the fact that a grave at Key West was purchased for reburial rather than for a regular interment might not have been recorded.

A VIEW OF THE THIRD STREET CEMETERY

We hoped that early images of the Third Street Cemetery would help us to envision the layout of the grounds and to understand the way the available space on the bluff was used. Unfortunately, neither Samuel Root nor Ephraim Cutter, nor any other photographers who documented the landscape of nineteenth-century Dubuque, chose the Third Street Cemetery as a subject for their work. Or if they did, the photos have long since disappeared. The bluff appears in two surviving images of Dubuque, a lithograph produced by John Caspar Wild in 1845 and the *Perspective Map of the City of Dubuque* sketched in 1889 by H. Wellge. In Wild's artwork Thomas Kelly's lead-mining operation is visible, but there is no hint of the cemetery. Wellge's *Perspective* depicts the cemetery area as level ground with a vague outline, perhaps representing a fence. A few small dark blots and a large piano-shaped spot occupy the ground within the outline. Neither artist gave us very much to go on. Our own artist, Deanne Wortman, had to combine ample imagination with the schematic information we provided to create a concept drawing of the cemetery circa 1877 (figures 6 and 7).

Fortunately, many newspaper articles addressing the neglect at the graveyard and the mining controversy provide details about the layout of the cemetery. We know the parishioners built a fence encompassing both the original cemetery and the later addition in the late 1860s. A respected gentleman named George Jones (a former Iowa senator) proposed an iron fence with stone foundations, but the fact that the fence was eventually built with volunteer labor suggests that the committee was unable to raise sufficient funds for such a substantial enclosure. Since D. J. Hennessy and Dennis Hartney destroyed part of the fence with an axe in 1867, it was

FIGURE 6. Conceptual drawing of the Third Street Cemetery ca. 1877
(illustration by Deanne Warnholtz Wortman).

probably constructed of wood, perhaps a post-and-rail fence. The fence
likely enclosed only the level ground, avoiding the steep slopes within the
cemetery's legal boundaries. The steps leading up to the cemetery would
also have been wooden. Locals recall that funeral processions ascended to
the burial ground via a path leading up the bluff from behind the cathedral to an east-facing gate. A pale line sweeping across the bluff in Wild's
picture may represent that path. None of the sources describe the gate, but
one can imagine it was as plain as the fence.

Today, the bluff rises steeply from behind the cathedral, and much of
the face appears to be sheer rock. One must bear in mind, though, that
years of erosion following the mining, deforestation, and grading of the
bluff have altered the landscape. In the old pictures, a more gradual slope

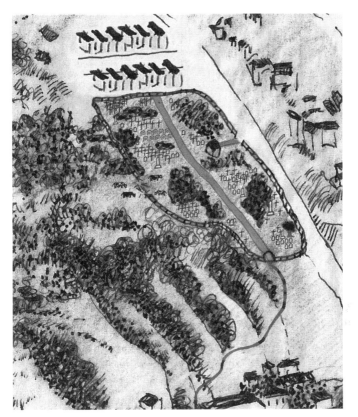

FIGURE 7. Bird's-eye view of the Third Street Cemetery as it would have appeared ca. 1877 (illustration by Deanne Warnholtz Wortman, redrawn by Tyler Perkins).

descends from the bluff top. Even with the harsher modern terrain, it is possible to hike, with effort, from St. Raphael's through one of the steep backyards on St. Mary's Street, which runs behind the cathedral, to the cemetery lot above.

In addition to the outer fence, newspaper articles mention individual lot enclosures, perhaps made of wood or ornamental wrought iron. We found no remnants of these during the excavation. In 1876 the sexton's house was added to the property. The committee raised just $418 for the construction, and, even then, that amount funded only a small and spartan house. To put it in perspective, consider that Josiah Conzett, a store clerk, paid $900 in 1870 for a five-room, one-and-a-half-story house that he described as "cheaply built." The cemetery building must have been sturdy, though, because it appears on aerial photographs from the 1930s and 1940s, despite being abandoned prior to 1900. In these photographs, a dirt track leads south from the steep section of Third Street to the small home, set back about 120 feet from the road. This two-track also provided alternate access to the cemetery.

Descriptions of the cemetery grounds consistently mention the tangle of vegetation thriving unhampered across the site both before and after abandonment. Though forgotten burial grounds often become overgrown, it is hard to picture an active cemetery covered with underbrush. At least one newspaper editorial (apparently written by a non-Catholic) blames the neglect of the grounds on the shameful laziness of the parishioners. However, lack of enthusiasm for maintenance may not have been the only reason for the condition of the property. An 1888 treatise on funeral customs in Ireland offers the following insight: "It is accounted a sacrilege to disturb or pluck up any plants growing in a churchyard, and as a consequence the cemeteries ar [sic] overgrown with grass and weeds, excepting in the cities, where modern ideas ar bringing about a change."[8]

In 1939 the *Dubuque Telegraph-Herald* published a photograph of four military headstones grouped together in an area reserved for veterans and fallen soldiers. The houses on Cardiff Street, to the west of the cemetery, are just visible in the background. The perspective in the photograph allowed us to roughly locate the military section near the center of Outlot 723. Nine military stones now stand in the Third Street section of Mt. Olivet Cemetery and may have stood together in the bluff cemetery as well. Annual articles in the Dubuque newspapers indicate that the Civil War soldiers' graves at Third Street continued to be visited on Decoration Day even after the cemetery fell out of use.

Despite the lack of monuments on the site, we can get an idea of how the cemetery looked by examining the markers in the Third Street section of Mt. Olivet. A few obelisks stand in the rows, but the majority are tablet-style stones of marble or limestone. Some bear the uniform shield of military markers, while others present flowers, shamrocks, a willow tree, clasping hands, and, of course, the ubiquitous cross. One can imagine the inscriptions illuminated by the morning light, with the sun rising over the Mississippi and casting long shadows from the stones and wooden crosses on the bluff. Maybe the dark blots in Wellge's *Perspective* portray these shadows.

Having exhausted the historical resources, we turned to our excavation data to build a clearer picture of the graveyard. Limited by the constraints of our project area and the effects of twentieth-century disturbance to the site, we were unable to investigate documented features such as the fence and the sexton's house. However, we found a road running through the cemetery, a linear, twenty-foot-wide area without graves, parallel to Third Street. We noted an attempt to create orderly rows of graves on the eastern part of our project area, though the densely packed graves on the western edge of the cemetery appear disorganized. Two particularly crowded areas had high proportions of children's and infants' graves, almost to the exclusion of adults. Either of these concentrations may represent an intentional "Garden of Innocents" or simply a public area that was in use during a period of high childhood mortality. A combination of spatial data, historical research, and osteological analysis led us to identify two groups of graves as family burial plots, which we describe in detail in chapters 8 and 9. A third possible family plot encompassed a group of individuals who all had fillings or dental prostheses. Given the rarity of professional dental work in this cemetery population and the proximity of these graves, it would be strange if these people were not somehow related.

The question of how many people were originally buried at Third Street remains unanswered. In a long editorial from 1870, signed "Grumbler," a person who appears well informed about local matters gives the number of graves as 3,000 to 4,000. If the number of burials per year stayed constant for the remaining ten years of the cemetery's use, then the final count would be around 3,800 to 5,100.

We made our own calculations using the excavation data and a computer model of the site. Much of the property consists of steep slopes, and of the 5.29 acres encompassed by the cemetery boundaries, only a 3.9-acre expanse of fairly level ground was suitable for burial. Subtracting the area of the road through the cemetery, where no burials occurred, and multiplying by the minimum and maximum grave density observed during excavations, we arrived at an estimate of 4,400 to 7,900 graves. This estimate assumes that the cemetery was full, as reported, at the end of its approximately forty-seven years of use. To ascertain whether or not our estimate falls within the realm of possibility, we looked at numbers gleaned from the 1855–75 burial records of the nondenominational City

Cemetery of Dubuque. A rough comparison with the average number of interments per month at the City Cemetery indicates that our estimate is realistic, with the actual number of graves at Third Street probably falling in the middle of the given range.

How is it possible that thousands of people lay forgotten for so many years? Who were they, and how did they die? We spent many hours in libraries and dusty courthouse records rooms trying to answer these questions.

THREE

Slumbering on the Bluff

––––––––––

ALTHOUGH WE LACKED complete cemetery records for Third Street, we were able to cobble together a substantial list of names of the people buried there by using the St. Raphael's burial register, lot sale records, newspaper obituaries, and the memoirs of Josiah Conzett. Other sources include early twentieth-century accounts of the abandoned cemetery, headstone readings compiled by the Daughters of the American Revolution, and headstones and coffin-lid crosses found during the archaeological excavation. We also gathered names from the forty-one remaining headstones moved to Mt. Olivet Cemetery in the 1940s. Local residents contributed a few more names based on sources like family Bibles. The murder of James Leyden, for instance, was well documented in the newspapers, but his burial place was not specified. A descendant provided the information that he was buried at Third Street. At the end of this volume, readers will find an appendix that provides the name, age at death, and date of death (or date of funeral or obituary) for all persons discovered during our research. While this list is far from comprehensive—and, in fact, may include people who were *not* buried at Third Street—it provides 914 more names than we had at the beginning of the project.

The names by themselves offer little information besides clues to their ethnic origin. To learn more about the people buried in the cemetery, we consulted census records and early histories of the town. The profile of the Dubuque population changed gradually over time, as did the profile of the Catholic community. The male-to-female ratio evened out by the mid-1860s. The percentage of foreign-born residents declined to 42 percent of the population in 1860 and just 28 percent by 1880. And Catholics, who were the minority at 25 percent of the population in 1839, became the majority. The exact ratio of Catholics to Protestants and Jews (a very small minority) is impossible to calculate, since census collectors did not record religious denomination. However, an 1860 newspaper article offers numbers gathered from the three Catholic and eleven Protestant churches in Dubuque. The Protestant congregations claimed 1,462 members and 1,047 Sunday school members, while the Catholics claimed 6,200 members and 1,400 Sunday school members.

St. Raphael's Cathedral and St. Patrick's Church, which was built less than a mile to the north of the cathedral, both hosted mainly Irish congregations. As mentioned previously, Bishop Loras encouraged Irish Catholics to settle in Dubuque through a series of letters sent to newspapers back east. Many of these settlers first arrived on America's shores as part of the vast wave of immigrants who fled the Great Famine in Ireland in the mid-nineteenth century. The famine, which eventually caused the death of approximately one million Irish and the emigration of another million, led to overcrowding in poorer quarters of large cities on the East Coast of the United States. Representatives of the Catholic Church in New York encouraged many of these immigrants to continue moving westward rather than putting down roots where they landed. The impoverished residents of Dubuque's Little Dublin were not the only members of the two churches, however. Many prominent citizens and enterprising businessmen of the city were Irish, and the majority of the men who joined the cemetery fence-building committee and the St. Raphael's Cemetery Association had Irish surnames.

The 1856 Iowa state census recorded equal numbers of German and Irish immigrants, but not all of these Germans were Catholic. The German Holy Trinity Church had twelve hundred adult members in 1860, compared with three thousand at the cathedral and two thousand at St. Patrick's. Though German Catholics buried their dead at Third Street prior to the founding of their own cemetery in 1861, they were the minority in the graveyard as well as in the cathedral. The German-speaking community retained its ethnic roots, producing multiple German-language newspapers and dwelling in close-knit neighborhoods primarily in the northern part of town. Interestingly, the histories of Dubuque do not report any German slums or a "Little Berlin."

Little has been written about the French Catholics of Dubuque. French names are well represented in the St. Raphael's burial register, but these listings may include individuals who were recent immigrants from France, French Canadians, French-speaking Swiss natives, and former residents of

French-settled areas like St. Louis and New Orleans, as well as Americans with French last names. It is likely that all of these people were considered "French" at the time, regardless of where they were born. A history of the Archdiocese of Dubuque mentions that the French population of the city was already declining in 1849 and that the remaining families stayed at the cathedral when the German congregation split off. Josiah Conzett mentions several prominent French citizens in his recollections, including Mayor Peter Lorimier and Bishop Mathias Loras.

In 1840 people of African descent—then known as "coloreds"—made up 2.4 percent of the county population and 8.6 percent of the city's population. The proportion of black to white residents fell over the remaining years of the Third Street Cemetery's use as the mining industry, which had drawn many black men to the community, declined. Due to the small size of the population, other studies have lumped all of the "colored" individuals together or separated them into "slave" and "free" categories, with no regard for birthplace or religious belief. Four entries in the burial register and two newspaper obituaries provide the only historical evidence that there were black members of the Catholic community in Dubuque.

Of these recorded deaths, one was an unnamed individual, described only as a colored man who was baptized on his deathbed and therefore not a part of the living Catholic community. Three of the other people had French names. Jean Baptiste Cibaut was described as a "free colored man" who "died at Snake Diggings" and was presumably a miner. Victoire Bassien was from St. Genevieve, Missouri. Sarah Tebeau is referred to in her obituary as "an old resident and very highly respected." The remaining two women had English names. Mary Margaret Williams was "a colored maid," though it is uncertain whether the priest who wrote the entry meant "young woman" or "servant." Mary Ann Aaron died in 1876, and her obituary praises her good character. A short history of the Aaron family can be found in chapter 10.

Native Americans were not enumerated in the census records for Dubuque. A number of newspaper accounts suggest that while they may not have been permanent residents, Native Americans frequently passed through the Dubuque area. One recorded incident occurred near the Third Street Cemetery. In 1866, not long before his own death, Thomas Kelly found a dying Native American man on his bluff property. When the man expired, he was buried with his pipe and blanket and a bottle in the city-owned cemetery instead of the Catholic one. Fabella Caliceur, the woman listed as a "half breed" in the burial register, is the only Native American known to have been buried at Third Street. Conzett mentions only one specific Native American in his recollections, a lawyer named Reed whose wife was the beauty of the town.

A discussion of who was buried at Third Street should also touch on who was not buried at Third Street. Father Charles Van Quickenborne, the first priest in Dubuque, and Father Samuel Mazzuchelli, who designed St. Raphael's Cathedral, are buried elsewhere. While the first two bishops of Dubuque, Loras and Smyth, were probably interred in the grounds originally, they were moved to the mortuary chapel built under St. Raphael's Cathedral at the request of Archbishop Hennessy, who also rests in the chapel. All of the religious orders that established themselves in Dubuque during the active period of the cemetery maintained their own burial grounds or buried their dead in Key West or St. Mary's Cemetery. Though the parish probably buried their priests at Third Street, the only member of the clergy known to be interred there is Reverend Wheeler, a priest from Bellevue, Iowa, who died of an apparent heart attack on the buggy ride to Dubuque. Sister Mary Francis O'Reilly died just before the Sisters of Charity of the Blessed Virgin Mary opened their motherhouse and associated graveyard in 1846. She was also buried at Third Street, though her sisters attempted on more than one occasion to reclaim her remains. Their efforts were thwarted by the disappearance of her grave marker and the confusion following the abandonment of the cemetery.

HOW DID THEY DIE?

The city of Dubuque started keeping death records in 1880. Prior to this, cause of death for individuals was recorded primarily in newspaper obituaries and on the mortality schedules of the federal census. Since the majority of the obituaries in the Dubuque papers did not mention cause of death and the mortality schedules list fatalities for only one year out of each decade, historical records have little to tell us about the mortality of the people buried at Third Street. As mentioned previously, entries in the burial register rarely provide cause of death, except in cases of cholera, homicide, or accidental death.

Out of the 957 named and unnamed individuals believed to be buried at Third Street, existing records provide cause of death for only ninety-five. Of these, sixty-nine deaths were due to disease, many of which were listed merely as "long illness." In the disease category, cholera's numbers are inflated—eighteen deaths—due to the bias in data from the burial register. Thirteen fatalities are attributed to consumption. Twenty-six deaths were due to various kinds of accidents and injuries. Four of these individuals drowned, and one burned to death, but the remaining twenty-one experienced trauma at or around the time of death (perimortem) that would have left evidence on the skeletal remains. Six people died from falls, two from unspecified accidents, and three from gunshot wounds. Two murderers were executed by hanging. A blow to the head killed one man, and another was stabbed to death. A steamboat explosion killed a man, and his son was hit by a train. Another man was crushed between cars at the grain elevator. One man was killed by a sand collapse while digging a privy, and another bled out from a leg amputation following a horseback riding accident. A veteran who was impaled by a metal hook in a lumber mill accident was buried with the hook still imbedded in his chest. Unfortunately, due to poor preservation and the fact that only a small portion of the cemetery was excavated, we were not able to identify any of these people based on skeletal evidence. Two excavated individuals appeared to have perimortem gunshot wounds, and one may have been stabbed, but the historical sources do not provide enough detail to match the observed trauma with the reported wounds.

Because we found little information about those buried in Third Street, we turned instead to comparative data from the City Cemetery, where the majority of the non-Catholic population of Dubuque was buried. An ordinance passed in 1855 required the sexton of the City Cemetery to keep records of all interments, including the name and age of the deceased, the date of burial, and the cause of death. The sexton had to present a monthly report to the city council in order to justify his billing. Some of these reports survived and were transcribed and compiled by a local genealogist. More reports turned up after the initial publication of the records, but we used the first edition, which provided 2,679 entries from 195 months between May 1855 and October 1875.

The records are not perfect. Sometimes cause of death was omitted or illegible. In some cases the sexton perhaps misremembered the details, since the City Cemetery record and the mortality schedule entry for the same individual report different causes of death. Also, we have no way of knowing when the information represents official medical diagnosis and when it is simply family opinion. Doctors may have gotten it wrong as well. Dubuque had a coroner as early as 1838, but autopsies were reserved for unidentified bodies and victims of foul play. Additionally, cause of death may have been misrepresented to the sexton in some instances in order to spare the family embarrassment in the case of something like syphilis or a secret pregnancy.

These caveats aside, the records speak loud and clear. Consumption, now known as pulmonary tuberculosis, killed more people than any other cause, just as in the rest of nineteenth-century America. Consumption accounted for almost 12 percent of the City Cemetery deaths. Nonspecific diarrhea held second place, followed by dysentery (an inflammatory condition causing bloody diarrhea), miscarriage/stillbirth, and lung fever (pneumonia). Though 120 causes of death are listed in the City Cemetery records, these first five causes account for 35 percent of the attributed fatalities. While consumption and pneumonia affected Dubuquers of all ages, diarrhea and dysentery primarily caused the deaths of infants and young children in Dubuque. Entries in the historical sources do not consistently specify whether infants were miscarried prematurely, were stillborn, or died during the birthing process. For the purpose of our research, all individuals who did not survive past birth were counted together as "miscarriage/stillbirth."

Other common causes included cramps (colic), inflammation of the bowel (enteritis), scarlet fever, typhoid, and inflammation of the brain. Inflammation of the brain or spine, known today as meningitis, was the tenth most common cause of death in the City Cemetery. Three other brain-related causes of death appear in the City Cemetery records. Unfortunately, sources on archaic medical terminology indicate that the names do not consistently correlate to modern medical conditions. Brain fever claimed thirty-one individuals, fifteen of whom were infants; congestion of the brain claimed twenty-four individuals (thirteen infants); and "brain disease" claimed fifteen individuals (ten infants). Though not as common as other diseases, the frequency of these conditions, particularly among infants, proved to be important when analyzing the data from the Third Street human remains (see chapter 5). Unlike most of the common causes of death in Dubuque, some brain conditions can leave evidence on the skeletal material.

Surprisingly few people died from childbirth, childbed fever, smallpox, malaria, influenza, rabies, or tetanus. The expected frontier health issues took far less toll than mundane diarrhea. Despite early Dubuque's reputation for lawlessness, only five murder victims were buried during the covered period. Lead poisoning resulted in only three fatalities, though a substantial portion of the population must have been coming in contact with lead on a daily basis. And contrary to local lore, cholera did not sweep through the city on an annual basis, dragging hundreds off to the afterlife prematurely.

Both tuberculosis (TB) and cholera thrived in the nineteenth century, with TB alone causing around 25 percent of deaths in Europe and North America. The causes of both diseases were misunderstood, and antibiotics had not yet been invented to combat them. Unfortunately, better-off people came to associate these illnesses with the poor, without understanding that crowded living conditions and limited access to clean water created breeding grounds for contagion. Big-city newspapers reported that the poor were more prone to disease because of their low morals, intemperate behavior, or cultural inferiority. For most of the 1800s, tuberculosis was believed to be hereditary. Identification of the bacillus in 1882 verified it as a contagious disease, but people did not understand that the disease could be transmitted through the air or contaminated cattle products, primarily milk.

A person could be actively ill with TB for years, allowing for its spread to many others and potentially leaving evidence on his or her skeletal remains. Pulmonary TB attacks the lungs and can cause a buildup of bone on the inner surface of the ribs. Cholera, on the other hand, kills quickly and leaves no mark on the bones. Transmitted through fecal contamination of drinking water, it causes rapid dehydration as a result of diarrhea and vomiting, leading to death in a matter of hours or a few days. The cholera bacillus was not identified until 1883. Epidemics usually occurred during the summer months; current research suggests that the reason for this is that the bacterium is dormant in cool water. Cholera and tuberculosis eventually subsided toward the end of the nineteenth century, probably due in part to major improvements in sanitation and understanding of the causative bacteria and possibly as the result of natural selection.

Though tuberculosis took a considerable toll on the early citizens of Dubuque, cholera did not. In fact, just twenty-two deaths from cholera are listed in the City Cemetery records and the mortality schedules from 1850, 1860, and 1870. Cholera infantum appears more frequently, but this condition is a noncontagious form of gastroenteritis, not the disease caused by the bacterium *Vibrio cholerae*. These records contradict the popular wisdom about mortality in nineteenth-century Dubuque generally and in the Third Street Cemetery specifically. An oft-repeated story about the cemetery asserts that the burial ground filled up as a result of cholera epidemics. So many people died and so quickly that mass graves needed to be dug to keep up with the overwhelming necessity to inter the dead. Variations of this story were told to us by many local residents, including a gas station attendant and the superintendent of Mt. Olivet Cemetery.

We encountered no mass graves during excavations at the site and discovered no historical documentation of the kind of deadly cholera outbreaks that persist in local lore. The major outbreaks in Dubuque occurred prior to the records of the 1850s, 1860s, and 1870s, but details of the episodes appear in histories of Dubuque County, particularly the volume written by Franklin Oldt in 1911. Oldt, whose work draws on city council minutes and other primary sources, mentions seven outbreaks of cholera. During the first epidemic in 1833, Dubuque suffered for three months, and about fifty people died countywide. The next notable outbreak occurred in the summer of 1849, when the disease killed at least eleven people in the city. Oldt does not specify the number of dead from the 1850 and 1851 outbreaks, but the cathedral burial register lists nine cholera deaths for those two years. The generally high mortality rate recorded in the burial register for the summer of 1851 points to a greater number of cholera fatalities, perhaps as high as forty-five, even though cause of death is not listed for most entries. In 1852 the city saw between ten and twenty deaths from cholera. In 1854 an article published in the *St. Paul Express* claimed that the prevalence of cholera was driving people out of Dubuque. The writers of the *Dubuque Weekly Observer* responded that only a few cases had appeared in the city, mainly among boat passengers. Oldt reports no cholera deaths that year. He does not mention cholera in 1855 or 1856 either, though the City Cemetery records indicate a generally high mortality rate for these two summers, perhaps suggesting cholera fatalities. During the last cholera "epidemic" in 1866, several individuals on two steamer ships arrived in the city already sick with the disease. Three of these people died, but the outbreak did not spread to the local population.

Though unfortunate, these deaths hardly add up to the numbers required to fill a cemetery, and the rate of death would not have outpaced a few strong grave diggers. The mass graves of cholera victims that feature in popular memory apparently never existed. Yet Josiah Conzett writes in his memoirs of the terror that gripped the city each summer, with citizens afraid to go to bed at night and hundreds dying each year from 1849 to 1857. Perhaps the number of cholera victims was exaggerated in proportion to the horror of the illness itself. The disease strikes people of all ages, felling the healthy as well as the weak. Symptoms appear without warning, and life can drain away in a matter of hours, with most deaths occurring within two days. Contemporary reports from other cities may have contributed to the mistaken memory as well. In St. Louis, 651 cholera victims succumbed in a single week in 1849. Around 3,500 New Yorkers died of the disease in a two-month period in 1832.

While there were no mass graves, the reported crowding at the cemetery definitely occurred in some areas where coffins were packed close together and stacked. Sometimes the stacking appeared intentional, with the coffins placed neatly within a single grave shaft. In other cases, overlapping grave shafts caused multiple levels of burials. The disintegration of wooden grave markers and the reselling of plots likely caused the intrusive grave digging. The dense concentrations of children's graves on the western boundary of the cemetery could be interpreted as cholera burials, but since the mortality profile of the disease includes people of all ages, this is unlikely. In another area, eight individuals, stacked two and three deep, were interred so close together that separate grave shafts were not discernible. The coffins of the three men, one teenage boy, two children, and two infants displayed no common features that would suggest a family grouping. Initially we believed this cluster might represent a mass grave of sorts. However, the lowest coffins rested at different levels, which indicates they were not placed in the bottom of a large pit during a single burial episode.

Instead, much of the crowding in the cemetery can be explained by its length of use by a large community with relatively high mortality rates by today's standards.

Another aspect of the local cholera mythology, that of surreptitious burials, has some basis in fact. The burial register includes nine entries concerning twenty-three burials made without formal arrangements, such as "2 children have been buried by the parents without giving notice of it to the clergy." Some entries, like this one from 1849, make a clear connection between the disease and the nonconforming burials: "Note 4 persons have been buried in the graveyard and no names were given. They were newcomers and they died of the cholera." Nothing in the burial register implies that these individuals were not Catholics or that the burials were furtive. This aspect of local lore seems to arise from an article published in the 1930s in the Loras College literary magazine, the *Spokesman*. Author John Frantzen relates the story as told by Mrs. James Sullivan, who places the cholera epidemic around 1870 and claims that Bishop Hennessy closed the cemetery because of all the non-Catholics buried just anywhere, even in the paths. Mrs. Sullivan did not witness these events personally; her information came from her parents' stories.

Documentary evidence confirms that some burials occurred without payment or formal ceremony, but the idea that people were sneaking bodies into the cemetery in the dead of night is not supported by facts. Nowhere did we find bodies that were dumped into shallow pits in nothing but winding sheets. In every grave we observed, the living had taken care in burying the dead. All the cemetery inhabitants were buried in coffins placed in level-floored grave shafts. Many coffins contained artifacts indicating formal burial. Osteological analysis cannot identify or exclude cholera as a cause of death, since the disease kills too quickly to leave any mark on the bones, but we have no reason to believe any particular group of graves was epidemic-related.

Despite abundant evidence to the contrary, local newspaper articles about our excavations at the cemetery regularly mentioned some version of the cholera story, unauthorized burials, and mass graves, attributing the information to such authorities as the archdiocese archivist and the superintendent of Mt. Olivet. These publications reinforced the tales already familiar to locals. After all, if it's in the newspaper, it must be true!

The image of grieving immigrant families dragging limp corpses up the bluff by moonlight is much more interesting than the humdrum truth and perhaps much easier to remember. Interestingly, no one ever bothers to explain why the sorrowful non-Catholic families would make the arduous trip up to the Third Street Cemetery instead of sneaking their dead into the City Cemetery on the floodplain just north of downtown.

In some cases, repetition of the cholera-related tales may have been motivated by embarrassment. With the land developer's lawsuit against the Sinsinawa Dominicans proceeding, the strongly Catholic community was perhaps anxious to offer an innocent explanation for why so many of the dead still rested on the bluff. If the burials were unrecorded, then the authorities charged with moving the graves would have had no idea they were there and could not have been expected to move them. And certainly the sisters could not be expected to know about graves that even the archdiocese did not know existed. The flaw in this logic, of course, is that the archdiocese workers had no map of the plots to guide them when they moved some of the graves in the 1940s. They had no idea where *any* of the unmarked burials were, so whether or not the deceased appeared in the very incomplete burial register proves irrelevant.

Just as cholera did not play the outsize role regularly attributed to it during the cemetery's usage, the number of deaths from accident or injury also seems low, particularly when compared to the frequent reporting of such incidents by the contemporary local press. Many of the gruesome train accidents and tragic suicides described in detail in the news occurred elsewhere in the region and were included mainly for the purpose of boosting newspaper sales. Only 7 percent of the deaths recorded in the City Cemetery records fall into the accident/injury category. Accidents, including falls, boiler explosions, factory mishaps, mine collapse fatalities, railroad accidents, house fires, accidental scalding, and injuries from horses and runaway wagons, claimed only ninety lives. Drowning claimed seventy-six lives. Twelve people committed suicide by hanging, shooting, poisoning, or drowning themselves. Five people were murdered, two of whom were shot, and one of whom was poisoned. The exposure category—freezing, sunstroke, and lightning—claimed eight lives. Three died of war wounds. The remaining two were listed as "died in jail" with no cause specified.

Though the City Cemetery records reflect the mortality of the portion of the population that was definitely *not* buried at Third Street, there is no evidence that living conditions were any different for the Catholics and non-Catholics of Dubuque. In both populations, some families were well off, while others lived in squalor. From the 1830s through the 1860s, everyone in town lived with the same rudimentary municipal sanitation. The entire city relied on wells for water prior to the creation of the public waterworks in 1870. The city installed sewers prior to 1852, but it seems these were merely storm drains. Privies serviced most homes until 1886, when a sewer system was created to carry wastewater away from downtown homes. Who was responsible for animal waste removal? The histories are silent on the subject, but by 1865 the streets had become so filthy in general that a group of citizens formed a brigade to clean them. Unclean water, spoiled food, and the unhampered spread of contagious diseases all contributed to the death toll in the city.

The level of medical care available to the sick probably depended on the wealth of the family. Patent medicines—widely advertised "cures" that often consisted of narcotics or stimulants in an alcohol base—were as plentiful, varied, and affordable as they were useless or even detrimental. The first doctor arrived in Dubuque in 1833, and practitioners formed a county medical society in 1852. The city established its first hospital in 1845, and several others opened during the years, including temporary hospitals for cholera in 1852 and smallpox in 1856. Mercy Hospital, which was still operating at the time of our excavation, opened in 1879. Unfortunately, even the best medical care available at the time would not have helped those who were dying from consumption. The antibiotics required to cure tuberculosis were not developed until the twentieth century.

The 1880s mark the end of the use of the Third Street Cemetery and the beginning of the modernization of the town. That decade saw the rise of Dubuque as a manufacturing center, as well as the introduction of gas, water, and electric utilities city-wide. In 1880, out of all the U.S. states and territories, Iowa boasted the highest percentage of people over the age of ten who could read. The 22,000 citizens of Dubuque were focusing on the future and the dawning of the next century. The graves of the laborers, miners, farmers, boatmen, tradesmen, businessmen, shopkeepers, saloonkeepers, merchants, politicians, and veterans in the overgrown lot on Third Street were, perhaps understandably, a low priority.

FOUR

Abandoned to Desecration, 1880–2013

FROM THE END OF THE ACTIVE PERIOD to the summer of 1939, the cemetery appeared in numerous newspaper articles decrying the disgraceful state of the property, once again an overgrown wilderness where livestock roamed free. In addition to the ravages of nature and domesticated animals, the cemetery suffered from perennial vandalism by boys who delighted in tipping over grave markers. The residents of the houses on Cardiff Street, on the western boundary of the cemetery, dumped trash on the abandoned grounds and occasionally dug trash pits into the graves. The tract, which had been unkempt even during its use, had become a nuisance property.

Two newspaper items illustrate the kind of mischief that occurred from time to time on the bluff. One Sunday night at eleven o'clock, the neighborhood awoke to shrieks coming from the graveyard. The next morning, a pool of gore and bloody fingerprints on the fence hinted at a violent event. Four nights later, two women were seen on the bluff squabbling over possession of a bloody shirt that belonged to the stabbing victim, Mike. Both women claimed to be the object of Mike's affection, and they tore the shirt in two during their fray. In 1901 members of a high school fraternity used the burial ground for their initiation rites. They blindfolded four candidates, marched them to the graveyard in the middle of the night, and left them tied to fallen tombstones. If these incidents made the papers, one can only imagine the kind of everyday shenanigans happening in the graveyard.

Some of the people who disturbed the cemetery were motivated by dreams of treasure, probing the soil on the bluff in search of the fabled chest of gold. During the excavation, "Have you found Kelly's gold yet?" was a common refrain among the people who visited the excavation or learned that we were the ones conducting it. We heard a variety of stories about Thomas Kelly. Later, we came across newspaper articles and other resources recounting his infamous life and death. That Kelly was a lead miner was true, and he did own the property on the bluff top south of the cemetery and also the land including Outlot 723, which his sister eventually sold to the diocese. One story claims that he refused to pay his miners, hoarding their wages (in gold?) for himself. He died a miser, and before his death he buried his gold somewhere on the bluff. Another version claims that he buried the treasure to spite his siblings and deny them an inheritance. Yet a third version argues that Kelly hoarded his personal wealth rather than wages withheld from his workers. If we had found Kelly's gold, we swore we would share it with everyone who ever asked us about it, with equal amounts spread among the crew members. No such luck.

Born in Ireland in 1808, Thomas Kelly worked in New York and New Orleans before coming to the mining region of Galena, Illinois, in 1830. He began sneaking across the Mississippi River to mine in the Dubuque area in 1832, before the beginning of the Black Hawk War, spending his nights digging lead ore and his days hiding out on one of the many islands in the river. In 1833 he began mining the area that became known as Kelly's Bluff, was wildly successful, and made oodles of money. He patented his land claims in 1843 and 1845. The estimated value of his property upon his death in May 1867 ranged from $50,000 to $200,000. Despite his apparent wealth, he did not pay his taxes, nor was he charitable to any needy soul or organization within the city of Dubuque. He never attended church, and he lived in what was little more than a shack on Kelly's Bluff.

Kelly was even reputed to have killed a man around 1850 in St. Louis or Albany, depending on which version of his life story one believes. In the Albany version, Kelly spent one or two years in an insane asylum, from which he escaped and returned to Dubuque. Perhaps what describes Kelly most clearly is that "while few could say he had done the world any particular good, all agreed that he was a bright example of a continually honest man, and that he had no vices."[1] Three of his six siblings survived his death and lived in or near Dubuque, inheriting his property and the back taxes owed. Because he was not a practicing Catholic, when Kelly met the end of his days at age fifty-eight, he could not be buried in the Third Street Cemetery, even though it was right next to his humble residence.

But what of his accumulated wealth? Where did all the gold go? He reportedly buried it in a secret location—on Kelly's Bluff or one of his other properties—down an old mine shaft or in a secretly excavated hole in the ground. Many people believe it's out there somewhere and are still looking for it. There might be as much mythology built up around Thomas Kelly as there is around the Third Street Cemetery. Oral tradition provided by the Dubuque County Historical Society maintains that locals have unearthed four portions of his buried treasure over the years. A boy named Peter Fortune reportedly found $1,200 in gold in a can while the Kelly heirs were still alive. He turned the money over to one of the brothers and was rewarded with a watch. The next find, $1,800, was also turned over to the Kelly family. Two boys tending cattle supposedly found a trunk containing $10,000 in gold coins but received no reward. Finally, in 1914 workmen digging the new reservoir uncovered $500 in silver coins.

Whether or not the legend of the gold is true, we found possible evidence of the eager search for it. Pits dug into the cemetery grounds, sometimes intruding on grave shafts, may have been the result of the fruitless quest for the hoard. At the edge of one grave we found a buried iron pot, but—alas!—it was filled with only dirt and cinders. Like so much of the mythology that surrounds the hermit miner, Kelly's gold may be more fantasy than fact.

THE FADING OF THE THIRD STREET CEMETERY

Over the years, the archdiocese considered several different plans to improve the cemetery or to use the land for another purpose. In 1896 the newly elevated Archbishop Hennessy announced that a seminary was to be built on the bluff property just south of the cemetery. A newspaper reporter mused that the cemetery would probably be converted into a park for the seminary students. Whether or not this was actually part of the plan, the archdiocese did not remove the graves at this time. In fact, the construction of the school barely got under way before the project was canceled and the land was placed in a trust for the establishment of a future seminary. The footprint of the completed seminary foundations can be seen on the 1906 city plat (figure 8), which shows the cemetery occupying its original lot only.

FIGURE 8. 1906 map of Dubuque, Iowa, showing the location of the planned semi-nary in relation to the Third Street Cemetery (redrawn by Tyler Perkins from the *Map of the City of Dubuque,* Iowa Publishing Company, 1906).

Meanwhile, detailed descriptions of lengthy funerals and lavishly deco-rated coffins printed in the Dubuque newspapers demonstrate that the beautification of death movement had reached its height in the city. As a consequence, the Catholic community focused on improving the newer, rural cemetery to the south of town. In January 1901 the new archbishop, John Joseph Keane, announced his plan to enlarge and beautify Key West Cemetery and place it under the control of a corporation, the Mt. Olivet

Cemetery Association, which would also manage the Third Street Cemetery. Within months, the association announced plans to remove as many
bodies as possible from the old cemetery, grade the land to make a "proper
and sightly lawn," and erect a monument to the pioneers on the bluff. This
proposal was modified to a self-service program within a few months; the
sexton of Mt. Olivet sent a work crew to clear the brush from the Third
Street Cemetery so that those wishing to remove their dead could find the
graves. The Mt. Olivet Cemetery Association announced in 1904 that it
planned to erect a large marble cross at the Third Street Cemetery to hon-
or the pioneer Catholics buried there. This plan also fell by the wayside.

In 1908 the issue of who owned the bluff-top graveyard was finally
resolved when Congress passed a bill granting title to St. Raphael's Cemetery to the archbishop of Dubuque. The decision of the Committee on
Public Lands was based largely on the 1838 plat map, which showed the
lot as a Catholic cemetery, and the fact that the General Land Office had
no records of further actions regarding the property. In 1922 Archbishop James J. Keane (no relation to John Joseph Keane) obtained a patent,
as corporation sole, for the original cemetery lot. Finally in possession
of legal title to the cemetery, the archdiocese apparently made its first
attempt to sell the land in 1925. A surveyor created a plat dividing the bluff
top into 116 residential lots. We never discovered why the subdivision plan
was abandoned; however, two issues still stood in the way of a land sale.
The first problem, of course, was the continued presence of a large number
of graves on the property. The second was the trust established by Archbishop Hennessy when his dream of a seminary was put on hold.

A real estate agent approached the archdiocese in 1939 with a potential buyer and a proposal. The buyer would purchase the entire bluff top,
except for the 5.29 acres encompassing the cemetery. At $600.00 an acre,
the total price came to $9,239.40. The sale never went through, but in
1945 the archdiocese offered the property to the Dominican sisters at Sinsinawa, Wisconsin, at a deep discount. The order was looking for a site
on which to build a rest home for elderly sisters, and the bluff location
provided easy access to Mercy Hospital. And the sale was quite a bar-
gain at $8,000, around $500 per acre for land described as being about
sixteen acres. When the sale went through in 1946, the Dominican sisters received a deed to the entire 20.7-acre property, though it seems the

cemetery portion had been subtracted from the price calculation. A plat produced around the time of the sale once again shows only the original cemetery lot, without the addition.

The vicar-general for the archdiocese, Monsignor D. V. Foley, worked with a team of lawyers to overcome several legal impediments to the sale. They spent almost a year compiling an abstract for the various lots, working around Bishop Hennessy's seminary trust, and ensuring that lateral heirs had no plans to make claims on the property. Meanwhile, Monsignor Foley was also making arrangements for the removal of the few graves he believed remained on the property, having assured the sisters that the land would be cleared when they took possession. He applied to the Department of Health for a disinterment permit, providing a list of twelve names gathered from headstones still in place in the cemetery. In 1948 Ashworth and Bennett Funeral Residence presented a bill to the archdiocese for the removal and reinterment at Mt. Olivet of eleven bodies. No other record of the reburial exists. Since the headstones listed on the permit (and many others) ended up in the Third Street Cemetery section of Mt. Olivet, we assume the human remains were reburied in the vicinity as well.

As far as the general public was concerned, that was the end of the cemetery. Archbishop Henry Rohlman turned the first spade of earth at the ground-breaking ceremony for the St. Dominic Villa in April 1948. The Villa, which operated from 1949 to 2000, occupied the scenic platform to the south of the cemetery, facing a grassy, level lawn to the north.

At the beginning of our project, we had only archaeological evidence of a serious disturbance to the cemetery. The large, level spot at the center of the project area was completely devoid of burials, and the graves on the edge of the void were truncated, some missing heads on the eastern edge and legs on the west. Comparisons of aerial photographs from the 1930s, 1940s, and 1950s led us to believe the disturbance occurred around the time of the Villa construction. Later, we gained access to eyewitness testimony collected in depositions taken for the recent lawsuit over the site, which provided unsettling details concerning activity on the property during the fall of 1948.

Two Mercy Hospital nursing students who visited the building site that autumn recalled seeing a mound of human remains and loose bones scattered haphazardly across the ground. They returned to the site many times over the course of several weeks, their interest kindled by their anatomy studies. Each time, they saw new piles of bones. The shallow excavation they observed suggests that these graves were disturbed during the earth-moving that leveled the lawn area rather than the digging of the Villa foundations. Two other eyewitnesses, a steelworker employed at the site and the son of a contractor, gave testimony supporting the nurses' story.

All four witnesses repeated the same story about a metal casket unearthed on the site. The child-sized casket was intact, and through the viewing pane they could see a little body in a white dress and bon-net. When the casket was removed from the ground, the viewing pane cracked, and with the vacuum seal broken, the body disintegrated. Each witness claimed to have personally observed the casket, but all had heard from someone else about the moment when the body collapsed. The vivid image conjured by this magical returning to dust may explain why all of the witnesses recalled the event more than sixty years later.

Perhaps the staff of the archdiocese honestly believed that most of the burials had been previously removed. The discovery of perhaps hundreds of intact graves, then, must have been quite a shock to the workers. One can imagine the frantic phone calls that may have followed the first day of earthmoving at the site. Someone at the archdiocese made the decision to proceed with the project, and the vicar-general applied for a blanket disinterment permit in July 1948. The response from the Department of Health stated that a blanket permit could not be issued but that disinter-ments should be made without permits. That's certainly a confounding way to avoid responsibility.

This mass disinterment definitely occurred. But what happened to the remains? The eyewitnesses claimed that someone came at the end of each day to collect the bones and take them to a cemetery. Only one of them actually saw such a pickup, though, and he indicated that someone from Hoffmann Mortuary, not Ashworth and Bennett, came for the remains. Mt. Olivet Cemetery has no records of mass reburials, but forty-five grave markers from Third Street were apparently moved to the newer cemetery around this time. In 1976 two members of the Sisters of Charity of the Blessed Virgin Mary went to Mt. Olivet to relocate the grave of Sister Mary Francis O'Reilly, who they believed was moved from Third Street in the 1940s. The sexton of Mt. Olivet at the time gave them a wildly incorrect account of the removals, claiming that bones had not been preserved at Third Street and that boxes containing symbolic grave dirt had been buried in a grassy area, which he indicated with a vague gesture. The current superintendent of Mt. Olivet has stated that he does not know of any place on the property where hundreds of remains could have been deposited together without these bones being encountered during burials in the years since he took charge of the cemetery in 1991. Unfortunately, the narrow scope of our project did not allow for remote sensing (like ground-penetrating radar) at Mt. Olivet, which could have established whether or not there were large burial features in the Third Street Cemetery section or on the northernmost point of the grounds, another reported mass grave location. The question of where the skeletons unearthed in the 1940s went must remain unanswered for now.

After the St. Dominic Villa opened in 1949, the property remained unaltered until 1968, when the sisters sold a portion of the grounds they had never used. The land sale included the bulk of the original cemetery lot and the northern half of the cemetery addition. From the time of this sale onward, these land parcels were sold and resold, combined and subdivided and renamed, until only a tiny tract—one-fifth of an acre of the Villa property—still bore the name "Roman Catholic Grave Yard" on legal documents. When development of these land parcels finally began in the 1970s, the local newspaper reported that workers discovered two sets of human remains in the cemetery addition while preparing the grounds for the construction of Kelly's Bluff Condominiums. Hoffmann Mortuary transported the skeletal material to Mt. Olivet for reburial in an unspecified location, and the condos opened in 1978. The adjoining lot, which includes most of the original cemetery grounds, lay undeveloped until 1993. Viewed today, both properties are level. Flattening the natural slope would have required the removal of several feet of soil. And only two skeletons were found?

Again, the depositions for the lawsuit against the Dominican sisters tell the real story. When workers first encountered human remains at the condominium building site in 1972, the landowners contacted the director of the Catholic Cemeteries of Dubuque, who assured them that Catholic Cemeteries, Inc., would cover the removal and reburial expenses. He also expressed the opinion that the encounter would prove to be an isolated incident. Other factors, including the death of one of the developers, delayed the project for four years. In 1976, when work resumed, the director received another phone call from the developers, who claimed that there were bodies all over the site. According to the director's deposition, the landowner said there was no way to keep things discreet, because the equipment operators had gone down to a bar already and were probably telling everyone they could find about the skeletons. The director visited the site, saw the remains in a small area of excavation, and arranged for their removal by Hoffmann Mortuary. He was unaware of any other remains turning up at the site after this.

A subcontractor on the condo project picked up the story from there. He recalled encountering human bones while performing the cut-and-fill grading done prior to construction. Though he emphasized in the deposition that his memory was vague, he estimated that he saw bones during twenty or thirty days on the project and that the remains were found in an area measuring about three hundred by four hundred feet. His estimate seems fairly accurate, given that the leveled area on the condo property and the adjoining lot measures almost exactly 120,000 square feet. No one contacted Hoffmann Mortuary about these bones, however. The fill dirt, bones and all, was dumped at another construction site in town near the intersection of John F. Kennedy Road and Pennsylvania Avenue. Another deposed witness identified the dump site more specifically as the current location of the Hospice of Dubuque. We visited the site but found nothing, of course. If the remains of Dubuque's pioneer dead are resting beneath this location, they are well concealed under concrete and asphalt. There's a certain mordant appropriateness in the bones resting beneath a hospice.

The discovery of graves disrupted construction once again in 1994, when the current owner of the original cemetery lot told workmen to shave off some of the slope and build a retaining wall near his newly completed home. Four burials were exposed in the process. Because Iowa's Ancient Burial Protection Law had been passed since the last incident, this property owner had to consult the Office of the State Archaeologist and the Iowa Department of Public Health and obtain a disinterment permit. The OSA staff excavated the four burials, and the remains were reinterred at Mt. Olivet Cemetery in September 1994.

While the previous grave removals were kept relatively quiet, the excavation in 1994 attracted media attention. Two articles in the *Telegraph*

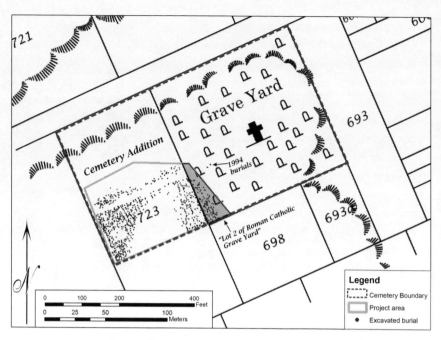

FIGURE 9. Map showing the original cemetery lot, the cemetery addition in Outlot 723, the location of the 1994 excavations, and "Lot 2 of Roman Catholic Grave Yard."

Herald provided detailed accounts of the project, as well as the (incorrect) history of the cemetery. One cannot help but wonder how the Dominican sisters continued to believe that the last of the graves had been removed from the cemetery in the 1940s. And why was the subsequent landowner, a Dubuque County native, surprised to find burials on the Villa property, which he bought in 2002 "as is," "where is," and "with all faults"? To be fair, both parties probably believed the graves had been moved previously, and neither could have predicted the *number* of burials that were eventually found. Since none of the maps available to them showed Outlot 723 as an addition to the cemetery, only the one-fifth-acre portion labeled "Lot 2 of Roman Catholic Grave Yard" appeared to have the potential for graves (figure 9). The discovery of over nine hundred burials surprised everyone, including the excavation team.

HOW COULD SO MANY PEOPLE have been left behind? we wondered. As our research progressed, our question changed: Why did everyone think the graves had been moved? In local lore, the moving of the graves usually follows the closing of the cemetery. The dates of the closing generally relate to the reasons given for why burials were no longer permitted. People believed the cemetery closed in 1856 because it was full of cholera victims or in 1867 because the bishop was upset about the presence of non-Catholics. The closing in the 1870s was thought to be due to the land dispute. In fact, Bishop Hennessy closed the cemetery for only one year, from 1867 to its reopening in 1868. No official announcement followed the last reported interment in 1880. The cemetery simply fell out of use.

Moreover, neither Bishop Hennessy nor the archdiocese ever issued an official request or demand that parishioners remove their loved ones from the cemetery. The subject of moving the graves came up when construction of the seminary began and again when the Mt. Olivet Cemetery Association took charge of the Third Street Cemetery. First, the cemetery association planned to coordinate the removals. Then they cleared the ground so that families could collect the dead themselves. A few graves were probably moved at this time, as well as earlier. Many headstones scattered throughout Mt. Olivet bear death dates that predate the opening of Mt. Olivet Cemetery, indicating that the individuals were buried somewhere else originally. Even while the Third Street Cemetery was still in use, some families may have chosen to move their dead to new family plots in better-maintained graveyards.

As late as 1904, anyone who read the Dubuque newspaper would have known from the cemetery association announcements that most of the graves on the bluff still lay undisturbed. A 1906 article about an outing to the burial ground states that visitors are "at every step treading upon the graves of Dubuque's earliest settlers."[2] Just eight years later, an article about the bluff-top cemetery states unequivocally that Bishop Hennessy ordered all burials to be removed in 1867 or 1868 but that many bodies "were not and have not yet been removed."[3] A 1931 article that attributes the cemetery removal to the seminary building period states, "Most of the bodies were removed, either by relatives—or if none were living any longer, by the diocese."[4] News items up to 1939 repeat the claim that most, but not all, of the dead had been disinterred.

The shifting details in the newspaper articles may have arisen from a simple lack of research on the part of the reporters. These misconceptions then became part of the oral version of the story. Alternately, the later articles may reflect the already-imperfect memory of the community, transmitted with slight alterations to each new generation. The fact that the stories appeared in print gave credence to the tales told by Uncle Ned or Great-Grandma.

Another, similar event in Dubuque's history may have contributed to the mistaken memory of the Third Street Cemetery. In the 1850s the city opened a new nondenominational graveyard north of town (now known as Linwood Cemetery) and closed the existing City Cemetery. The city council published a notice in the newspaper informing all persons who had friends or family interred in the old graveyard that the burials had to be removed. The city sexton and a crew of hired men disinterred the remainder of the dead, and the land became the public park called Jackson Square. Recollections of this official and orderly cemetery removal may have gotten mixed up with tales of the Third Street Cemetery. Of course, the City Cemetery story did not really end with the dedication of the park. Twelve years later, when the park was graded and remodeled, workers discovered that many burials had been left behind. The city council accused the contractor of leaving the bodies heaped together and exposed on-site for days at a time, as well as using soil containing bones as fill dirt on other construction projects, including a railroad berm. The scandal hit Dubuque just a few months before Mayor Knight's cemetery-mining fiasco, and at least one of the newspaper editorials mentions both desecrations. These circumstances may have led to further confusion of the details from the two separate burial grounds.

The lack of grave markers at Third Street also helped perpetuate the belief that most of the underground residents had been moved. In 1939 a visitor to the recently cleaned-up graveyard remarked that approximately forty headstones still stood on the grounds. Adding up the markers that were moved to Mt. Olivet, those documented in historical sources, and the fragmentary markers discovered during our excavations, we have evidence for just 113 headstones. This number seems extremely low for a cemetery with around six thousand graves, especially in an urban community with plentiful native stone and multiple stonecutters advertising monument-design services. A single preserved piece of wooden stake found at the head of a burial in 2007 suggested that graves at Third Street may have been marked with wooden crosses. However, archaeological excavations at contemporary cemeteries, such as Elmbank Catholic Cemetery in Ontario and the Old Irish Cemetery in Illinois, yielded evidence that a higher percentage of those graves had stone monuments than we found at Third Street. The surreptitious removal over time of stones from the derelict cemetery might explain the low numbers. Interestingly, we found documentation that the headstone of Sister Mary Francis O'Reilly disappeared as early as 1885. And unknown persons absconded with a grave marker resting in the alley beside the site during our excavation work in 2007–8.

The people of Dubuque had plenty of good reasons for thinking the cemetery was all but empty by the 1940s. The question remains: Why didn't the archdiocese know better? The vicar-general who coordinated the land sale, Monsignor Foley, had full access to the archdiocese archives. Yet his initial request to the Department of Health indicates that his investigation went no further than reading the twelve still-standing headstones and skimming the phone books and city directories for possible relatives. Once construction work began at the Villa, Foley would have been among the first to know that the story of grave removals was a myth. By keeping the discovery hushed up, he kept the myth alive and added a new chapter. Subsequent news articles claim that all burials remaining on the bluff in the 1940s were moved by the archdiocese.

Unwittingly, we, too, contributed to the local lore. Given all the media coverage of our project, the average person on the street in Dubuque is now doubly certain that all of the burials have been removed from the Third Street Cemetery. By notifying the Dubuque Planning Services Department and publishing our report and this book, we hope to spread the truth: some of Dubuque's pioneers still lie on Kelly's Bluff.

One hundred and eighty years ago, the story began with the funeral of the first Catholic who died in Dubuque, someone who perhaps hoped to mine the bluffs and ended up buried in them instead. The tale concludes, for the moment, in 2013 with the completion of our project, the publication of our technical report, and the reinterment of the dead. The history presented above, uncommonly tumultuous for a "resting place," required perseverance and healthy skepticism to compile. Local lore and misinformation thwarted our research at every turn. An issue as simple as establishing the boundaries of the cemetery was resolved only by ignoring common wisdom and legal documents and by delving deeper. Local myths about cholera epidemics, mass graves, and the buried treasure of a miserly miner all contributed to the confusion surrounding the cemetery. Slowly, through careful excavation and painstaking research, we have unraveled some of these tangled tales.

Having established as much of the Third Street Cemetery's history as the records allow and challenged a few of the myths that surround it, we now turn to the skeletal remains to discover what they can reveal. Lacking accurate cemetery records, we look to the skeletons and the objects in the graves to learn more about the people at Third Street and the families who laid them to rest.

FIVE

The Untold Story

STUDYING THE SKELETAL REMAINS, grave goods, and coffins makes it possible to limn a picture of life and death in nineteenth-century Dubuque. While each of these separate examinations is essential to our understanding, by combining them we can begin to see individual stories of life and death. Changes in coffins and grave goods (items buried with the dead) during the cemetery's half-century of active use reflect the influence of the beautification of death movement in the mid-nineteenth century. We can learn much about the cemetery population from general observations about age, sex, disease processes, and cause of death.

The greatest obstacle to our analysis of the Third Street Cemetery materials proved to be poor preservation. Burials with most of the remains complete yield detailed information about the individual's life and death. However, the skeletons were most often in moderate to poor condition, and the bones of young children and infants were particularly degraded. As a result, what we could learn from the bones was in many ways limited. The younger infant burials often contained little more than teeth, for example. The bones were in bad shape in part because the site's soils retained water, leading to more rapid degeneration. The soil was also acidic, again promoting decay. Burrowing animals such as groundhogs and pocket gophers, tree root infiltration, and burial disturbance in the past all contributed to the poor condition. Despite these limitations, we found some vestiges of flesh, including desiccated brain tissue and skin, in addition to head hair, pubic hair, and chest hair. The hair in a few women's burials retained the coiffure created for the funeral, with the tresses twisted or braided into a bun or chignon. These organic materials frequently survived because they were close to rosaries, religious medals, and other copper-alloy objects. The toxic salts from corroded copper discourage decomposition. But such organic remnants were the exception.

Those of us who study human bones use certain techniques to determine age, sex, and stature. Generally, age can be assessed in children by how much their baby (deciduous) and permanent teeth have developed or by the length of their bones. Estimating age for adults is much more complex, and one must take into account factors such as diet, which can affect tooth wear, and diseases that can mimic changes seen in older adults (e.g., arthritis). One way of estimating a more specific age for an adult involves evaluating two surfaces on the pelvis; another method notes changes in the ends of ribs. Most often, we are able to provide a general age range, such as young, middle, or old adult, by looking at a number of characteristics. The cranium and pelvis provide the best evidence for evaluating sex. The cranium of a woman is generally more gracile, or slight, than that of a man, but variation is often population-specific. Differences in the shape of the three bones comprising the pelvis (left and right innominates and the sacrum) distinguish men from women. In general, women's "hips" are broader and have a wider opening to accommodate the birthing process. We calculate stature based on measurements of long bones (the bones of the arms and legs) using formulae developed from people of known height.

Out of the 939 burials we excavated, 889 contained human remains.[1] The 393 adults include 205 males, 125 females, and 63 individuals for whom sex could not be determined. The 496 subadults (youths and children less than twenty-one years old) account for the larger portion of the burials. The reason why we found more children than adults could be simply that more young people were buried in the portion of the cemetery excavated, or perhaps because virulent diseases affected the city's youngest members disproportionately. The average man stood approximately five feet seven inches and the average woman five feet one inch tall. These heights are almost identical to average prefamine statures in Ireland in the mid-nineteenth century. Two nineteenth-century American cemeteries excavated in recent decades, the Milwaukee County Institution Grounds and Alameda-Stone Cemetery in Tucson, Arizona, yielded similar stature estimates for men and women. Poor nutrition or disease may account for why these Dubuque residents were on the short side, or it may reflect ethnicity. Irish and German immigrants constituted the majority of the Catholic community of Dubuque. Only one excavated person displayed evidence of being of non-European descent.

Based on adult age estimates, the Third Street Cemetery men lived longer than women. While 37 percent of the men died by the time they reached fifty years, over half of the women in this same age group had died. Three-fourths of the children had died by the age of two and a half years. Near-term fetuses and newborns were among the dead at Third Street. Why did so many infants and children die so young? Their small bodies were vulnerable to a number of factors, including the health of the pregnant mother, birthing trauma, disease, nutritional deficiencies, poor sanitation, and tainted milk. Many of these factors would afflict children at the time when they were weaned. Suddenly deprived of the natural immunities and nutrition supplied by their mothers' milk, children's health diminished, and drinking cow's milk or water exposed them to certain pathogens for the first time. It was likely an uphill battle to survive to early childhood in nineteenth-century Dubuque. Imagine the feelings of new parents as they feared that the odds of their infants' survival could be slim.

POOR DENTAL HEALTH

In the younger child and infant burials, teeth often were the only remains preserved and became an essential component for determining age. Dental remains also revealed much about the dental health of the adults and the population as a whole. The people of Dubuque generally had bad teeth. Nearly 60 percent of all people excavated had at least one cavity (carious lesion), while 44 percent of the adults suffered from dental abscesses. Over half of them had lost at least one tooth antemortem (before their death), and eight had lost all their teeth during their lifetimes. In the better-preserved dental remains, nearly all individuals displayed some degree of tartar (calculus) buildup, and this was likely true of the general Dubuque population. It was not surprising that Dubuquers (among many Americans) had poor dental hygiene. Toothbrushes had not come into common usage, and people did not go to the dentist for an annual cleaning. Mass production of toothbrushes in the United States began around 1885, after the Third Street Cemetery apparently no longer was in use. The number of cavities and dental abscesses we saw suggests that a large portion of Dubuque residents in this period had very bad breath and likely suffered from pain.

Over one-third of the cemetery's dead displayed what are called "enamel hypoplastic defects"—grooves or pits in the teeth where the dental enamel fails to form properly as the permanent teeth develop. Periods of disease or nutritional stress cause these defects. All teeth form from the chewing surface toward the root, backward from what most people imagine. Deciduous teeth begin forming as the jaws develop in the womb and start erupting around six months of age. The permanent teeth develop in the mandible and maxilla (lower and upper jaws) not long after birth, with the first permanent molar erupting at around age six. It is while these teeth are still in the formative stage that the laying down of the enamel can be disrupted. Since dental enamel forms at a relatively predictable rate, we can measure the location of a particular defect and estimate when the defect occurred within a six-month range. Therefore, we can tell that a particular person suffered a period of nutrition- or disease-related stress at a particular age, such as between 2 and 2½ years. In general, the more defects an individual displays, the more periods of stress he or she endured and survived. In the Third Street Cemetery population, defects most commonly occurred during the age range that coincides with weaning, supporting the idea that this was a very stressful period for young children.

Though the prevalence of tooth decay suggests few people could afford their services, several dentists worked in the area. The 1856 Iowa state census for Julien Township of Dubuque County lists five dentists, and the local newspapers and city directories ran their advertisements. We found archaeological evidence of their work, too—teeth containing gold fillings showed up in nine burials. Burial 64, identified as Susan Blake (see chapter 9), had nine fillings in six upper teeth. While people might also have cavities in their back teeth, the front teeth more frequently contained fillings, particularly the upper incisors.

Additional evidence of dentists at work came from the recovery of three different dental appliances. A middle-aged to older man had a ceramic false tooth replacing his upper right central incisor. The remains of a female adult included a gold or gold alloy partial denture with false upper lateral incisors. An older woman was buried with a complete upper jaw denture placed, oddly enough, under her right elbow. Her coffin had a hinged lid for viewing, so you would expect the denture to be placed in her mouth. Instead, it may have been a last-minute addition to the burial, hidden under the right arm. The denture was composed of vulcanized rubber, pinkish in color, with white ceramic teeth. A local dentist advertised this same type of denture in the 1856–57 Dubuque city directory. Like many of the gold fillings, these dental appliances improved the look of the individual's smile or the teeth that showed when they were talking, rather than simply serving the utilitarian purpose of making it easier to chew.

One of the more interesting dental findings was artificial wear on the teeth of ninety-six adults, or nearly one-fourth of the adult population. They all displayed cupped wear on the occlusal (chewing) surface of their teeth, a sign that they had habitually clenched a pipe stem in the mouth. We identified twelve of these adults as women and eighty-two as men. Pipe smoking must have been common behavior for both sexes. A few additional people with small notches in the upper front teeth likely held pins or nails in their mouths habitually.

Of the 145 adults displaying dental crowding and tooth rotation, the most commonly crowded teeth were those in the front of the lower jaw or mandible. Today, many people with crowded teeth seek out a good orthodontist to have those teeth straightened, but this option was not available in the nineteenth century. Dental crowding is particularly prevalent in the populations of the British Isles, and indeed, many of Dubuque's residents came from Ireland. We frequently observed another dental trait among the Third Street people—the congenital absence of third molars, or wisdom teeth. About 20 percent of people in modern populations exhibit this trait worldwide.

DISEASES LEAVING THEIR MARK

When disease or trauma affects bone, this tissue responds in one of two ways: by decreasing or increasing (destroying bone or laying down new bone). We may lose bone content, such as in the case of osteoporosis, or we may find our bones responding to trauma, such as a fracture or a systemic disease like tuberculosis, by laying down new layers of bone on top of the existing bone. Sometimes both processes can occur at the same time, depending on the disease or traumatic event. By examining bones in light of how they respond to stress, the trained skeletal biologist or physical anthropologist can suggest possible causes for any anomalies, such as disease, trauma, and general aging processes. However, because of the limited ways in which bone reacts, it is often difficult to attribute particular changes on a bone to a specific disease. Moreover, many disorders do not leave any signs of their presence on the bones. As anyone who has ever broken a bone knows, the healing process takes time. Short-term diseases such as dysentery and pneumonia leave no marks on the skeletal remains, so we found no evidence of these virulent diseases, even though we know from historical sources that they caused many deaths during the active period of the cemetery's use. According to the World Health Organization, dysentery and pneumonia are still two of the three leading causes of death in children under five years.

We noted evidence of disease on many individuals, particularly the adults. The condition we observed most often was degenerative joint disease, present in 163 adults. It manifests on the bones in the form of bony spicules called osteophytes, which can become quite large with continued stress to the joint. Also typical of this condition is the wearing down of joint surfaces. These pathologies / bony changes are usually associated with arthritis. The spine, hips, and hands were the most frequently affected areas of the skeleton. Generally, the degenerative changes we found were mild to moderate; we rarely saw severe arthritis. Degenerative joint disease can result from repeated, habitual physical activity, such as shoveling or swinging a pickax or typing at a computer. It can result from trauma as well. And unfortunately, it is also part of the aging process, as any older individual with creaky bones and sore joints can attest.

Another condition we observed on many people's bones was periostitis, a nonspecific infection that affected sixty-eight of the individuals. Inflammatory processes cause periostitis, and the bones respond by laying down new bone, creating a rough-textured surface. It can result from some systemic infection or be related to trauma, such as an infection following a bone fracture. Skeletal biologists most often observe this growth on long bone shafts. A bone fracture followed by infection can result in swelling, pain, and possibly pus on the skin surface. Once the infection sets in and starts affecting one bone, it can travel to other bones, so that a broken lower leg bone can end up affecting some or all of the bones of the leg and foot. Given the poor condition of the remains we found in the Third Street Cemetery, the occurrence of this medical condition was probably much higher than we observed.

Twenty individuals showed signs of osteoporosis, or loss of bone mineral density. People with this affliction often suffer from collapse of the vertebrae, leading to a humped back and stooped appearance. They are also extremely susceptible to bone fracture in response to even the most minor trauma, sometimes just in the act of walking. Usually we think of osteoporosis as a disease of old age. However, one of the cases from the Third Street Cemetery was a young adult female. She may have suffered from a disease or a prolonged period of hunger or malnutrition that weakened her bones.

We noted evidence for pulmonary tuberculosis, the often-fatal respiratory disease, in ten people. The chief signs are changes in the ribs and vertebrae, but these bones were rarely well preserved, if at all. Also, depending on the length of time a person suffered from this disease, the bones may not have been affected. Because of these limits, we believe that tuberculosis was likely much more prevalent than indicated by the osteological evidence, especially since tuberculosis, then called "consumption," was the most commonly reported cause of death in Dubuque in the mid- to late nineteenth century. Though people tend to think of "consumption" as an archaic cause of death, reported cases of TB have been on the rise in recent years. Because it's easily transmitted from person to person, public health officials are making great efforts to detect it and cure the patients.

Two adults exhibited evidence of gout, a condition in which the accumulation of uric acid crystals in the joints causes severe inflammatory arthritis. Symptoms include flare-ups of intense pain, particularly in the big toe. One of these individuals also displayed diffuse idiopathic skeletal hyperostosis (DISH), a degenerative disease in which the spinal ligaments turn into bone (become ossified), resulting in fusion of the vertebrae. Fusion of the back bones limits mobility, causes pain and discomfort, and inhibits one's ability to perform normal everyday tasks. Gout and DISH may result together from a common metabolic factor or obesity. Once known as the "rich man's disease," gout actually has a higher prevalence today than in preceding decades, probably due to a number of factors, including changes in what we eat.

We found two possible cases of tapeworm infestation, as evidenced by the presence of a mineralized cyst in the chest cavity. People are more likely to be infected by this parasite when they live in poor hygienic conditions and are involved in herding cattle and sheep, which can carry and transmit the disease. The larva of the tapeworm attaches by hooks to the wall of the intestines or other organs, eventually forming a cyst that becomes mineralized. Nausea, diarrhea, and weight loss often follow, and more severe complications sometimes occur. Tapeworm infestation in humans can be fatal. Poor street sanitation and a lack of knowledge of how tapeworms were transmitted to humans made infestation much more common in the nineteenth century than in the United States today. Herd animals are generally treated by veterinarians, and most people know to thoroughly cook meat. Today tapeworm infestation is a greater problem in regions of the world without public sanitation, such as areas of Africa and Southeast Asia.

The children of Third Street suffered from many common diseases, as well as nutritional deficits. While these conditions often killed too quickly to have any effect on the bones, we also observed three distinct signs of poor health in their skeletal and dental remains. The most frequently observed pathology in the whole subadult population is cribra orbitalia, found in the orbits (eye sockets) of 84 out of the 212 children who had intact or partially intact orbits (17 percent of the total subadult population). Cribra orbitalia manifests as spongy, porous bone in the upper wall of the eye socket. It results from disease or nutritional stress and has been linked to iron deficiency anemia in some cases. We also noted healed or nearly healed cribra orbitalia on the orbital walls of seven adults. Clearly, many of Dubuque's nineteenth-century residents experienced serious childhood malnutrition and illness.

Five children and two young adults had dental enamel defects known as mulberry molars and Hutchinson's incisors. Both can be signs of congenital syphilis, a condition passed to unborn infants by mothers who are suffering from primary or secondary syphilis.[2] Prior to the advent of antibiotics, infants born with congenital syphilis had a very low survival rate, and the chances of reaching adulthood were slim. The reasons why we saw so little evidence of congenital syphilis may be because the teeth of many of the buried children were poorly preserved and because the disease does not always affect the teeth. Given contemporary newspaper accounts of prostitution in the second half of the nineteenth century in Dubuque, it is surprising that we found no evidence for tertiary syphilis in adult skeletons. The infected mothers of the children with congenital syphilis could have been buried in other cemeteries, or perhaps they died before the disease affected their skeletons. U.S. agencies did not keep records of syphilis infection rates in the nineteenth century, but the disease was believed to be most prevalent from 1880 to 1920. The Centers for Disease Control and Prevention report that in 2013 more than 110 million men and women in the United States had a sexually transmitted disease, with 117,000 new and existing cases of syphilis. Syphilis was the eighth most prevalent sexually transmitted disease in the country.

Twenty-five children (as well as five adults) exhibited labyrinthine endocranial lesions—new bone growth on the inside surface of the cranial vault. From skeletal evidence, we can't tell exactly what caused such lesions. However, they might be caused by a myriad of diseases, including tuberculosis, meningitis, tuberculous meningitis, other inflammatory diseases, hemorrhage, epidural hematoma (a type of traumatic brain injury), anemia, scurvy, rickets, and venous drainage disorders (causing improper flow of blood to and from the brain). The bony changes we observed may also be a secondary effect of infections such as otitis media (middle ear infections), pneumonia, and bacterial influenza, and they may be associated with vitamin deficiency and bone tumors. After over a hundred years of research, osteologists are still uncertain which specific conditions create these labyrinth-like patterns on the skull. The fact that we saw a lot of these lesions suggests the younger population was at risk for one of these many diagnoses, including meningitis and tuberculosis. Both of these diseases, as well as the others listed here, can affect the blood vessels around the brain, particularly the meninges (the membranes around the brain and spinal cord). Once the disease process begins affecting these vessels, the bone on the inside of the cranium reacts by adding new bone to the inner surface. The longer the child lives with the disease, the more pronounced these bony deposits become and the more pressure accumulates around blood vessels and membranes surrounding the brain. Inflammation around the brain would ultimately prove to be fatal.

We discovered evidence for trauma occurring during an individual's life in fifty-three adults with healed or partially healed fractures. It's important to remember that the majority of trauma people experience during their lifetime affects only the soft tissue, leaving no mark on the skeletal remains. For example, think of all the bruises you manage to get without ever breaking or damaging a bone. The bone fractures we observed would have been the signs of only the more severe injuries that the Third Street Cemetery occupants suffered. Nearly three-fourths of the trauma victims were males, generally with broken lower legs. Females more often had minor fractures in their arms, hands, ribs, or the cranium. We found only one child with evidence for trauma, a healed fracture of the fibula. Again, the paucity of findings may be due to poor preservation of children's bones at this cemetery. The limited data suggest that men were more likely to be injured, probably as a result of their occupations. The most common fracture was to the fibula, the outer bone of the lower leg; the second most common was to the skull. In the nineteenth century, mining accidents and run-ins with a horse and buggy are likely scenarios for causing broken bones. Today, we still are subject to fractures through debilitating automobile accidents, modern mining cave-ins, and or just slipping on a wet floor. Life is probably no safer now in terms of trauma.

Five adults showed signs of osteomyelitis, an infection in the bone or bone marrow. This type of infection leads to expansion of the bone cortex (its outer layer), which becomes fairly thick along the shafts of long bones and sometimes includes the presence of cloaca, or drainage holes, there. A break in the bone or damage to soft tissue can produce osteomyelitis, as can bacterial infections and diseases borne by the blood. Swelling, warmth, and tenderness in the infected area eventually lead to severe pain and pus draining through the skin. Today, such infections can be treated with antibiotics and proper medical care.

Our studies revealed the cause of death for just a few people buried at Third Street. During the excavation and osteological analysis, we uncovered dramatic trauma that occurred at or around the time of death in a few cases. This perimortem trauma included two cases of possible gunshot wounds; cut marks on one individual's ribs; one unhealed trepanation; and cases of multiple fractures. Additionally, an older woman displayed a large lesion in her pelvis. Because none of these pathologies displayed evidence of healing, we could confidently say these individuals did not survive very long after the traumatic event that caused them. All of the people affected were adults, six men and one woman. These few cases reflect only a small portion of the numerous accounts of violent death reported in the newspapers of the time. However, determining cause of death with precision is not as easy as it may appear in modern-day mystery novels and TV crime shows with forensic pathologists. This is particularly true when dealing with skeletonized remains that are poorly preserved and have been in the ground for around 150 years. The "evidence" is often ambiguous.

During excavation, we found a .31-caliber lead ball resting in the right rib area of a thirty- to forty-five-year-old man. The presence of the bullet suggested he may have died from a gunshot wound, but we couldn't tell how badly the bullet might have injured him because the ribs and vertebrae were very poorly preserved. As a result, we can only speculate about whether or not the bullet contributed directly to his death. It may well have been that he was buried with a bullet in his pocket, since the soft lead projectile was not deformed as one would expect after impact with a human body.

In another case, an adult male forty-four to fifty-nine years of age had a hole on the right side of his skull in front of the ear on the temporal bone. The defect, almost perfectly circular in form, with two radiating fractures, completely penetrated the cranial vault. It is possible that a perimortem gunshot caused this wound, although we did not find an exit wound or a bullet. Without these things, we could not be confident of the exact cause of this hole in the skull, but its location in the right temple had us speculating that this person committed suicide.

The remains of a young man displayed very fine cut marks near the sternal end of a left rib, the end closest to the breastbone. Based on bone coloration, the marks occurred near the time of death, not during our excavation. The evidence suggests wounding caused by a sharp-bladed instrument. This young man may have been the victim of a stabbing. The St. Raphael's burial register lists at least one man who was stabbed to death and presumably buried in the Third Street Cemetery.

The next trauma victim, a thirty- to thirty-nine-year-old man, had undergone surgery, specifically, trepanation, the surgical removal of a portion of bone from the skull. A semicircular area of bone, about one inch in diameter, had been cut out of the right side of his cranium. The area around the removed bone was scored with deep cut marks, which had allowed for the removal of an additional, rhomboid-shaped section of bone. The missing bone was not in the burial. The reason for the surgery was unclear, as there were no signs of trauma on the cranial bones, neither fracturing nor a bullet wound. We saw no evidence of healing, which means that the trepanation either caused or contributed to this individual's death. Local doctors used trepanning as a treatment during this time period in Dubuque as they did elsewhere in the United States, typically to treat individuals with head wounds or those suffering from mental illness or conditions such as epilepsy, the latter poorly understood in the nineteenth century. In 1871 a *Dubuque Daily Herald* article reported that a four-year-old boy suffered a head injury after falling from a buggy while his family was returning from a funeral. The boy showed immediate improvement following a trepanning operation but died a few weeks later.

A middle-aged man suffered two perimortem fractures that may have resulted from a work-related accident. The left clavicle (collarbone) was fractured completely and broken in half. The left femur, or thigh bone, displayed a complete spiral fracture. Since neither fracture showed any sign of healing, we concluded that the trauma that caused them likely contributed to this individual's death. Perhaps he was crushed under falling rock in a mine collapse or else fatally injured in a horse accident.

One of the last burials we excavated contained the remains of a thirty-five- to forty-four-year-old man. This man suffered a terrible accident that broke his leg bones in several places. All the major leg bones—both femora, tibiae (the inner bone of the lower leg), and fibulae—were fractured at or near the time of death. His injuries ranged from a single complete fracture through the middle of his left fibula to numerous small and large fractures of both femora and the right tibia. The left tibia also contained a complete spiral fracture. However, his patellae (kneecaps) were unaffected, as were the bones of the feet, so we knew that he did not fall and land on his feet or knees. No injuries occurred to his skull, torso, or upper limbs. The observed fractures are much like those people suffer today in high-velocity car crashes when their legs hit the dashboard. A high-impact, probably twisting event caused the dramatic trauma that led to this man's early demise. The many dangers inherent in early Dubuque life led us to speculate that he might have been in an accident involving a horse-drawn buggy or wagon, a train or a mining cart, or perhaps a logging calamity.

An interesting contrast to the trauma evident in these men that seemed to be related to work accidents or violence is the case of an elderly woman. Her bones displayed several pathological conditions, including the loss of all her teeth and probable osteoporosis. Her left hip bone contained a large penetrating abscess that had almost completely destroyed the surface that joins with the sacrum, the bone at the base of the spine. The sacrum appeared to be deformed by bone loss probably associated with the abscess on the left hip bone. The most likely cause of the damage was either suppurative arthritis (a bacterial infection) of the sacroiliac joint or tuberculosis. She probably did not survive this large damaging lesion for very long, and she likely suffered a great deal of pain near the end of her life.

THE 1856 IOWA STATE census lists twenty-two self-proclaimed physicians for Julien Township in Dubuque County, but the rudimentary care they provided did not stop epidemics or properly heal broken bones. The trepanned cranium provides the most obvious evidence of medical intervention, and the results proved unfortunate for that patient. None of the healed fractures that we found appear to have been set professionally, and disease took a heavy toll on the children and many adults buried in the Third Street Cemetery. We also know that young children and the elderly were more susceptible to short-term diseases such as pneumonia, scarlet fever, and dysentery that leave no trace on the bones.

The number one observable medical issue in this population was poor dental health. The dental health issues we saw suggest that the likely causes were bad dental hygiene and the consumption of cavity-promoting (cariogenic) foods, the latter also associated with poor nutritional health. These foods include simple sugars and starches found in breads, potatoes, and some vegetables and fruits, for example. During the nineteenth century, a diet heavy in starchy foods would likely have been the norm for those with little access to or financial resources for meat and more healthful foods. Flour, a high starch product, was a common commodity. The people buried in the cemetery suffered from numerous cavities, tooth loss, and dental abscesses, and despite the presence of dentists in the county, few individuals sought dental care. Dental fillings and appliances were rare among the cemetery population.

Broken bones and arthritis highlight the rigorous and sometimes injurious lifestyle of old Dubuque, particularly among the men. Men likely suffered these injuries because they held more dangerous jobs, working in lead mines and factories or on trains and steamboats. The newspapers were filled with accounts of accidents and deaths occurring within town and on the river. Several of these casualties ended up buried on the bluff.

The physical demands of arduous jobs, the prevalence of disease and poor sanitation, and the lack of modern-day conveniences and medicine seem antiquated to many in present-day America. But all of these things still exist, both here and worldwide.

The Third Street Cemetery project is unique in that it is the largest Catholic cemetery excavation in the Midwest to date. The recovered individuals represent a socioeconomic cross section of a nineteenth-century urban American population. Many other large excavations that have taken place in recent decades have been of poor farm cemeteries. As the name implies, these contain the interments of those unfortunate souls who could not maintain or find jobs nor afford housing in the later nineteenth and early twentieth centuries. In general, the people buried in these cemeteries are not representative of their communities as a whole. Their populations include more men than women and more adults than children. Evidence of dental and other diseases was generally similar to Third Street, but their manifestation was often more virulent. A study of the adult remains from the Milwaukee County Institution Grounds, for instance, showed a much greater incidence of trauma than seen in the excavated portion of the Third Street Cemetery, and a significant number of those affected had experienced more than one traumatic event. Given their unfortunate circumstances, those poorhouse populations were somewhat more susceptible to the diseases and hazards of the nineteenth century than were the poor buried at Third Street.

The human remains tell only part of the story. Bones were not all we had to provide information about the people buried in the Third Street Cemetery. We also analyzed the coffins, coffin hardware, and all the items included with the remains in each burial—the things the dead took with them.

SIX

The Things They Took with Them

POOR PRESERVATION AFFECTED the artifacts just as it did the bones. Items such as coffin handles, hinges, and nails were corroded, and the more fragile decorative hardware items were frequently fragmented. The condition of coffin wood varied. At times it was fairly good, even when the coffin itself had collapsed from ground pressure. In other cases, no wood at all was present, and only nails defined the coffin outline. The condition of grave goods depended on what they were made of and whether the burial had been disturbed. Religious medals and crosses or crucifixes often contained copper and corroded over time. Fabric-covered and shell buttons fared poorly in most cases, while certain other button types were preserved perfectly.

The Third Street Cemetery was founded before the beautification of death movement reached the Midwest in the 1850s, and it continued to be used after the funerary trend took hold. As a result, we saw a definite change in the styles of coffins used to enclose the dead. They ranged from simple boxes constructed only of wood, nails, and plain screws to a few highly embellished caskets that reflected the height of the beautification movement. However, as with the bones, what we could learn depended on what survived. Wood preservation was poor in the majority of burials, making it difficult for us to discern the details of coffin construction. We found only three metal coffins. Over two hundred coffins were buried inside crudely constructed wooden outer crates, which served the dual purpose of shoring up the grave shaft and protecting the coffin by redistributing the weight of the backfill soil, just as concrete vaults do today. We drew on nineteenth-century funeral industry trade catalogs to identify the coffin styles and their hardware. This also helped us place some of the coffins into a specific time range, since elaborate coffins were not available during the earlier years of the cemetery's usage.

Unlike modern coffins, which are generally uniform in design, those produced in the nineteenth century ranged from austere to what now would be considered gaudy. At the Third Street Cemetery we found the full array of coffin types, but certain elements of wooden coffin construction appeared to be consistent. The lids, fastened by nails, gimlet screws, or more elaborate coffin screws or thumbscrews, were made of either a single lengthwise board, particularly for the smaller children's coffins, or four joined boards (figure 10). The coffin sides were affixed to the base with nails oriented horizontally, and the head and foot boards were positioned with the grain

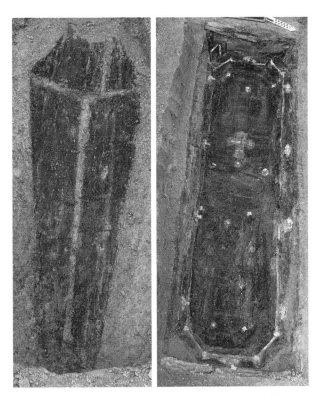

FIGURE 10. Coffins at the Third Street Cemetery ranged from plain hexagonal (*a*) to more expensive burial containers, like this heavily decorated, cloth-covered octagonal casket (*b*).

oriented vertically. We analyzed a small number of wood samples and found that both pine and walnut were used in coffin construction. They were available locally, with the pine floated downriver from Wisconsin. The use of locally available wood told us that many of these coffins were most likely manufactured by Dubuque cabinet and casket makers.

We determined the coffin shape for 704 burials, with 71 percent hexagonal. These are often referred to as the square-footed or toe-pincher types. Six coffins were gabled, having a peaked lid running the length of the coffin. Gabled coffin lids, popular in the seventeenth and eighteenth centuries, became less common in the 1800s. The few rectangular- or trapezoidal-shaped coffins were most frequently associated with infants' and children's burials. This pattern is familiar from other cemeteries. Archaeologist James Davidson notes that despite the increasing advertisement of rectangular coffins in the second half of the nineteenth century and their availability through local undertakers, many people chose to bury their loved ones in the hexagonal coffin as late as the early twentieth century. Artisan coffin makers today, such as the Trappist monks at the New Melleray Abbey south of Dubuque, continue to make beautifully crafted hexagonal coffins.

In addition to the many wooden coffins, we found three made of cast iron. A fourth coffin, excavated in 1994, was constructed of wood and at least partially covered by metal sheeting. The presence of the metal exterior suggests that the coffin was not of local manufacture. Enclosure in a metal casket was a common practice in the late nineteenth century when remains were to be transported over long distances. Shipping regulations for railroads and steamboats required all wooden coffins to be enclosed in bulky, expensive lead or zinc outer boxes to prevent leakage of decomposition fluids. No such extra measures were required for metal coffins, though they were sometimes shipped in wooden crates to preserve their appearance. The wooden crate lining this grave shaft was likely a shipping crate reused as a burial vault.

The three cast-iron coffins excavated at the Third Street Cemetery were clearly not locally made, since only a few manufacturers obtained a license for the Fisk patent that was required to produce these expensive metal coffins, and none of these companies were located in Dubuque. Two of the cast-iron coffins lay side by side and were nearly identical in size and decoration. The third metal coffin was found some distance away, along the western perimeter of the site. The coffin's metal viewing-pane cover was unbroken, and the burial case was intact. The "torpedo" shape and beveled lid were reminiscent of a Fisk Patent Case Model 3. Even the outer wooden crate was unique, being hexagonal in shape rather than rectangular like all the others found at Third Street. Because the seal was unbroken, the coffin likely still contained biohazardous materials from body decomposition. With safety in mind, we decided to have the coffin transferred to Mt. Olivet Cemetery for immediate reinterment. The process of removing this heavy coffin and placing it in the back of a pickup truck drew the rapt attention of every crew member. The remains stayed undisturbed and unknown to us.

Unlike modern "half-couch" caskets, which are hinged to expose the body of the deceased from the head to the waist, most of the Third Street coffins had only two options—lid on or lid off. Just nineteen coffins had hinges that allowed mourners to open the lid in the head or head and chest area to view the deceased. The upper portion of the lid flipped down toward the feet or opened from left to right or right to left. During the later period of the cemetery's use, viewing panes came into fashion. These glass panes set in the coffin lid allowed the mourners to view the remains while protecting them from the offensive odors of decomposition. Eighteen coffins had viewing panes, including an elaborate infant coffin with an intact teardrop-shaped glass. Due to the expense, only the most elaborately decorated coffins incorporated these panes in their designs. A protective wooden cover, usually in the same shape as the viewing pane, was fitted over the glass. This cover, adorned with white-metal caplifters, was lifted off for the viewing and replaced when the coffin went into the grave.

At least fifty-three wooden coffins had been painted or varnished. In some other burials, we found uncollectible tiny paint flakes, indicating that painted coffins were more common than the better-preserved evidence indicated. The most common color was a light cream, which originally was likely white. Indeed, nineteenth-century trade catalogs advertised "gloss white" as an option for many coffins. In a few cases, we saw coffins with a red undercoat; at least two coffins had a red outer coat. Eight coffins had originally been covered with exterior fabric, although very little of the fabric survived. In two cases we found traces of velvet (one sample identified as cotton) and in another wool velvet or velveteen with the pile dyed black or deep blue.

Coffin lining tacks, coffin lace, and the remnants of lining fabric gave us some clues about interior decoration. The tacks or coffin lace (a woven, copper-and-fabric tacking strip) rimmed the upper edge on the interior walls of almost 340 coffins. The fabric, preserved only as small remnants, appeared to be loosely woven, and three of the specimens were identified as wool. Contemporary trade catalogs also offered luxury options for lining fabric, such as satin, cashmere, brocade, and stamped silk, but we found none of these preserved in the excavated burials. Coffin furnishings included pillows and mattresses stuffed with wood shavings or excelsior. The shavings created the illusion of softness in coffin upholstery. We found evidence of mattresses in three coffins and pillows in only eight, but there may have been more that decayed and disappeared. In her book *Death in Early America*, Margaret Coffin relates a superstition once held by coffin makers regarding wood shavings. According to this folk custom, all small pieces of wood left over from the coffin-making process needed to be placed inside the coffin, because any stray shavings left on clothing or tracked into a house could mark a person for death.[1] One wonders if Dubuque's coffin makers shared this belief.

Various coffin catalogs and the 1882 records of Dubuque's Hoffmann Mortuary provided prices for coffins. A comparison of the Hoffmann records with price lists for untrimmed coffins shows that the funeral home added a markup on top of the charge for the addition of hardware. Depending on the size and whether or not a coffin included an outer crate, wholesale prices ranged from $1.25 for a plain child's coffin to $72.00 for an adult "extra size" metal coffin. The 1882 records from the Hoffmann Mortuary indicate a price range from $2.50 (about $59.00 in 2012 dollars, based on general inflation rates) for the plainest child's coffin up to $47.00 (about $1,100.00) for a child's finely trimmed wooden coffin. In addition, Hoffmann Mortuary provided other funerary accoutrements such as a hearse, drapes, gloves, and crepe.

Coffin Trimmings

Archaeologists often find mass-produced ornamental coffin hardware in excavations of American cemeteries in use from the mid-nineteenth to the early twentieth century. By the late 1800s, this hardware had become increasingly varied, having gone through numerous functional and stylistic changes. We saw these changes in the items we unearthed from the Third Street Cemetery (what we call an "assemblage"), though much of the hardware we recovered was corroded or fragmented. Almost half of the excavated burials had some type of hardware besides nails, utilitarian screws, and common coffin lining tacks. Decorative fittings used to personalize the coffin included lid plaques, handles, decorative screws used to fasten the lid in place, and stamped-metal adornments fastened to the lid and sides. Handles were composed of two parts: the bail, which was the portion grasped for carrying the coffin, and the lug, the part or parts attaching the bail to the coffin. Escutcheons, or flat metal base plates, were paired with decorative screws of complementary design. Caplifters, in shapes such as flowers or crosses, were affixed to the wooden covers protecting viewing panes.

Coffin handles serve both functional and ornamental purposes and are thus one of the most common types of mortuary hardware. Almost 10 percent of the coffins excavated from Third Street had handles, ranging from purely functional to extremely ornate. We found thirty-nine different handle types in the assemblage, and historical archaeologist Cindy Nagel developed a typology to aid in analysis of hardware collected in future cemetery projects.[2] The iconography of these handles, mirrored on the other types of hardware, reflects the sentimental tastes of the time. Floral and geometric designs, crosses, clasping hands, angels, torches, wreaths, stars, books (probably Bibles), and urns were common motifs. Lambs and cherubs usually decorated the coffins of infants and young children. Other themes, such as the crucifix and the miter and crozier (bishop's hat and staff), were specific to the Catholic community. Several handles and coffin-lid crosses were decorated with shamrocks, likely a nod to the Irish heritage of the deceased person's family. Like handles, coffin-lid crosses and plaques were both ornamental and practical. In addition to beautifying the burial case, they memorialized the deceased by recording the name, date of death, and age at death.

While the Catholic Church does not expressly forbid the inclusion of secular items and mementos in the coffins of the deceased, the practice has long been discouraged. The custom of including only items related to devotional and funerary traditions was evident at Third Street, where we recovered very few nonreligious artifacts besides clothing fasteners. Almost 20 percent of the excavated burials contained one or more items related to the religious practices of the deceased or, in the case of infants, their families. The religious artifacts we found fell into four categories: rosaries and chaplets, religious medals, crosses and crucifixes, and funeral wreaths.

A Catholic rosary consists of a string of beads used to count prayers recited in honor of the Virgin Mary while meditating on events in the life of Jesus Christ and his mother. The word "chaplet"—meaning "little crown"—is commonly applied to shorter (or longer) strings of beads used to count prayers to the Virgin Mary, the angels, or a particular saint, usually asking for intercession or protection. Even in Catholic literature, disagreement arises over the use of the words "rosary" and "chaplet," with some claiming that only the Dominican rosary (fifty-nine beads) can truly be called a rosary. For the purposes of our analysis, we designated all sets of beads that were arranged in ten-bead "decades" as rosaries and all others as chaplets. Many items classified as chaplets were probably full rosaries when they were placed in the grave, but burial disturbance and deterioration had reduced the number of beads by the time we found them.

The graves of men, women, children, and even infants included rosaries and chaplets, though adult women were more often buried with rosaries than anyone else. The placement of the rosaries varied, with most found in the right or left hand or in both. The modern prohibition against wearing rosaries around the neck did not yet exist, and several individuals wore them this way. Rosaries and chaplets placed in infant graves often lay over the baby's chest or abdomen. Of the six commonly produced types of rosaries, we identified three at Third Street: the four-decade Rosary for the Dead, the five-decade Dominican rosary (figure 11), and the six-decade Bridgettine rosary. Rosaries with seven, ten, and fifteen decades are often associated with the clergy and members of religious orders. Since our project area did not include the portion of the cemetery closest to the

FIGURE 11. Five-decade rosary with japanned wooden beads and a pendant crucifix. This rosary was designed without a center medal joining the circlet of beads to the pendant string.

cathedral where the clergy were likely buried, it is probable that we excavated only the graves of the laity.

Most rosaries and chaplets were composed of wooden beads and copper links, though we also found beads made from Job's tears (the seeds of *Coix lacryma-jobi*), glass, ceramic, vulcanized rubber, gutta-percha, and early celluloid plastic beads. Charles Goodyear patented vulcanized rubber, also known as vulcanite or Ebonite, in 1844. Items made from this material are usually black with a glossy finish, so the rubber beads were similar in appearance to japanned (black enameled) wooden beads. Gutta-percha, the moldable sap of the Malaysian gutta tree (Palaquium gutta), arrived in the European market in 1845 and quickly became a popular material. The gutta-percha rosary beads found at Third Street were mostly brown or a dull black. John Hyatt invented celluloid plastic in the 1860s, though he did not receive a patent for the product until 1870. The few plastic bead rosaries found were usually light green in color. We found one disintegrating rosary with beads that may have been made from compressed rose petals. The most unusual chaplet recovered during the project included natural garnet crystals strung with green glass and gray stone beads.

Most rosaries included both a center medal and a pendant cross or crucifix, as did many chaplets. A few of the center medals had been repurposed, with holes drilled through the original design to allow for suspension from the rosary instead of a chain. Standard iconography appears on most of the crucifixes, but the reverse of one copper cross was embossed with a collection of objects associated with the crucifixion: the rooster, the crown of thorns, the flaming heart, four nails, pliers, the ladder, the spear that pierced Jesus's side, the sponge of vinegar, and a chalice. This object was unique within the cemetery collection, and we found nothing similar in books of Catholic art and artifacts nor in antique sales listings. Three women were buried with Rosaries of the Immaculate Conception, a variation with a Miraculous Medal (see below) in place of the crucifix. Others had additional medals attached near the crucifix. In some cases, the pendant portion of the rosary was missing altogether. This phenomenon has an interesting parallel. During the excavation of a small part of the nineteenth-century Second Catholic Grave Yard in St. Louis, archaeologists noted that all of the rosaries included in the coffins were missing the pendant portions. Researchers on that project suggested that the families of the deceased may have customarily retained the crucifix as a memento. Perhaps some Dubuque families did likewise.

Religious medals are coin-like objects struck or cast to commemorate the Virgin Mary, Jesus Christ, various saints, famous shrines, miracles, apparitions, pilgrimages, religious associations, or historic events. The images serve as a reminder to honor the subject displayed on the medal, and today Catholics almost always wear such medals around the neck. In addition to those medals recovered with rosaries and chaplets, we also found medals alone, often near the neck with remnants of a cord, but also pinned over the heart. A few appeared to have been sewn into small pouches. All were made from copper-based alloys except for two white-metal examples.

Nearly all of the religious medals were heavily corroded and had to be cleaned by electrolysis. Even after cleaning, many remained illegible. We were only able to make out the images on 54 of the 123 medals we recovered from the cemetery. Almost 85 percent of the medals we could identify turned out to be the same type, the Miraculous Medal (figure 12).

FIGURE 12. Miraculous Medal recovered from the grave
of the man with the mummified thumb.

This medal, still popular today, commemorates three apparitions of the
Virgin Mary witnessed by Sister Catherine Laboure in Paris in 1830. On
the obverse of the medal, Mary stands on a globe with a serpent crushed
beneath her foot and rays of light emanating from the fingers of her out-
stretched hands. The reverse is stamped with a large letter M surmounted
by a cross; below the M there are two flaming hearts: the heart of Jesus, surrounded by the crown of thorns, and the heart of Mary, pierced by a sword.
The design on the reverse is surrounded by twelve stars, while the design on
the obverse is surrounded by an inscription. A slim majority of our medals were inscribed in French: "O MARIE CONÇUE SANS PÉCHÉ, PRIEZ
POUR NOUS QUI AVONS RECOURS À VOUS." The English translation,
found on many of the medals we recovered, reads: "O Mary conceived
without sin, pray for us who have recourse to thee." We found Miraculous
Medals inscribed in two other languages, one in German and one in Italian.

The prevalence of the Miraculous Medal is not surprising, given that the
active period of the cemetery coincides with the height of its popularity.
From the original casting of two thousand medals in France, Miraculous
Medal production reportedly had risen to almost ten million worldwide
by 1836. The circulation of the medal was both geographically widespread

and socially diverse. Some religious orders were distributing these medals to the poor at the same time the queen of France was wearing one.

The remainder of the Third Street medals were varied, with almost no repetition of design. Two were commemorative rather than devotional. A white-metal medal indicated that the older gentleman buried with it was a member of the Catholic Temperance Association. An elderly woman's medal celebrated the jubilee of Pope Pius IX in 1847. A middle-aged woman wore a Mary of the Seven Sorrows medal, which depicts Mary with seven swords piercing her heart, with a crucifixion scene on the reverse. The woman in Burial 868 (described in detail in chapter 7) was buried with a medal inscribed to "St. Lewis of Gonzague," commonly known as St. Aloysius; the reverse shows an angel and child surrounded by the words GUARDIAN ANGEL GUIDE ME.

Two medals reflect devotions specific to particular regions of Europe. In the coffin of a petite middle-aged man, we found a medal dedicated to Notre-Dame de Fourvière, a statue of Mary and Child in a chapel on a hilltop in Lyon, France. Locals credit the statue with keeping plague away from the city in 1643. The obverse of the medal shows the statue as it appears in the chapel, standing under an arch and flanked by angels, and the inscription reads "N.D. DE FOURVIERE PRIEZ POUR NOUS" (Our Lady of Fourvière pray for us). The reverse has a crucifixion scene with city walls in the background.

Another unusual medal, buried with a middle-aged to older woman, is dedicated to St. Pellegrino and St. Bianco, two saints whose bodies are preserved in a glass tomb in a chapel in the Garfagnana Mountains near Bagni di Lucca, Italy. The obverse bears an image of St. Benedict standing with his inscribed shield, surrounded by the words "CRUX ST BENE" (Cross of St. Benedict). On the reverse, parted curtains hang beneath a crown. Below the curtains, two figures lie within a stylized tomb. Surrounding this image are the words "S PEL I BIANC RE DI SCOZ," meaning "St. Pellegrino and Bianco, King of Scotland" (figure 13). The word *pellegrino* is Italian for "pilgrim," and the saint is also known as Peregrine or Peregrinus. Tradition holds that he was the son of the king and queen of Scotia—believed to be part of modern Ireland or Scotland—and that he lived out his days as a hermit in Italy after making a pilgrimage to Jerusalem and Rome in the seventh century. St. Pellegrino is a locally venerated

FIGURE 13. Medal showing the preserved corpses of
St. Pellegrino and St. Bianco in their glass tomb.

saint who is also recognized by the Catholic Church. St. Bianco, however,
does not appear on any official lists of saints. Because the devotions of
Notre-Dame de Fourvière and St. Pellegrino and St. Bianco are localized,
it seems likely that the two individuals in these burials had some connection to Lyon and Bagni di Lucca, respectively.

Like the medals, some crosses and crucifixes were found with rosaries
and chaplets, and some were found alone, usually at the neck or over the
chest. Those found with prayer beads were usually stamped from sheet
metal, while the independent crucifixes were often more substantial, with
the Christus cast separately and riveted to the cross. A one-year-old child
was buried with an unusual mold-blown black glass crucifix. Six crucifixes were composites, combining an ebony or mock-ebony cross with a
cast-metal Christus, skull and crossbones, and other decorative elements.
Nine of the crucifixes in the collection included the words "SOUVENIR
DE LA MISSION," or some variation thereof, stamped on the back. These
crucifixes differed in design, though they were all cast from copper-alloy
materials. While these items could be tokens from any pilgrimage site, the
time period makes it likely that their bearers brought at least some of them
home from Lourdes. The apparitions of the Virgin Mary at the Grotto at
Lourdes occurred in 1858, and the spot quickly became a major pilgrimage

site. The Grotto would have been open to visitors during the second half of the cemetery's period of active use.

In addition to demonstrating that Dubuque's Catholics maintained ties with European communities, the religious items in their graves link them to local and national markets. The presence of thirteen identical wooden-bead rosaries suggests both mass production and local purchase. Other multiples in the collection—five identical floral crucifixes, two identical celluloid rosaries, two Job's tears and glass bead rosaries—indicate that the materials were reaching the community through the same supplier, if not necessarily the same shop. In his memoirs, Josiah Conzett mentions a Catholic books and notions shop owned by J. J. E. Norman. Mr. Norman, coincidentally, was also buried at Third Street before being moved to Mt. Olivet Cemetery.

Archaeologists expect to find rosaries, medals, and crucifixes in Catholic cemeteries. The final type of religious grave good we encountered, though, proved more of a mystery. At first, no one knew what to make of the little bits of twisted copper wire we discovered around the heads of some infants and children. In some cases, we found a perfectly circular pattern of wire preserved in the grave, and two children were buried with ferrous metal bands instead of the bits of copper wire on their heads. It seemed logical that these objects were the inorganic remnants of garlands of flowers or greenery. But what did they mean? Approximately 10 percent of the infant and child graves we excavated held these wreath remnants, although in a few cases they were placed over the abdomen instead of on the head. An elderly woman and two teenage girls were also buried with wreaths. Many Latin American cultures follow the tradition of dressing dead children as *los angelitos* (the little angels), all in white with floral wreaths. However, nineteenth-century records offer no evidence of a Hispanic population in Dubuque.

At first, our attempts to delve into the historic funerary customs of the predominant ethnic groups in Dubuque yielded little useful information. No one in the Irish Folklore Studies Department at University College Dublin had ever heard of placing wreaths on the heads of dead children. An article on funeral customs in Ireland, published in the *Proceedings of the American Philosophical Society* in 1888, mentions that the corpses of children were sometimes adorned with flowers for the wake but gives no further details.[3] Historians at the Musée Funéraire National in Paris found a reference to placing wreaths on children who were victims of violent or accidental death, but this tradition was rarely followed and was found only in western France.

Intriguingly, we discovered that during the sixteenth through the eighteenth centuries in Germany, it was customary to place funeral wreaths on the heads or chests of children. Practiced by both Protestants and Catholics, this custom was part of the funeral-wedding tradition, an indication that the deceased was a virgin. While the initial similarities to what we found at the Third Street Cemetery seemed promising, the wreaths described in a German archaeological study were far more elaborate than anything recovered in Dubuque.[4] The German wreaths featured ornamental wire and fake pearls and rarely incorporated organic materials. Reportedly, the tradition died out in the nineteenth century in Germany, though an article about German bridal customs published in a British literary magazine in 1868 refers to it.[5] Possibly the twisted wire found at Third Street represents a New World variation of the German tradition, but relatively few Germans should have been buried in our project area, since they opened their own cemetery just a few years after the excavated portion of the Third Street Cemetery came into use.

American mortuary photographs contemporary with the active period of the cemetery indicate that the practice of placing a wreath of flowers on a child's head in the coffin was not uncommon in this country. Was this perhaps a custom that developed here rather than being a tradition imported with Dubuque's immigrants? Were these wreaths one of the trappings that came with the beautification of death? We are sometimes left with more questions than answers. Regardless of the origin of the custom, we consider the wreaths religious grave goods insofar as they are specific to the funeral ritual and not everyday items incidentally included in the graves. It is to the latter that we now turn.

SECULAR GRAVE GOODS

The nonreligious or secular items found in burials sometimes can tell us about the person interred there or about the culture of the time, place, and community. Certain items can be used to give an approximate date of death. If a particular object in the grave was patented, we know that the burial occurred no earlier than the patent date. The arrangement of items on the body, such as buttons, helped us identify specific articles of clothing.

Of the 1,764 secular grave goods we recovered from slightly more than half of the graves, the vast majority relate to clothing or shrouds: buttons, buckles, hook-and-eye sets, copper pins, and so forth. Clothing varied from items requiring buttons, such as simple day-wear shirts and dresses, to more elaborate attire with ribbons and beadwork. Shrouds were simple robes or gowns that were pinned or tied closed in the back. If we found multiple types and sizes of buttons, we concluded that the deceased had been buried wearing an outfit including multiple items, such as a jacket or coat, shirt, and pants. Buckles, all of the cinch type, indicated vests, belts, or pants. The position of fabric recovered from a few of the burials also suggested dresses and trousers.

Buttons and Fasteners

We found buttons in over one-third of the burials, for a total of more than twelve hundred buttons. Men, on average, had more buttons than women, because men's clothing often included suspenders, jackets, pants, and shirt cuffs and fronts. Women with just a few buttons in their burials probably were interred in a simple garment that may have been the burial norm at that time for females. If we found buttons on top of, under, or around the head, we assumed the individuals were buried in hats, caps, or bonnets. These were most often found in the burials of children. One baby's cap or bonnet was trimmed with nine plain white Prosser buttons.

Seventy-five percent of the buttons were Prosser buttons, which were made of ceramic material and first patented in England in 1840. They arrived in the United States after 1849 and remained popular until the mid-twentieth century. They are distinguished from other ceramic or glass buttons by the orange-peel texture on the back. Most of the Prosser buttons from the Third Street Cemetery were a plain white type. They were no doubt cheap and easily accessible thanks to mass production.

We also recovered a variety of other buttons. Among the metal buttons were cloth-covered, shank, and sew-through types. Most of these indicate the presence of a jacket, vest, or pants. Nearly three-fourths of the metal buttons were associated with men. The largest number of metal buttons recovered from one burial was found in the interment of a teenage boy.

Seventy-seven wood and bone buttons came primarily from adult male burials. Although shell buttons had decomposed within some of the graves, we did recover thirty-seven of them. The largest number of shell buttons recovered from a single burial was seven from the well-preserved interment of a young adult male (see chapter 7, Burial 818). Sixteen buttons did not fit the classifications described above and include vulcanized rubber, glass, porcelain, and composite buttons.

Seven burials yielded metal grommets. In three cases, the grommets lay in the area of the waist, suggesting they may have come from corsets or waist cinchers, garments many women wore in this time period. Thirty individuals had hook-and-eye sets. Two burials contained infants probably dressed in some form of gown fastened by hooks and eyes along the back.

The three types of pins found in the burials served different purposes. We recovered two diaper pins from two infant burials. One of them was engraved with the words "Woodward patent," indicating a pin design that was registered in 1842. This pin was replaced in popularity by one patented in 1849. By identifying this object, we established that the child died in the 1840s or perhaps early 1850s, assuming that this particular pin was not reused for more than a few years. Ten hairpins adhering to preserved head hair fastened braids or chignons upon the heads of seven females. However, the copper-alloy straight pin was most ubiquitous: 270 of them turned up in the graves, with nearly two-thirds found in infant and child burials. These pins fastened clothing, shrouds, diapers, and children's bonnets. Most likely they were inexpensive and readily available in Dubuque. Indeed, the mass production of pins started in the United States in the 1830s based on a system patented earlier in England.

Fabric and Clothing

Many of the numerous coffin supply catalogs of the nineteenth century advertised burial garments with prices ranging from $0.50 for a child's lawn robe to $12.00 for a man's merino wrapper. In contrast to daywear, the burial-specific garments usually lacked buttons and were closed by ties or pins instead. They were often unhemmed, but the raw edges were pinked to give them a prettier look than unfinished edges.

The number of copper straight pins recovered suggests that many Dubuque families buried their loved ones in plain burial garments or shrouds. However, several burials included evidence of daywear in the form of clothing and shoes. A few men were apparently buried wearing neckties. One young man (see chapter 7, Burial 818) was buried with a silk herringbone tie. The collar fabric, brown twill cotton, was also preserved, along with a thin stiffener (possibly made of bone). The interment of a boy in his mid- to late teens included dark green or black fabric recovered from the neck area, likely also the remnant of neckwear. A middle-aged to older adult male had green fibers in the area of his neck, on his left clavicle (collarbone), and on the back of his skull. The fibers may be remnants of a tie or ribbon.

Twelve individuals were buried with fabric that could be identified as part of regular clothing. A man thirty-five to forty years old was buried in what seems to have been a dark blue-green coat, as well as a shirt and pants made of different fabrics. The coat's hem reached the thigh bones, and the long, stepped lapels suggested this may have been a frock coat. We found large quantities of blue-green fibers, probably wool, covering the chest and arms of another old man, extending to his hips. The same blue-green material covered the buttons found in this burial. The man was also buried with a harmonica. In another case, we judged the sex of the deceased based on the fragments of silk dress fabric with a wool undergarment we found in the chest area. Remnants of velvet or velvet-like fabric from an outer garment and fabric pieces from a simpler underdress or shirt were recovered from the burial of an infant aged six to eighteen months. Though fragmentary, such scraps tell us something about the funeral customs of the time, the resources the deceased's family could command, and also, occasionally, the gender of the individual.

Sixteen burials contained shoes: ten children, three women, two men, and one adult of indeterminate sex. The shoes associated with child burials were generally slipper or slip-on types, two decorated with buckles or beads. These appear to be "fancy" shoes rather than everyday wear. The adults' shoes were generally in poor condition, with only the soles or scraps of the shoe leather preserved. A nearly complete pair recovered from an adult disinterment appeared to be classic Victorian style, possibly a style that was worn on a daily basis, depending on the social status of the owner. We found it odd that all that was left behind of this person was a pair of fancy shoes.

Jewelry and Personal Adornments

Jewelry was extremely rare, seen primarily as finger rings recovered from twelve burials. Eleven of these people were adults, and one was a child between 10½ and 12½ years old at the time of death. The majority of the rings either were plain copper-alloy bands with no discernible inscription or had a plain bezel (a wider section of the hoop with a flat surface). An adult woman had four rings on her right hand. One, a coral-colored and clear striped agate ring, included a raised, ovate bezel. The other three rings were corroded copper alloy with oval or heart-shaped bezels that were not raised. Finger rings were recovered from both the left and right hands on both men and women. In European tradition, people tended to wear their wedding rings on the right hand. The paucity of rings may reflect a tradition of keeping these objects in the family to pass down from mother to daughter or father to son, rather than burying them with the deceased. Similarly, only eight rings were recovered from over a thousand burials at the nineteenth-century Alameda-Stone Cemetery.

One fairly complete and one partial brooch turned up in two separate burials, both adult women. Also found were a set of cuff links and two collar studs. A teenaged boy had a copper collar stud recovered from the chin area. Another teenaged boy was laid to rest with a gold-plated collar stud and set of red glass cuff links.

Two small children were buried wearing earrings. The grave of a child less than six months old included two plain hoops made of thin, flattened copper less than an inch in diameter. The burial of a toddler, 2½ to 3½ years old, contained metal earrings made for pierced ears. This child was also buried with shoes on. A third infant, aged approximately two to three months, was buried with a necklace composed of ninety-four turquoise and ninety-five white glass seed beads in an alternating pattern. These grave goods suggest the children were likely female.

An adult woman's burial contained a bone-like object found at the back of the head. It appears to be a comb or some kind of hair fastener likely made from tortoise shell. We also found a curved vulcanized rubber hair comb in the fill with the commingled incomplete remains from two disinterments. The curved shape of the comb suggests that a woman used it as a hair ornament. Perhaps these combs were functional items, like hairpins, meant merely to keep the deceased's hair in a comely fashion, or perhaps they were treasured possessions.

The majority of the Third Street dead were buried with few, if any, grave goods. This absence reflects the financial means of the families of the deceased or early nineteenth-century standards of simple interments with the body dressed in a shroud or plain gown. The appearance of jewelry, shoes, hair fasteners, fancy buttons, and so forth indicates the shift in the mid-nineteenth century to individuals interred in daywear or fancier apparel within more ornate coffins.

Unusual Grave Goods

Despite church restrictions on the inclusion of personal items in burials, a few people were interred with unique objects that were neither functional (related to apparel) nor religious (like rosaries). What particular reasons would the family have for including them in the burial of their loved one? Did they symbolize something significant about the deceased or define that person's role in life? The meaning isn't always clear.

Two graves included coins. In the case of one older juvenile boy, someone had placed two Seated Liberty quarters dating from 1856 and 1858 on his eyes. Maybe they symbolized "paying the boatman," a vestige of an old pagan tradition of placing money with a body so the dead could pay Charon to take the soul across the River Styx. It was interesting to find this tradition being carried out in the nineteenth century. Another individual was buried with a quarter and a dime that were probably inadvertently left behind in a jacket or pants pocket.

We recovered two pocketknives in very different contexts. One was a corroded item found in the fill of a disinterred adult grave. Possibly it was left behind by the person who dug up the body, or it may have belonged to the person originally buried there. In another case, we found a pocketknife at the top of the left thigh bone of an adult man, likely in his left-hand pocket. Like the pocket change, it may have been an inadvertent inclusion. But other objects had been purposely placed.

For instance, we discovered plates in two burials. A burial containing the remains of an infant who died before reaching six months of age included a thin metal plate approximately 2.5 inches in diameter. It lay on the left side where the chest would have been if it had been preserved. The silver-plated object was round, with a raised rim and an embossed radiant cross in the center. It appears similar to a Communion paten, but we don't know what purpose this small plate served in this burial. Burial 749, described in detail in chapter 7, contained the remains of an adult woman interred with a ten-sided whiteware plate at the left elbow. This was a surprising find and left the crew baffled as to its meaning.

An older juvenile girl was interred with a pair of scissors, probably dress shears, placed above her left shoulder. Remnants of a dress with ribbons and heart-shaped beadwork lay on her bones (see chapter 7, Burial 206). The interment of another teenage girl included an ambrotype, a photographic image made on a glass surface. In a frame measuring approximately four by four inches, the photo had been placed to the right of the girl's head. Unfortunately, the photographic image did not survive. The brass filigree frame was painted gold, and the scabbard case was constructed of "cigar box" mahogany and leather. Ambrotypes reached their peak of popularity in the mid-1850s and 1860s but were produced until 1880, so we can't positively date this one. One wonders what image faded from view: A wedding portrait? Children? Parents?

And, as we mentioned earlier, a harmonica, ferrous and badly corroded, lay directly below the lower jaw in the grave of an older man, the one interred in a blue-green wool jacket. The significance of this object defies knowing, but we may suppose that this man loved his music.

MOST OF THE PEOPLE BURIED in the excavated portion of the Third Street Cemetery had been interred in plain, hexagonal coffins with few grave goods of any kind. Though the cemetery included members of all levels of Dubuque society, it was difficult to determine social status from the coffins and the items buried with the dead in most instances, since funeral trends and family preferences have to be taken into account. We discovered that a few of the older teenagers, both male and female, went to the grave wearing relatively elaborate clothing with collar studs, cuff links, and ribbons. Nonreligious items tucked into their coffins, such as scissors and a photograph, added a personal touch we did not see in most burials. Perhaps this is purely coincidence, but it may speak to the way death at an age close to or just at adulthood caused families to take extra care with the preparation of the body.

The bits and pieces, clues and speculations needed to be pulled together so that we could puzzle out information about the lives and deaths of people from the Third Street Cemetery. In the following chapter, we provide a few portraits gathered from the burial evidence.

SEVEN

Humanizing the People of Third Street

————————

WHILE ALL THE ANALYSES involved in studying the Third Street Cemetery resulted in data and counts and specifics about coffins, hardware, and grave goods, it is only by combining these details that we can begin to glimpse the stories of individuals in the cemetery. The following portraits do just that, allowing us to see everything at once and gain a greater understanding of some of the people of Third Street.

THE CROWDED GRAVE

The person in Burial 206 was interred in one of the more elaborate burial containers. An outer crate enclosed a hexagonal coffin of tulip poplar with traces of red paint and primer coats of white, olive, and beige. The upper portion of the lid included a teardrop-shaped viewing pane. Unfortunately, the white-metal lid cross had degraded to the point that no engraving was visible, so we do not know the deceased's name. Ten urn-shaped thumbscrews, set in geometric escutcheons, fastened the lid. Five large ornamental tacks with geometric designs decorated the coffin lid. We recovered twenty-five additional diamond-shaped tacks, but because the coffin's wood had collapsed, we don't know where the tacks were originally placed. Six swing-bail handles with cross-shaped lugs, each decorated with an open book in the center of the cross, were attached to the coffin sides. A feather design decorated the handle bail. The original coffin must have been a beautiful thing to behold.

We estimated the person in Burial 206 to have been approximately eighteen to twenty years of age at the time of death. We can assume from the grave goods that this individual was female. She was interred on her back, with her elbows slightly bent and her hands on her pelvis, left over right. A large pair of scissors rested to the left of her head. The viewing-pane glass helped preserve the fabric covering her ribs and breastbone. The fabric had become dark brown in color as it decayed, and we can't now discern its original color. However, we do know that it included an arrangement of thirty-five clear glass seed beads sewn into a heart shape. Silk ribbons of a lighter brown color also survived under the viewing glass and probably served as decorative elements on the garment. Two pieces of sewn, pleated ribbon formed a circle or rosette over the left ribs. Beneath the fabric on the breastbone we found a heavily corroded religious medal. A metal button rested in the area of the pelvis, while three Prosser buttons were also recovered.

The quantity of fabric and ornaments we found was not the only unusual feature of this burial. The fabric and the area around the young woman's teeth contained insect larvae, suggesting a longer than average interval between death and interment. We did not encounter larvae in other burials. From local historical newspaper accounts, we know that burial usually occurred within a few days after death. Viewings and funerals generally were held in the home of the family or a friend, followed by interment in the cemetery. Perhaps this young woman had a loved one who was out of town at the time of her demise, and burial was postponed until he or she arrived. Although embalming began during the Civil War, this practice did not reach Iowa until late in the nineteenth century. Little could be done to preserve the bodies of the dead aside from storage in an ice casket, or "corpse cooler."

A particularly distinctive feature of this burial was that the commingled remains of three other individuals lay between the coffin and outer crate and on the lid of the coffin. Likely what occurred was that all or portions of these three burials were disturbed when the grave shaft for Burial 206 was being dug. The disturbed remains included the skulls of all three individuals, which had been carefully placed in one corner. Perhaps the disturbed burials were unmarked at the time of this young woman's interment. It is unusual that the bones were placed inside the young woman's lidded crate rather than simply deposited in the soil in the grave shaft.

The young woman's bones were in good condition, and her skeleton was nearly complete. She probably stood about five feet five inches, considerably taller than the average of five feet one inch for the women buried at Third Street. She had lost two teeth before she died. Although it seems uncommon these days for such a young person to have missing teeth, unfortunately it was not unusual, given the generally poor dental health observed at the Third Street Cemetery. Twenty-seven enamel defects on her teeth showed that she had suffered four periods of disease or nutritional stress, resulting in enamel growth disruption; two of these periods occurred when she was between 2 and 4 years of age, and two more occurred between 5½ and 6½ years. She had cavities in five teeth. Two upper molars had been completely destroyed, and the sockets contained abscesses.

This young woman displayed degenerative changes in seven vertebrae, suggesting some form of trauma to the spine. These changes were relatively mild compared to the other evidence of disease we observed. She had periostitis on the lung or visceral surface of seven of her left ribs. Both eye sockets contained cribra orbitalia, a pitting of the bone. Lesions were present on the inner surface of the frontal bone of her cranium. Periostitis in conjunction with cribra orbitalia and endocranial lesions suggests she probably suffered from early-stage tuberculosis, showing that even the wealthy were not immune to this disease.

Speculating on the life of the young woman in Burial 206 is easy to do, but actual facts are hard to prove. She likely came from a well-to-do family, based on the expense involved in her elaborate coffin. Her fancy dress suggests something other than casual daywear. She suffered periods of disease or nutritional stress as a child and possibly died of tuberculosis as a young woman just starting her adult life. But what did the scissors mean?

THE LADY WITH A PLATE

Burial 749 consisted of a hexagonal coffin with the lid secured by six coffin screws. Little of the coffin wood survived. The skeletal remains ranged from poor to good condition. Grave goods included four Prosser buttons, two in a row on the chest and one at each wrist. A bone button was found near the left elbow. A religious chaplet lay between the left hand and the breastbone. So far, this appeared to be a relatively unremarkable burial.

But then we found a ten-sided whiteware plate, which had been placed between the left elbow and the left hip. We deciphered the registration mark on the back of the plate and learned that it had been manufactured in Great Britain on June 10, 1851. The plate was plain, with the exception of one raised decorative line on the rim, and it was about dessert plate in size. The exact reason for the placement of such an object in this burial is unknowable. Perhaps it was the last object touched by the deceased. Sometimes, ceramic dishes placed on the body of the deceased may have held some degradable substance. During traditional Irish wakes, it was customary to place a plate with tobacco or salt near the deceased or even on top of the chest. However, there is no documentation to suggest these plates were left in the coffins for burial.

We determined that the individual was an adult female, middle-aged or possibly older based on her poor dental health. She stood about five feet one inch tall, average for the time and place. Oddly, the remains were not all in normal anatomical position. First, the arms were tightly flexed, with the hands resting on the corresponding shoulders, a position observed in only two other burials. Second, the legs and feet were in unusual positions as well. The lower legs and left foot were out of place in the grave, as if they were not attached to the rest of the body when the woman was placed in her coffin. However, we did not see any trauma on the bones. Perhaps the burial of this woman had been delayed for some reason, resulting in differential decomposition prior to interment. This could have resulted if portions of the body were exposed to cold, such as partial submersion in a snowbank or a frozen river, delaying decay, while the rest of the body went through normal decomposition. The more likely explanation is that taphonomic (environmental) factors were involved. Forensic anthropologist Stephen Nawrocki suggests that the legs may have been slightly flexed upward at the time of burial, and when the soft tissue decomposed, the shin bones (tibiae) dropped down over the lower end of the thigh bones (femora).[1] What about our local burrowing animals? Groundhogs certainly could have created some if not all of the disturbance.

Even more than most Dubuquers of the time, this woman had extremely poor dental health: she had lost eighteen teeth before her death, she had cavities in nearly all the teeth present except two, and she had four abscesses. She must have been in considerable pain all the time.

The left and right arm bones displayed bony crests, indicating moderately well-developed areas of muscle attachment, particularly the supinator brevis muscle on the ulnae (one of the two lower arm bones). This muscle allows for the outward motion of the lower arm and hand. Many of the day-to-day tasks performed by most women in the nineteenth century involved use of the arms and arm muscles. Imagine scrubbing clothes by hand, kneading bread, knitting and sewing clothing, cooking and house cleaning without any electric appliances! It's also interesting that she had six, rather than the normal five, lower (lumbar) vertebrae, a trait found in only six other burials at Third Street Cemetery.

The unusual positioning of the remains of the older woman interred in Burial 749 may be explained away by normal decomposition along with disturbance by groundhogs or pocket gophers. It's much harder to account for the plate, though. Possibly her family held with an older European tradition. Even though her health was poor, she clearly led an active life. Whatever caused her death left no skeletal markers that we could see.

AN EARLY DEATH

Burial 818 held the mortal remains of the person we fondly referred to as "Bow Tie Guy." His exceptionally well-preserved coffin still bore traces of two colors of paint, red and cream. One may have been an undercoat or some form of sealant. Coffin trimmings included lining tacks, a viewing pane, and an incomplete coffin-lid cross. The six handles had cross-shaped lugs with an open-book motif at the center of each cross with an additional grapevine decoration. A floral vine motif adorned the bail of the handle. Also decorating this coffin were ten thumbscrews, ten escutcheons with a cross motif, three urn-shaped caplifters over the viewing pane, and a minimum of twenty-four decorative tacks. The tacks were star-shaped, with a six-pointed star in the center and floral designs around the edges. Though not as elaborate as Burial 206's coffin, this one was richly embellished.

Two Prosser buttons found near the upper end of the largest lower leg bones (tibiae), one on each side, probably came from pant cuffs. Seven shell buttons extended from the neck to the lower vertebrae, telling us there used to be a shirt here. A nearly complete silk herringbone bow tie was preserved at the front of the neck and included part of the cotton collar inside it.

The remains were in excellent condition and nearly complete, probably because the grave floor was located in a silty sand lens that allowed for good drainage, in contrast to the soil in most of the Third Street Cemetery. Markers on the skeleton identified this individual as male. He was interred on his back with his arms extended along his sides, and he was probably in his late teens to early twenties at the time of his death, with the age more likely at the lower end of this range. He stood about five feet six inches, a little short of average.

His dental remains were in good condition. All the upper teeth were present. In the lower jaw, both wisdom teeth were congenitally absent (had never formed), as was the left second molar. The young man had three cavities at the time of his death. One of these was in a deciduous tooth that hadn't fallen out on schedule. He had the distinction of having the most enamel defects of any person we found in the cemetery, though this was probably due to the excellent preservation of his teeth rather than any unusual health problems. Twenty-two of his teeth contained sixty-two defects, indicating that he experienced nine episodes of enamel growth disruption from the time he was about six months old until he was five. The front lower teeth were very crowded, a problem characteristic of people from the British Isles. His ancestry, however, is unknown to us.

While the enamel defects indicated repeated health problems in his childhood, evidence on his bones pointed to medical issues closer to the time of the young man's death. His skull showed early-stage lesions in the form of small areas of porosity and white discoloration on the interior surface. Both femora exhibited mild periostitis on the shaft surface and on the neck. Despite having a rough childhood, the young man survived all the periods of disease or nutritional stress that had affected enamel growth on his teeth. Sadly, he did not live very long after that period, probably succumbing to a disease such as meningitis or meningeal tuberculosis. His ornate burial container and fine apparel tell us he had a family willing and able to pay the expense for a fancy funeral. This burial also occurred during the latter half of the cemetery's active use, when elaborate funerals were more common.

THE WOMAN IN THE RED DRESS

The best-preserved wooden coffin encountered during the excavation was found in Burial 868. The solid construction of the crate protected the coffin from ground pressure, so that only the central panels of the lid collapsed. The preservation of the coffin, in turn, promoted the preservation of organic materials *within* the coffin, so the grave also had the distinction of being the only one with any remnant of decomposition odor.

The coffin itself was unique within the Third Street Cemetery, being the only "octagon" or "canted rectangular" burial case we found (see figure 10). The outside of the pine box was completely covered with wool velveteen tacked down by strips of rounded, gold-painted molding. The pile of the fabric was originally dyed dark blue or black. Other than the ostentatious cross-shaped handle lugs, the silver-plated coffin hardware followed a secular theme, with geometric and floral designs, and rose-shaped cap-lifters over the large glass viewing pane.

The collapse of the coffin lid brought the viewing pane to rest directly on top of the bones. Because the glass cracked in only a few places, it created a sealed environment that preserved small amounts of fabric and straw from the mattress and pillow that furnished the coffin. We even found a flower that was pinned to the person's right shoulder. Other plant remains, including juniper greenery, had been placed around the head and on top of the chest. Fragments of red, very fine weave, pleated fabric also survived on top of the remains, remnants of a silk dress that buttoned all the way down to the ankles. Blackened skin still covered some of the ribs, and, eerily, two stains on the glass showed where the eyes had decomposed.

The same unusual burial environment that preserved the organic materials contributed to the disintegration of the mineral component of the bone, similar to the way the acidic, anaerobic conditions of peat bogs preserve the skin and clothing of "bog bodies" while the bones dissolve. The bones in Burial 868 were little more than crumbs, and we could learn nothing from them. We assume the individual was female, based on the clothing. Measured in the grave, she was 4 feet 11½ inches tall, a little shorter than average. Her teeth, which survived in fairly good condition due to the density of dental enamel, provided a little more information. Though she had lost several teeth before death, there was not a great deal of wear on the chewing surfaces of the remaining teeth, suggesting she was neither young nor particularly old. Three of her wisdom teeth had gold fillings.

The ornate coffin-lid cross was not as well preserved as the coffin, so her name was not legible. She was buried with a crucifix and an illegible medal under her right shoulder and a wooden rosary in her hands. Three additional medals were attached to the rosary, two Miraculous Medals and one dedicated to "S. Lewis of Gonzague," who is more commonly known as St. Aloysius Gonzaga in English-speaking countries and Saint-Louis-de-Gonzague in French-speaking areas. This woman's veneration of Aloysius, the patron saint of victims of plague and other incurable diseases, may be a clue pointing to her own long illness or to that of a loved one.

For the moment, the only thing certain about this woman is that she died toward the end of the cemetery's use; her coffin type and the associated hardware would not have been available prior to the mid-1870s. The presence of gold fillings and the elaborately decorated coffin suggest a person or family of some wealth.

A DISTANT DEATH

Burial 897 lay on the far eastern side of the project area, and the foot end of the coffin ran nearly up to the eastern fence line. The eastern end of the burial lay under about three feet of overburden full of construction trash such as gravel and brick fragments. Coffin hardware included lining tacks, coffin-lid cross fragments, four handles, and six coffin screws. Large pieces of wood charcoal had been placed inside the coffin near the legs and waist—not at all typical for Third Street burials. Another unusual feature was the mismatched hardware; the coffin had two different kinds of handle lugs, and one handle had a lug of each type. We found four Prosser buttons in the area of the chest or near the wrist. The lack of pants buttons and the few shirt buttons indicate the man was interred in a simple burial robe or nightshirt. Fabric had been preserved on top of a rosary cross and the back of a religious medal. The rosary was wrapped around the right hand, and the religious medal was resting just below the breast bone.

The remains were in good to fair condition, with some preserved skin. We even found some chest hair adhering to the cloth attached to the back of a religious medal. The individual was interred on his back, with his arms along his sides and hands resting on his pelvis. The long bones were in good condition, but the skull had broken in situ because of ground pressure. Some of the smaller elements, such as hand and foot bones, were not as well preserved. However, the presence of the rosary's copper salts mummified his right thumb, including the fingernail. This man was twenty to thirty-five years old with a stature of 5 feet 8½ inches.

The dental remains were well preserved but showed the usual signs of poor health. Nine teeth each contained a cavity, two so large that the tooth crowns were completely destroyed. Nine enamel defects present on six teeth showed us that he experienced an episode of enamel growth disruption when he was about three, possibly due to weaning or nutritional stress.

Two of the unusual features of Burial 897—the large pieces of wood charcoal and the mismatched coffin handle lugs—hint that this individual died away from Dubuque and had to be shipped back there for burial. The charcoal would have served to reduce the smell of his decomposing body. The lack of matching hardware suggests that whoever procured his coffin may have had to do so hastily. Intrigued by the possible clues in this burial, we searched the historical records for a death with similar circumstances. The local newspaper reported that one Dubuque resident, Charles H. Mix, had died in San Antonio, Texas, prior to January 26, 1870. His remains did not arrive in Dubuque until February 8, and he was buried at Third Street Cemetery on February 9, more than two weeks after his death. There is no direct evidence that the man in Burial 897 is Charles Mix, but it is a possibility. Chapter 10 details what is known about the life and death of Charles H. Mix.

A WOMAN OF MULTIPLE MISFORTUNES

Burial 1022, on the eastern boundary of the project area, was the deepest, and therefore probably earliest, of a group of crowded, overlapping burials. The plain hexagonal coffin was covered with planks rather than being enclosed in a crate. The individual was lying on her back with her arms extended at the sides, hands resting on the upper femora. No grave goods were included with the remains, not even buttons, indicating burial in a simple gown or shroud. Her plain clothing suggests either that she was buried early in the cemetery's existence, before the beautification of death movement, or that there was little money available for her funeral arrangements.

Bone preservation was good, with the skull complete and all elements present. We believed that the person was female based on all observable pelvic features and overall size, though some of the cranial markers were indeterminate for sex. She was probably twenty-five to forty-two years old at her death. Unusually, she was markedly prognathic, especially compared to all the other people we excavated at Third Street. In other words, her lower face projected forward, suggesting that she was of African descent, though the remainder of the cranial features placed her in the Caucasian or intermediate range. She was the only person of African descent we identified in the cemetery.

We calculated that she was about 5 feet 1½ inches tall, but she probably seemed shorter in life because her spine was misshapen from scoliosis. Her upper spine deviated first to the right and then to the left, but the lower vertebrae did not appear to be involved. We did not find any of the traits typical of congenital scoliosis, so the cause of the deformity was probably some kind of trauma or a neuromuscular disorder. The position of the ribs in the grave suggests that she had a rib hump, a hallmark of scoliosis. During excavation, we also found a curved piece of bony material—probably ossified cartilage—overlying the neck of the right femur. Ossification (or hardening into bone) of the cartilage that holds the head of the femur in the hip joint commonly occurs in modern patients with spinal deformities and can cause pain and a limited range of motion.

The woman had lost three teeth during her lifetime. We observed ten enamel defects on six teeth, with the locations suggesting three periods of poor health between 2½ and 4 years. Just like so many other Dubuquers, she had very poor dental health, with ten cavities, three of which had completely destroyed the crowns of the teeth. She also had four active, perforated abscesses at the time of death.

As if these aching teeth were not enough, we also noted that she had two fractures on the right side of the cranium. Radiographic images of the two areas in question show that the defects are consistent with blunt force trauma, and we saw no evidence of healing. If in fact this woman suffered trauma to her head, the event occurred very close to when she died, the last in a series of misfortunes that marked her life.

THESE SKETCHES are just a sample of the lives and deaths we pulled together from the material evidence from the cemetery. Unfortunately, all of these people are nameless to us. However, we were able to give names to some of the residents of the Third Street Cemetery despite the lack of grave markers. Historical archaeologists thrive on small clues left behind, and in the next chapter, we follow these hints from the unknown to the lives of some of our cemetery's citizens.

EIGHT

The Kindhearted Gunsmith's Family

BECAUSE THE Third Street Cemetery had few burial records, no map of the individual graves, and no standing grave markers in situ, we held out little hope that we would be able to identify any of the skeletons recovered during the project. As work progressed, though, a few clues emerged. Excavators found that some of the coffins (about 12 percent) had metal crosses or plaques on the lids. These lid ornaments were originally engraved with information such as the name of the deceased, the date of death, and the age at death. Unfortunately, the thin, cheap metal did not survive well in the acidic soils of the bluff top. More often than not, we found only gray metallic powder in the shape of a cross.

Out of all of the crosses collected, only five had legible names, and four of these were incomplete. One belonged to a child, "M—— Cochran / died January 11th 1860 / aged 3 years." Because he or she was born and died between censuses, and because that spelling of the surname was not found on any records for Dubuque, nothing could be learned about this child or the family. The remaining four crosses led to the identification of two family burial plots and possibly thirteen people.

FINDING THE MURPHYS

"Well, you just never know what's going to happen when you answer the phone," remarked eighty-year-old James T. Lynch after being informed that the graves of his great-great-grandparents had been identified during the Third Street Cemetery excavation and subsequently relocated to Mt. Olivet Cemetery. Prior to the phone call, Mr. Lynch had no idea that he was related to anyone named Murphy, let alone that his ancestors had been resting for more than a century on the bluff in Dubuque.

ONLY ONE COFFIN-LID cross recovered from the excavated portion of the cemetery bore legible first and last names. The silver-plated cross of "Wm. P. Murphy" was also inscribed with a date of death, July 25, 1871. The age at death was unfortunately obscured by corrosion. Also unfortunate was the condition of the bones in the coffin. Though the lid cross was almost perfectly preserved, the bones were in sorry shape. The cranium had been crushed by soil pressure, the surface of the long bones had been damaged by contact with wet, acidic soils, and the vertebrae and ribs had completely decayed. However, the biographical information on the lid cross gave us a unique opportunity for historical research to find out more about Mr. Murphy.

Mr. Murphy's passing was marked by an obituary in each of the competing local newspapers. The "Mortuary" item in the *Dubuque Daily Herald* offers a wealth of information.

Mortuary—Another old settler has departed from our midst. W. P. Murphy expired at the residence of his son-in-law, on 4th street, last evening at 5 o'clock, after a short illness. Deceased was the father-in-law of John Lynch and Lawrence Corcoran of this city, and for a year or more has been unable to leave his residence although he was able to walk from one room to another, a feat he performed last Sunday. Old age crept over him and his feeble frame gave way all at once resulting in death. W. P. Murphy was a man who has filled many important positions in life. For a number of years he was a gunner at the United States armory near Boston, where heavy ordnances were cast and tested which latter business was his special duty. After moving to Dubuque his love for machinery and tools prompted him to open a shop on 8th street, where small jobs such as filing saws, mending locks, fitting keys, &c, occupied his attention for several years. A little over a year ago his consort preceded him to that "bourne from which no traveler ever returns," and thus has passed away another generation. Two children remain of the family, a son residing in Chicago and a daughter, wife of John Lynch. Mr. Murphy's age was 81 years.[1]

The shorter obituary in the *Dubuque Daily Times* describes him as a gunsmith and a kindhearted man who would be missed by a large circle of friends. A small death announcement on the same page states that he died in the eighty-first year of his age. As was often the case in nineteenth-century America, different ages are given for Mr. Murphy in various accounts. All of the available records place his birth somewhere between 1790 and 1800.

According to the U.S. census records, William P. Murphy was born somewhere in Ireland around 1795. His wife, Cecelia, was also born in Ireland around the same time. Exactly when the two married or arrived in the United States is unknown. Their older daughter, Mary, was born in Ireland around 1826. The younger daughter, Cecelia, born between 1830 and 1836, appears on some census records as having been born in Ireland and on others as having been born in Massachusetts. Given this information, it seems likely that the family emigrated in the 1830s. Their point of entry is unknown, but the Murphy family appears to have settled in Massachusetts, since Mr. Murphy's obituary mentions that he worked for a number of years near Boston. After his daughters grew up and married, both women stayed in Massachusetts as well. Two of Mary's children and one of Cecelia's were born in Massachusetts in the late 1840s and early 1850s. Because the name of the Murphys' son is not given in William's obituary, and because the son is not listed as living with the family in any census records, we were unable to gather any information about him.

U.S. military records provided only one likely match for William Murphy, a man who enlisted in New York City on May 1, 1837. Many details of the enlistment match the William Murphy who ended up buried at Third Street. Described as a forty-year-old "whitesmith," the man was slated to work in military ordnance. However, his place of birth is given as Liverpool, England. Perhaps Mr. Murphy misunderstood the question and gave the location he had sailed from rather than his birthplace; Liverpool was the port of departure for many of the Irish sailing to America. It may be that he intentionally lied about his birthplace in an effort to avoid the prejudice against Irish Catholics that was prevalent in America at the time. Alternately, since William Murphy is a common name, this simply may not be the correct individual. The service records for this William Murphy indicate that he spent part of his enlistment at Fort Monroe, Virginia, and there is no mention of his work in Massachusetts. He is described as being 5 feet 4½ inches tall, with a dark complexion, gray eyes, and black hair. Records indicate he was discharged in January 1840, a few months before the end of his initial three-year commitment, due to an unspecified disability.

In November 1851 a patent was granted on a military bounty-land warrant for 160 acres located approximately twenty-five miles southwest of Dubuque. This particular warrant was issued to "William Murphy Laborer in Captain Hanger's [spelling unclear] Company, United States Ordnance." The warrant likely belonged to the William Murphy buried at Third Street, since he was known to have worked in ordnance. We could not confirm the connection, because we found no records of "Captain Hanger's Company." At that time, the U.S. government issuance of bounty-land warrants served two purposes. First, and most importantly, the warrants served as an incentive for enlistment and as a reward for military service. Second, according to public lands historian Benjamin Hibbard, the warrants were issued to veterans in hopes of creating a frontier of battle-hardened pioneers between the displaced Native Americans and the civilian settlers.[2] As such, these warrants went to men who had provided service during wartime—in the War of 1812, the Mexican-American War, one of the many Indian wars—or who had experienced combat of any sort. What service did Mr. Murphy perform to earn such a warrant? His military records do not provide that information. Many recipients of these warrants transferred or sold the warrants themselves or patented the land and sold the acreage. Mr. Murphy probably did the latter, as we found no record of his family ever living in the countryside. The Murphys may have occupied the property briefly between census years, but they had clearly relocated to the city of Dubuque by the early 1850s, since they are listed on the 1854 Iowa state census.

THE MURPHYS IN DUBUQUE

A "Wm. Murphy" is listed on the 1854 Iowa state census as living in Julien Township, which encompassed the city of Dubuque. He was the head of a household including himself and two females. Since no other information is given, the identity of the second female remains unknown. Both of his daughters were married, so it seems unlikely that one of them would have come west without her husband and children. However, both daughters must have brought their families to Dubuque soon after their parents relocated, since both gave birth to children in Iowa in 1855.

The 1860 census shows William Murphy and his wife (name transcribed incorrectly as "Alice") sharing a house with their daughter Cecelia Lynch's family. The Dubuque business directories for 1865–69 list Mr. Murphy as a gunsmith with a shop just five blocks from his residence off Bluff Street. He was also one of the founding members of the local St. Vincent de Paul Society, established in Dubuque in 1858. Daughter Mary Corcoran's family is listed in the census as a separate household but was perhaps not too far away, since the Corcorans were household number 410 and the Murphys were 446.

William's wife, Cecelia, died in 1870. Her death announcement, which appeared in the *Dubuque Daily Times* on February 27, gives her age as seventy-eight and states that the funeral was to proceed from "the residence on Fourth Street, west of Bluff." According to the 1870 mortality schedule, Cecelia was born in Ireland around 1792 and died in March 1870 of intermittent fever, the archaic term for malaria. This entry demonstrates the inaccuracies of the mortality data collected during the 1850–1900 federal censuses, in which households self-reported resident family members who had died in the preceding twelve months. Hazy memories sometimes incorrectly recollected the exact date of death and age at death. Sometimes the cause of death given to the census taker differed from what was listed in the person's obituary. In this case, intermittent fever is the only cause of death recorded for Mrs. Murphy. As it happens, malaria was an uncommon cause of death for the area, accounting for less than 0.5 percent of deaths in the records we examined from Dubuque in the 1850s through 1870s.

William Murphy appears on the 1870 census as a seventy-five-year-old widower and retired gunsmith still living with his daughter's family. We searched courthouse records but failed to find a deed showing that Mr. Murphy or Mr. Lynch had purchased a city lot on Fourth Street, west of Bluff Street, which is the address given in the obituaries. The intersection of Fourth Street and Bluff was a dead end in the 1870s. Since Fourth Street now continues west past Bluff Street, the city lot that was the most likely location of the Murphy home, Lot 611, now lies under the road.

William Murphy's grave was identified by the presence of the well-preserved, engraved coffin-lid cross. After we discovered that his wife preceded him in death by only eighteen months, we took a second look at the materials excavated from the graves around his burial. One of the burials nearby contained a skeleton that showed severe signs of aging. The coffin-lid cross was not complete, and corrosion obscured some of the writing, but the "Cec" and "urp" of Cecelia Murphy were legible.

Buried side by side, the Murphys lay in a plot beside the road that ran through the cemetery, with William's grave to the left (north) of Cecelia's. The two were buried in hexagonal walnut coffins with nearly identical coffin hardware, including handles with cross-shaped lugs, filigreed thumbscrews, floral-motif escutcheons, and crucifix tacks. Both coffins had hinges near the head of the coffin, but the construction of the lids was different. Mr. Murphy's coffin included two sets of hinges on the left side, indicating that the head of the coffin lid could be opened from right to left. Mrs. Murphy's coffin had a set of hinges on each side, near the shoulders, so that the upper part of the lid flipped down from the head, rather than across, for viewing. We found nine metal upholstery buttons in the portion of the coffin that would have been visible with the lid flipped down, which gave us the impression that Mrs. Murphy's coffin interior was a little fancier than her husband's.

Mr. Murphy was laid in his coffin on his back, with his arms extended at his sides and his hands resting on his upper legs. He held a five-decade rosary with wooden or possibly gutta-percha beads and a copper crucifix wrapped around his right hand. He appears to have been buried in clothing from his daily life, since six Prosser buttons were recovered from his grave, found in the configuration one would expect for a shirt. Shrouds purchased specifically for funeral purposes were usually fitted with few, if any, buttons.

Mrs. Murphy also rested on her back in her coffin, with her hands placed on her abdomen. The six-decade, wooden-bead rosary worn around her neck had a plain, stamped, sheet-metal cross. No buttons, pins, or any other clothing fasteners were recovered with her skeleton, which suggests she was buried in a simple shroud or robe. A *Harper's Bazaar* article published in 1886—slightly later than the Third Street Cemetery—makes the following recommendation concerning preparations of the dead: "In dressing the remains for the grave, those of a man are usually 'clad in his habit as he lived.' For a woman, tastes differ; a white robe and cap, not necessarily shroud-like, are decidedly unexceptional."[3]

The coffins and artifacts associated with these two burials reflect exactly what one might expect to find in the graves of a well-respected small businessman and his wife, both members of the Catholic community. The coffins, though trimmed with decorative hardware, do not fall within the highest tier of burial containers found at the site, since metal caskets and coffins with viewing panes represent the greatest expenditure on burial cases. Nevertheless, the cost of the Murphy coffins would have been well above average for the excavated portion of the cemetery.

The location of the graves, immediately adjacent to the east–west road running through the cemetery, may also indicate status, as plots that were easily accessible may have cost more than remote plots. Unfortunately, with few sales records available, we were unable to determine whether or not the cathedral staff used this modern pricing scale. During the process of preparing the grave for Mrs. Murphy, the grave digger unearthed an older coffin containing a middle-aged man. The bones of this unknown man were deposited haphazardly on top of and around Mrs. Murphy's coffin. This preferential treatment of Mrs. Murphy's remains may have been a reflection of the family's standing in the community. More likely, it merely resulted from overcrowding in the cemetery. The Murphy burials occurred during the last decade of the cemetery's use, so the lack of empty lots is not surprising.

OSTEOLOGICAL ANALYSIS

Physical anthropologists perform osteological analysis independent of historical research so that information from written sources does not influence their findings. This blind analysis sometimes brings important discrepancies to light. In some cases, the skeletal examination shows that the historical records are incorrect; the following chapter concerning the

Blake family offers an example of osteology exposing a 136-year-old lie. In other cases, accurate historical records demonstrate the limitations of osteological analysis, especially when dealing with poorly preserved and incomplete bones.

The skeleton in Mr. Murphy's grave was easily identified as male based on characteristics of the skull and pelvis. However, many of the surfaces that osteologists examine in order to determine age had deteriorated in the grave. Based on what was present and observable, the analyst classified him as a middle-aged adult, despite the fact that all but five teeth were lost before death. This age estimate was supported by the fact that his remaining teeth had little wear, usually an indication of a younger individual who has not abraded the surfaces of the teeth through decades of chewing. Additionally, only mild age-related changes were seen on the joint surfaces, except for the left shoulder. The preponderance of the evidence from the bones pointed to a middle-aged man. These findings do not imply that the wrong person was resting in Mr. Murphy's coffin. Aging methods can be unreliable when human remains are not in good condition. The lack of tooth wear can be attributed to early loss of the opposing teeth, which left the remaining teeth with nothing to grind against. The fact that we found little evidence of arthritis was mainly due to the poor preservation of the vertebrae and other joint surfaces most often affected by age-related degeneration.

Little other information could be gleaned from the analysis of Mr. Murphy. Enamel defects observed on some teeth confirmed a period of illness or health stress between the ages of 2½ and 3 years. The stature estimate, based on long bone lengths, is 5 feet 4½ inches, which correlates with the measurement taken of the skeleton while still in the grave. Though this height is below average for males in the Third Street Cemetery population, it is within the observed range. Interestingly, this estimate precisely matches the height given on the military records of the William Murphy who enlisted in New York in 1837.

The bones of Cecelia Murphy fared even more poorly than her husband's. Many joint surfaces were degraded or completely absent, and the vertebrae, ribs, and pelvis were represented only by small bone fragments. Evaluation of sex relied entirely on a fragmented skull with the outer surface peeling away. Three of the cranial characteristics indicated a male, and two were intermediate (midway between male and female in appearance), so the osteologist recorded the individual as a possible male. While this determination was reasonable given the evidence on the surviving bones, there was nothing about the skeleton that would rule out the possibility that the individual was female. The evaluation of sex of poorly preserved remains frequently yields ambiguous or even incorrect results.

The skeletal remains provided much clearer evidence of Mrs. Murphy's age than her sex. The appearance of the pelvis and the extent of cranial suture closure—the fusing of the individual bones of the skull—indicated an age of sixty years or older. All but four teeth were lost before death. Severe degenerative joint disease was observed in the bones of the neck, on fragments of the lower vertebrae, and on the few other joint surfaces present. Thinning of the outer surface of the long bones suggested osteoporosis, and a buildup of bone on the internal surface of the skull, known as hyperostosis frontalis interna, indicated advanced age. This thickening of the frontal bone of the skull is common in postmenopausal women and causes no symptoms.

Osteological analysis also provided tantalizing clues about Mrs. Murphy's life. There was evidence of three possible cysts on the bones of the right and left wrists. These may have been ganglion cysts, commonly known as "Bible" cysts, fluid-filled lumps that are harmless and often painless. Two small, smooth bone growths, probably benign tumors, were found on the outer surface of the front of the skull. A circular indentation near the back of the skull appeared to be a well-healed depression fracture. One of the canine teeth exhibited the kind of notch that is usually related to pipe smoking in the Third Street population.

Unfortunately, the historical record offers few details about Mrs. Murphy's life to compare with the osteological findings. Questions of when and how she received her head injury remain unanswered. We have no way of knowing if her cysts caused her discomfort, though her advanced arthritis almost certainly did. Since malaria leaves no mark on the bones, we were unable to confirm the recorded cause of death. Her pipe smoking would not have been remarkable, though as a middle-class woman she might not have done it in public. Bone length measurements were not possible in the lab due to the condition of the remains, but approximate measurements taken during the excavation yielded a stature estimate of 5 feet ½ inch. Her husband may have been short, but she could still look up to him.

Two other members of the Murphy family may also have been interred in the family plot. Mary Corcoran, the older daughter of William and Cecelia, died on October 29, 1865, at the age of forty-two. Her obituary specifies that she was buried on the bluff with a daughter who preceded her in death. The name and age of the daughter are not given, but it was likely Mary Anne Corcoran, who was born in 1855 and died sometime prior to the 1860 census. Immediately to the south of Mrs. Murphy's grave, excavators found the burial of a woman interred with a child's coffin covering the foot of her coffin. Based on the developmental stage of the teeth, the child was estimated to be about two years old. The adult skeleton was estimated to be between thirty and forty-four years old, and her stature was calculated at 5 feet ¾ inch, which is consistent with the expected height of a daughter of the Murphys. She had a small, healed depression fracture on the right side of her head and evidence of an injury to her back. Her left arm and right hand had also been fractured before her death; the breaks had healed, but signs of infection were still present. We observed cribra orbitalia, porotic hyperostosis, and periostitis of the clavicles and lower legs, likely evidence of some type of systemic infection or chronic illness. This suite of medical conditions could have been compared to biographical information, if such information were available. Unfortunately, nothing is known about the life of Mary or her daughter. The adult coffin was somewhat ornate, but no similarities in the hardware connected her coffin to those of the Murphys. The coffin-lid cross was well preserved but bore no name. Without any further information, the identifications of Mary and Mary Anne Corcoran are tentative at best.

THE DESCENDANTS

Now that we had identified the Murphys, the next big question was whether or not we could find any living relatives. There is a tendency to think of modern American society as being unsettled and nomadic in comparison with previous generations. In fact, in the nineteenth century this country witnessed constant westward migration. This mobility is one of the many reasons that historic graves have come to be forgotten. The dead were left behind as the families moved on to new land and fresh opportunities. Therefore, tracking down descendants is not always a simple task.

Census records are an excellent resource for following a family's off-spring through time, but three major limitations exist. The first limitation is related to mobility. If a family moves away from a known location between census years, how does one know where to look next? Fortunately, computer search engines have made this a surmountable problem, provided that the cluster of names representing a family is unique enough to be distinguished from other families and that other basic information, such as birth dates, is known. The second problem is that daughters become untraceable through the census once they leave the family home and take on a new surname. Unless additional information is available from marriage records or other sources, only sons can be followed from one census to another. The third issue is that U.S. census records remain sealed for seventy-two years. At the beginning of the Third Street project, the 1930 census was the most recent one available, and many of the people listed in those records had already passed away.

William and Cecelia could not be found on census records from the 1830s and 1840s, when their children would have been living in the same household, so other sources had to provide the names of their offspring. According to Mr. Murphy's obituary, the couple had three children who lived to adulthood. The name of the son who lived in Chicago is not mentioned in the article, but the married names of the two daughters are given.

Daughter Mary, who died in 1865, was married to Lawrence Corcoran, a pressman at the newspaper. The couple had two children who survived to adulthood, Thomas W. and Cecelia. Thomas took up his father's trade and remained in Dubuque most of his life, but just before the turn of the century, Lawrence and Cecelia Corcoran moved to Janesville, Wisconsin. Retired father and spinster daughter are shown living together on the 1900 census, with "Washing & Ironing" listed as forty-eight-year-old Cecelia's profession. An obituary shows that Lawrence died in 1903, and Cecelia could not be located on any subsequent census records.

Thomas Corcoran appears on the 1895 Iowa state census, where he is listed as a patient at the Iowa Hospital for the Insane in Independence, Buchanan County, Iowa. In 1900 he still resided at the hospital. By 1905 he had returned to Dubuque. The 1910 census marks his last appearance on any obtainable records; he is shown as a roomer in a hotel, still single and working for the newspaper. This census entry is the last evidence of the Corcoran branch of the Murphy family.

William and Cecelia's younger daughter, Cecelia, married John Lynch, a tailor. The Lynch family stayed in Dubuque after the Murphys died. They had four children who survived to adulthood: Andrew William, Sarah A., Cecelia, and James Thomas. The two girls could not be tracked in the census records, presumably because they married. Andrew William Lynch, another newspaper pressman, and his wife, Minnie D., are shown on the 1900 census as residing in Dubuque with their two children. This branch of the family had moved to Chicago by 1910, and no living descendants could be tracked down.

The remaining Murphy grandchild, James Thomas Lynch, continued to appear on the federal and Iowa state census records as living in Dubuque up to 1925, first as a bookkeeper and later as a sidewalk inspector. He and his wife, Elizabeth, had at least six children, but only one of them was recorded as living in the area after reaching adulthood. George T. Lynch—William and Cecelia's great-grandson—appears on the 1915 Iowa state census as a twenty-five-year-old telegraph operator in Dubuque. The 1920 census records list George T. Lynch working as a telegraph operator for the railroad and living in Savanna, Illinois, about fifty miles south of Dubuque. By 1930 he lived in Minneapolis and worked as a freight agent for the railroad. He was married to Ida Lynch, and they had a six-month-old daughter listed in the census records as Dona [sic] J. Lynch.

Efforts to find living descendants of the Murphys were stalled for several months while we waited anxiously for the release of the 1940 census. After that information was made public in 2012, we discovered that the Lynch family had moved to St. Paul by 1940 and had added another child, James, who was born in 1932. Donna Jean and James T. Lynch were the great-great-grandchildren of William and Cecelia Murphy.

At this point, it would have been impossible to go any further were it not for the combination of uncommon names and the magic of Internet search engines. An Internet search including the terms "Ida Lynch,"

"Donna," and "obituary" produced an obituary that gave us Donna's married name (Putney) and the 1980 residence of James T. Lynch, which was Burlington, Iowa. Sadly, Donna had already passed away.

James Lynch had put down roots in Burlington and was listed in the phone book when we went looking for him in 2012. Though surprised by a phone call about ancestors he had never heard of, Mr. Lynch talked with us at length about the project. He willingly shared information about the rest of his family and put us in touch with his daughters and nieces, who were also kind enough to take the time to answer our questions. We mailed out a packet including all the information collected about the Murphy family and their graves, as well as maps showing the location of the Third Street Cemetery, the location of Mt. Olivet Cemetery, and the location of the grave in Mt. Olivet where the Murphys have been reburied. Mr. Lynch and his daughters expressed interest in seeing the final report on the excavation and gave permission to have their names included so that the genealogical record would be complete.

Donna Lynch married Glenn Putney, and the couple had two children, Linda Mancini and Laurie Gerding. Laurie and her husband, Bill, have a daughter named Jillian Gerding. James Lynch married Patricia Ann

FIGURE 14. Murphy descendants (*clockwise from top left*): George T. Lynch (as a young man, with two unidentified women), George T. Lynch (later years), Donna J. Putney, Jillian Gerding, Laurie Gerding, and Linda Mancini.

FIGURE 15. Murphy descendants (*from left*): James T. Lynch, Juli Weiss, Rachel Weiss, and Angela Keyserling, with husband Michael Keyserling.

Dannies, and they had two children, Juli Weiss and Angela Keyserling. Juli and her husband, Bradley, have a daughter, Rachel Weiss. Jillian Gerding and Rachel Weiss are the great-great-great-great-granddaughters of the Murphys. At the time of publication, six known descendants of William and Cecelia Murphy were still living in Iowa, Florida, and South Carolina (figures 14 and 15). Sadly, James Lynch passed away in 2014.

The outcome of the search for the Murphy descendants was a pleasant one, but the situation could have been different. In other cases where abandoned cemeteries have been relocated to make way for development, descendant families have protested and even initiated lawsuits, as was the case with an abandoned African-American cemetery on a landfill property in Clayton County, Georgia. Though the courts dismissed the lawsuits and a district attorney's investigation found that the Clayton County Commission had acted within the law in issuing the disinterment permit, the episode stirred up many hard feelings in the community. Relocation of a Euroamerican settler cemetery in Ooltewah, Tennessee, halted midexcavation when locals demanded that the Hamilton County Commission reexamine the disinterment permitting process. Again, no wrongdoing was discovered, and the project went forward. In this instance, the individuals who initiated the investigation did not claim any relation to those buried in the cemetery. Notifications had been placed in the local newspaper in an effort to locate descendants who might have an interest in the fate of the burial ground, and none of the relatives had offered objections.

The situation of the Third Street Cemetery was a little different. By the time the Murphys were identified and the relatives located, the human remains had already been excavated, analyzed, and reburied. What would have happened if the descendants were upset by our work? The disinterment permit was legally obtained, with the Iowa District Court, Dubuque County, ruling that, "due to the passage of time, the lack of burial records and the abandonment of the graveyard . . . there are no surviving spouses or ascertainable next-of-kin of the decedents buried in the unmarked graves." The two institutions that oversee enforcement of Iowa's burial protection laws, the Office of the State Archaeologist and the Iowa Department of Public Health, approved the disinterment order. Perpetual care was not offered when the Murphys paid for their plots, so the Archdiocese of Dubuque could also claim exemption from liability. If the Lynch family had wanted to claim the Murphys' remains, who would have paid for the work of disinterring them again? Heavy equipment would be required to unearth and open the concrete vault, and someone would have to look through more than three hundred labeled containers of remains to find William and Cecelia. The archdiocese paid for all of the reburials, but would it be willing to accommodate a particular family for a re-reburial? These are issues that should be considered ahead of time when the decision is made to relocate a cemetery in the name of progress.

Fortunately, we did not encounter any negative reactions from relatives of the dead in the cemetery. The Murphy descendants were content to learn that their forebears had been well cared for and reburied at no expense to them. Though all of the family tree information has been given to the superintendent of Mt. Olivet Cemetery in case other descendants come forward, future problems seem unlikely. And it is nice to think that members of the Lynch line might visit the grave site in Mt. Olivet one day, if only out of curiosity.

NINE

The Brick Maker's Unfortunate Family

APPROXIMATELY TEN YARDS northeast of the Murphy plot, close to the old road through the cemetery, we discovered a cluster of graves we believe belonged to the Blake family. One of these burials contained a partially legible coffin-lid cross engraved with the name "SUSAN [B] LAK[E]" and "Age 28" (figure 16). According to the local newspaper, a woman named Susan Blake died at the age of twenty-eight in 1876, and her obituary specified that she was buried in the Third Street Cemetery. The obituary also states that Susan was the daughter of the late John Blake, brick maker and former city alderman. Archival research using the church burial records, newspaper obituaries, and census records revealed that John Blake himself and eight of his children were probably buried at Third Street. These materials, in conjunction with courthouse documents and baptism records, allowed us to compile a history of the family and to

FIGURE 16. Coffin-lid cross of Susan Blake.

gather enough personal information to make tentative identifications of the people buried in the vicinity of Susan Blake.

DEATHS IN THE BLAKE FAMILY

The brief biography of John Blake Sr. printed in the *Dubuque Daily Times* after his death in 1870, states: "About twenty-four years ago, Mr. Blake purchased a lot in the 3d Street Cemetery and near the same period of time buried three of his children there, and two more recently."[1] The deaths of the first three children, John, Julia, and Charles Blake, were recorded in the St. Raphael's Cathedral burial register. All died in the 1840s. According to Bishop Loras's day book, John Blake Sr. purchased a cemetery lot on October 15, 1843, just five days before the death of the first child, John. Of the two more recent burials mentioned in the biography, one was that of John's son William Blake, whose obituary appeared in January 1868.

John Blake Sr.'s death in August 1870 was followed two months later by the death of his youngest child, John Joseph. Susan Blake's obituary in 1876 was the last mention in the newspapers of a Blake being buried at Third Street. However, two other children of Mr. Blake, Ellen and Eliza, disappeared from the census records during the active period of the cemetery. Ellen Blake is listed on the 1850 federal census but not on the Iowa state census of 1856. She does not reappear in subsequent records. Between 1850 and 1856 Ellen would have been seventeen to twenty-three years old. While this is a common age for marriage, we found no record of her marriage license at the Dubuque County Courthouse. Few newspapers from this time period have survived, so we found no obituary for Ellen. She is not listed in the cathedral burial register, but those records are incomplete, especially for the years 1855 and 1856. Since she is not listed as one of the heirs in her father's will, it is likely that she died before he did. Her grave was probably the other recent burial mentioned in the biography of John Blake Sr. Eliza Blake disappeared from the records between the 1870 and 1880 censuses, a period during which she would have been in her twenties. No marriage license or obituary was found for Eliza either.

The biography of Mr. Blake states that he was distressed by the city council's decision to lease the Third Street Cemetery for mining purposes, and "the very last act of his life was the purchase of a new lot, less likely to future disturbance, and the removal of his children. . . . A few days since Mr. B was buried in the same lot." Since Mr. Blake's obituary specifies that he would be buried at Third Street, it appears that he did not remove his children's graves to the cemetery outside of town. Rather, he moved them from their plot in the original Roman Catholic Grave Yard lot and reinterred them in Outlot 723, the later addition to the western side of the cemetery. The bishop had a clear legal title to Outlot 723, so there was no danger that the city council would sell the mineral rights to this property.

Based on the information gathered thus far, we determined that nine members of the Blake family were likely buried in Outlot 723 of the Third Street Cemetery. The graves of John (1840–43, three years), Charles (1845, ten days), Julia (1846, three weeks), Ellen (1833–1850s, age unknown), and William (1831–68, thirty-seven years) would be reinterments. John Sr. (1808–70, sixty-two years), John Joseph (1851–70, nineteen years), Eliza (1843–1870s, age unknown), and Susan (1837–76, thirty-eight years) all died after the new burial plot was purchased in 1870.

FAMILY HISTORY

John Blake was born in County Cork, Ireland, on June 24, 1808. The date of his marriage is unknown, but his wife, Ellen, née Murphy, was also born in County Cork circa 1810. The Blakes' son William was born around 1831. Between the birth of William and the birth of daughter Ellen around 1833, the family immigrated to New York, where Mr. Blake was engaged as the superintendent of an ironworks. According to census records, daughter Mary was also born in New York around 1835.

In 1836 the family relocated to Dubuque, where John Blake established himself as a manufacturer of bricks, "by which business he had amassed considerable property," according to an article in the *Dubuque Daily Herald*. He served as a city alderman for several years beginning in 1844. Courthouse deed books show that during his residence in Dubuque, Mr. Blake bought and sold dozens of properties and mineral rights to properties. One deed from August 10, 1867, bears both John Blake's signature and an "X" labeled "Ellen Blake's mark." From this deed, it may be assumed that Mrs. Blake could not read or write, though she was never listed in the census records as illiterate.

The location of the original family residence is unknown, though the family may have settled on Mineral Street immediately upon arriving in Dubuque. In his memoirs, fellow Dubuquer and contemporary Josiah Conzett states that the well-known Blake home was already standing when Conzett's family arrived in town in March 1846. The earliest directory that could be located during research, the 1857 city directory, shows the family residing on Mineral Street. On a 1906 map the block of their residence is labeled "Ellen Blake's Subdivision." The house is described in the *Dubuque Daily Times* biographical sketch of Mr. Blake. "Mr. Blake displayed much taste in the erection of a residence on Mineral Street. Shaded and adorned with beautiful, thrifty trees, it is indeed a sylvan retreat, where 'Eternal greens the mossy margin grace, Watched by the sylvan genius of the place.'"[2] The house was, of course, constructed of brick.

Mr. Blake brought his family to Dubuque at the urgings of his brothers William and Charles, who had left Ireland before him and were among those lead prospectors who began mining in the vicinity of Dubuque in 1832, before the land was officially opened to American settlement. Records from the 1836 territorial census list seven residents in Mr. Blake's household, including himself, his wife, three children, and two additional adult males who were probably his brothers William and Charles. The 1840 census shows a household of nine, which includes the Blakes' daughter Susan, who was born around 1837. Two men in their twenties are listed as part of the household, but these are not Mr. Blake's brothers, since William and Charles are listed as heads of their own households. The two unnamed men may have been boarders or laborers. A female between the age of ten and fifteen may have been a boarder or a servant.

According to records from St. Raphael's Cathedral, John and Ellen Blake's son John was born around 1840 and died on October 20, 1843. Daughter Helene, who is listed in census records with many name variations, was born on February 17, 1841, followed by daughter Eliza on March 23, 1843. A son named Charles was born on January 26, 1845, and died ten days later. Daughter Julia, born February 19, 1846, died at the age of three weeks on March 13.

The 1850 census records show the eight members of the Blake family sharing a household with nine unrelated individuals. Of these, eight were men born in Ireland. They may have been workers in the brick-making concern, since they were all between the ages of twenty-four and thirty-eight, and they were listed as laborers. No profession is given for the eighteen-year-old woman, Margaret, but she may have been a servant. The family could certainly afford a servant. John Blake's real estate was recorded as having a value of $4,500 that year, the equivalent of about $120,000 in 2012. According to cathedral records, the youngest child of the Blake family, John Joseph, was born on July 10, 1851.

The Iowa state census of 1856 shows the Blake family living with a different female servant, H. Dergan, and two unrelated male laborers in their twenties. Daughter Ellen is not listed, presumably having died. Eldest son William was either living away from home or accidentally omitted from the records. He may have joined his uncle Charles Blake, who headed to California during the gold rush. Charles died en route, and the location of his grave is unknown. By 1860 William had returned to his father's home and was listed as a "day laborer." The value of Mr. Blake's real estate that year was listed as $35,000, while the value of his personal estate was $500. Only one unrelated individual is shown in the household in the 1860 census records, a forty-year-old servant named Anna. It is interesting to note that all of the unrelated individuals who resided with the Blake family over the years were born in Ireland.

William Blake died of consumption (tuberculosis) on January 19, 1868, at the age of thirty-seven. His obituary in the *Dubuque Daily Herald* explains that he was prostrated with sickness for several weeks. This death announcement also states that his remains were to be taken to Key West Cemetery for interment. Why would he be buried in Key West when his brothers and sisters were buried at Third Street? It is possible that the plans for his funeral were misreported. During the course of research, we found several instances in which newspaper retractions of incorrectly reported burial locations were printed after the funeral occurred. No such retraction appeared for William Blake, though. Another explanation for his burial alone in Key West is that his death occurred during the year that the Third Street Cemetery was officially closed. His father may have exhumed his coffin from Key West and buried him in the family plot after the cemetery reopened later in 1868 or after the purchase of the new family plot in 1870. In any case, there is no headstone for William Blake in Key West (Mt. Olivet) Cemetery.

The census of 1870 lists John Blake Sr. as a retired manufacturer living in the Fifth Ward of Dubuque with real estate property valued at $12,000 and personal property at $800. This estate valuation illustrates a substantial reduction in the family's fortune, down to one-quarter of the 1860 appraisal, taking postwar inflation into account. They were, however, still quite well off, as evidenced by the other estate values listed for Dubuque in the 1870 census. No unrelated individuals are listed as living with the Blake family that year. Though two members of the family passed away in 1870, both died after the mortality schedule was compiled for the census, so little information is available about their deaths. John Blake Sr. died on August 11, 1870, at the age of sixty-two. The obituary in the *Dubuque Daily Herald* gives his cause of death as a "malignant type of fever" and states that the illness lasted a few weeks. The *Dubuque Daily Times* death notice states that he expired after a long and painful illness. The funeral began at the family residence on Mineral Street, followed by services at the cathedral and burial at the Third Street Cemetery. Reportedly, over fifty carriages took part in the funeral procession. Two months later, John Joseph died in St. Louis just a few weeks after moving there to attend college. According to the obituary in the *Dubuque Daily Herald*, his death followed a brief illness. The body of the nineteen-year-old was brought back to Dubuque and interred at Third Street.

The probate records for John Blake Sr. show that he left all of his personal and real estate property to his wife, to be divided after her death between John Joseph, Mary, Nancy (Helene), and Eliza. To Susan he bequeathed "the sum of one dollar." No reason is given for her disinheritance. Susan Blake died on March 4, 1876. The age given in her *Dubuque Herald* obituary was twenty-eight, and cause of death was not reported. As mentioned previously, Eliza Blake disappears from the census records sometime between 1870 and 1880.

Of the seven Blakes listed on the 1870 census, only three remained in the household by the time of the 1880 census: the widowed Ellen and her two unmarried daughters, Mary and Anna (formerly recorded as Nancy). The records list Ellen as "keeping house" and the two daughters merely as "at home." Estate value estimates no longer appear on census records after 1870, so it is unknown whether the family was living in reduced circumstances. The 1885 Iowa state census shows the family living at 367 W. Locust Street, because Mineral Street was renamed in the 1880s. Helene/Nancy/Anna is listed as Nellie. The 1890 census was destroyed in a fire, but the family appears on the 1900 census. Ellen passed away sometime in the intervening fifteen years, but the two unmarried daughters were still living at 367 W. Locust, with Helene/Nancy/Anna/Nellie listed as Nettie.

After 1910 the two Blake sisters no longer appear in the census records. Nettie is last shown living on Locust Street in the 1918 city directory. Her obituary appeared in the *Dubuque Telegraph-Herald* on December 15, 1919, with the name Nancy.

The house numbers in Dubuque were changed in 1920; based on the shifting of the neighboring house numbers, the Blake house should have had an odd number between 601 and 637. Apparently the house was unoccupied after the death of the last Blake, since no house number in that range was listed in the 1922 city directory. The home, which was one of the finest houses in Dubuque when it was built, no longer exists. According to Josiah Conzett, Mr. Blake's wealth "was spent and dissipated By his two Sons—leaving his Widow and her Daughters nothing but The Home and that almost a ruin."[3] At the time of our research, a Dollar General store and parking lot occupied the spot where the Blake home probably once stood on Lot 7 of Ellen Blake's Subdivision.

A PECULIAR FAMILY TRADITION

During the review of census records, we noticed a peculiar trend. The Blakes always lied to the census takers about the ages of their daughters. While it was common for heads of household to give only approximate ages of their children, the misreporting of the Blake girls' ages was so egregious that it appears deliberate (see table 1).

The result of this reporting is that Mary and Helene both "age" only twenty years in the fifty years between 1850 and 1900. By contrast, William's age appears to be reported correctly in 1850 and given as three years too young in 1860. John Joseph's age is reported correctly on all records. More than a decade after their mother's death, the two remaining sisters

TABLE 1. Ages reported in federal census records for the daughters of the Blake family

Name	Age in 1850	1860	1870	1880	1900
Mary	15	19	27	25	35
Susan	13	17	25		
Helene	11 (Nancy)	15 (Nancy)	23 (Annie)	23 (Anna)	30 (Nettie)
Eliza	7	13	20		

finally gave the census taker somewhat accurate ages; the 1910 census lists Mary as sixty-nine and Nettie (Helene) as sixty-seven.

Perhaps the parents hoped younger ages would make their unmarried daughters more appealing to potential suitors. In the case of Susan, it is clear that the charade was not for the census takers alone; both her obituary and her coffin-lid cross give her age as twenty-eight, though she was probably around thirty-eight when she died. None of the five Blake daughters who survived childhood went on to marry, an unusual circumstance in the nineteenth century, particularly for a prominent and well-to-do family. We did not find any of the family's personal papers during research, so the reason behind the public age misrepresentation and the unmarried daughters remains a mystery.

DESCENDANTS

All four of the male heirs born to John Blake were dead by the end of 1870. Only William had reached marriageable age, and we found no record that he ever wed or produced legitimate offspring. Of the female children, at least one died in infancy, three died while relatively young and unmarried, and two died as old spinsters. As far as can be determined, all descendants of John and Ellen Blake were dead by 1920.

THE FAMILY PLOT

Five graves were found in the vicinity of Susan Blake's burial. Viewed on the site map, the grouping appears to be separated from the surrounding graves, though this impression is artificially enhanced by the fact that all the burials to the south were removed by land grading decades prior to archaeological fieldwork. The graves were arranged in two rows, running approximately north-northwest to south-southeast. The western row included (in order, from northwest to southeast) Burials 64, 287, and 101, and the eastern row included Burials 36, 30, and 24, as well as the disturbed remains of at least two infants placed between Burials 30 and 36. We noted that these graves included two of only three metal coffins found during the excavation and two of only nine individuals with gold dental fillings.

Armed with information from historical sources and the data from the independent osteological analysis, we began looking for connections between the members of the Blake family and the human remains excavated from the two rows near Susan. We first compared age and sex and then looked for more specific details that would link the graves to the individual Blakes.

We knew from the coffin-lid cross—silver plated and engraved with shamrocks, her name, and her age—that Burial 64 contained the remains of Susan Blake. We couldn't confirm female sex from the poorly preserved skeletal remains, but the age at death was evaluated as somewhere between thirty and forty-four years. This estimate is inconsistent with the age of twenty-eight years given on the coffin plate and in her obituary but corresponds to her historically documented age of thirty-eight. Thus, our analysis helped expose a 136-year-old lie! Susan had nine gold fillings, and she was buried in an elaborately decorated coffin with a glass viewing pane. These expenditures seem at odds with the image of a daughter who was cut from her father's will. Perhaps her alienation ended after her father died. Or perhaps the strange clause in the will was not a reflection of disfavor but rather a matter of practical necessity due to some unknown legal or financial situation.

The lid cross on the coffin in Burial 101 was so degraded that we could not read the name or date of death. Since the unusual bouquet-motif coffin handles were patented in 1867, though, the individual had to have been buried at some point after that. The skeleton belonged to a middle-aged man, thirty to fifty years old, who was approximately five feet eight inches tall. His dental health was relatively good, but enamel defects indicated that he experienced three distinct episodes of illness between the ages of one and five years. All four third molars (wisdom teeth) were congenitally absent. This absence is a relatively common finding in modern European populations. Minor compression fractures were observed on some of the lower vertebrae, but we could not determine the extent of his spinal injuries because of poor bone preservation. A lesion, or hole, in the bone behind the right ear indicated that the man suffered from mastoiditis. This inflammatory condition is sometimes found in children with severe ear infections today but was a common secondary infection in tuberculosis patients in the nineteenth century. Since William Blake died of tuberculosis in 1868 at the age of thirty-seven, Burial 101 was likely his grave. Interestingly, he was the only Blake buried with a religious object, a small French Miraculous Medal.

Burial 36 was the designation for the remains of three people, an adult in an elaborately decorated, hinged wooden coffin and two infants whose commingled bones were found between the coffins of Burials 30 and 36. The adult was a man between the ages of forty-five and sixty years. He was somewhere between five feet eight inches and five feet ten inches tall in life. He had poor dental health, with numerous cavities. Both of the lower wisdom teeth were congenitally absent. Unusually, the left maxillary lateral incisor, the tooth to the left of the "two front teeth," also appeared to be congenitally absent. This lack of tooth formation is often a hereditary trait. Both Schmorl's nodes (signs of disc protrusion) and compression fractures were noted on his vertebrae. Compression fractures can be caused by traumatic injury, by indirect stress due to heavy labor, or by loss of bone structure due to osteoporosis. All three of these conditions were likely for a nineteenth-century brick maker who had surpassed the age of sixty. The individual was tentatively identified as John Blake Sr. because the skeletal remains were consistent with those of a sixty-two-year-old man and the coffin was appropriate for a prominent local businessman.

The incomplete bones of at least two infants were found jumbled together between Burials 30 and 36, with no coffin materials of their own. Based on size and development, the bones were separated into two individuals aged 1½ to 2½ years and newborn to 6 months. The older child had cribra orbitalia, a condition often associated with anemia and chronic illness. This child is believed to be John Blake Jr., based solely on age and the fact that the remains were found within the Blake plot. Also, historical documents show that the family had sufficient warning of the child's impending death to buy a burial plot in advance. The skeletal signs of chronic illness are consistent with this scenario rather than a sudden death. The younger infant is believed to be Julia or Charles Blake, based on age alone. We did not find any remains representing a third Blake infant, who should have been buried with the others. However, the newspaper biography of Mr. Blake states that the graves of the three infants were moved to the new family plot decades after their original interment. Preservation was probably poor, and many bones may have been left behind in the original graves, which is not uncommon in disinterments. The remains were disturbed again when Burial 30 was interred, and more bones were probably lost at that time. It is not surprising that the third Blake infant was missing or else rendered unrecognizable in the handful of bones recovered from the narrow space between the coffins.

Burial 30 contained one of only three metal coffins found in the excavated portion of the Third Street Cemetery. The lid cross was identical in design to Susan Blake's, right down to the shamrocks. The name "Eliza" was inscribed at the top, but only the first two letters of the death date were legible, "Ju." The first digit of the age at death was "2." The skeleton inside the coffin was female, though some of her bone measurements fell within a range typically assigned to males. Her stature was around five feet six inches, which is above average for women in this cemetery population, and she appeared to be about twenty to twenty-nine years old. We found evidence of a mild pathological condition in the temporomandibular joints, where the lower jaw attaches to the cranium, but the nature of the problem was not identified. Her dental health was poor, and she had four gold fillings. Enamel defects indicated periods of illness recurring regularly through early childhood; similar evidence of recurring illness was also noted on Susan's teeth. Eliza's lower wisdom teeth and one of her upper premolars (which dentists call "bicuspids") were congenitally absent. The left maxillary lateral incisor—the tooth missing from John Blake Sr.—was also absent. This young woman is presumed to be Eliza Blake, though no obituary could be found to confirm a June or July death date. Eliza was in her late twenties to early thirties when she disappeared from the census records, and that age is consistent with both the osteological age of the remains and the age given on the lid cross. Her lid cross was identical to Susan's, and her metal coffin was identical to Burial 24 (below). Her gold fillings, observed on only nine individuals in the excavated portion of the cemetery, are another strong tie to Susan, and her congenitally absent teeth connect her to the rest of the family.

The metal coffin of Burial 24 was identical to the one in Burial 30 in every detail except that no lid cross was recovered. Though the two coffins were buried side by side, it does not appear that they were buried at the same time, since the head of one coffin was offset to the west. The individual in the coffin was a young man approximately 15½ to 18½ years old. A variety of buttons and some preserved fabric suggest that he was buried in a jacket, shirt, and pants, with a cravat or bow tie at the neck. His dental health was good. Enamel defects indicated only a single period of illness at the age of 2 to 2½ years. Both maxillary lateral incisors were congenitally absent, instead of just the left lateral incisor, as seen in the other Blakes. All four wisdom teeth also appeared to be congenitally absent. The young man was tentatively identified as John Joseph Blake, since the estimated age is consistent with the age at death reported in his obituary. Also, we know that the youngest son of the Blake family died away from home, in St. Louis. The use of a metal casket does not always indicate that a body travelled after death, but it certainly raises the possibility. Additionally, the congenitally absent teeth connect this young man to the rest of the Blake family.

Burial 287 held a plain hexagonal wooden coffin with no decorative hardware. The lack of buttons, fasteners, or pins indicate the individual was buried in a shroud or gown. Skeletal markers suggested the person was female. In life, she stood about five feet five inches tall. We estimated that she was between fifteen and twenty-four years old when she died. One of her lower vertebrae was slightly compressed. Enamel defects on the teeth showed that she, like Susan and Eliza, suffered from regularly recurring periods of illness up to the age of five. Also like them, her dental health was poor, with many cavities and an abscess but no gold fillings. Interestingly, she had something else in common with Eliza. Her left maxillary lateral incisor was congenitally absent. This trait connects the young woman to the family biologically, though her plain coffin and clothing set her burial apart from the others. We tentatively identified her as Mr. Blake's daughter Ellen. Historical research did not provide an exact death date for Ellen, but she disappeared from the census records between the ages of seventeen and twenty-three. This age matches the biological profile of the skeleton.

EVIDENCE OF FAMILY GROUPING

Does this group of burials really represent the Blakes, or is it just wishful thinking on our part? Certainly, there are many similarities. Two coffins are identical, two coffins have the same lid cross, and two people have gold fillings. Susan Blake's identification is positive, and the presence of an "Eliza" name plate is also solid evidence. The age and sex information gathered from the analyses matches what is known about the Blakes, and there is osteological evidence supporting the known cause of death for William. The disturbance of the infant remains matches the historically recorded circumstances of their relocation. Stature could only be calculated for two of the men and two of the women, but all four were found to be on the upper end of the male and female ranges for the cemetery. Heights calculated for the two men were identical.

The individuals in Burials 24, 30, 36, and 287 all lacked one or both maxillary lateral incisors. No other individuals excavated from the Third Street Cemetery were missing these teeth congenitally. In modern northwestern European populations, the prevalence of congenitally absent maxillary lateral incisors is 1 to 2 percent. The congenital absence of third molars, or wisdom teeth, is a much more common finding, with a prevalence estimated between 9 and 20 percent in modern populations. The incidence in the presumed Blake plot is particularly high. Four out of six adults are missing two or all four of their third molars. A fifth person, Susan, may also have exhibited this trait, but because she lost so many teeth before death, it is impossible to determine whether she lost all four third molars or never had them.

GLIMPSES OF BLAKE FAMILY LIFE

Much of the data gathered from the analysis of the bones and artifacts in these graves support what was already known about the Blakes from historical sources. This information helped us identify the individuals. But did we learn anything new? Susan had bad teeth, and Ellen may have had an injury to her lower back. John Blake Jr. was chronically ill before he died, and there was something wrong with Eliza's jaw. Unfortunately, poor bone preservation limited the amount we could learn about any one individual.

However, some of the evidence falls into patterns that invite speculation on aspects of the Blake family's life. For instance, both William and John had evidence of occupational stress on their spines, but John Joseph did not. Was this simply a matter of age? Or was this because the elder son, William, had to work hard to help his father establish the brick-making concern, while the late-born son had the privilege of going to college instead? All three of the adult daughters had some long bone measurements that placed them within the male range, and Susan's cranial features ranged from ambiguous to male. Could a robust or even masculine appearance have been part of the reason none of the Blake daughters ever married? Enamel defects observed on the teeth of Eliza and Susan indicate health stress around the second half of 1843. Could this health stress be related to a communicable disease, one that perhaps also took the life of their brother John in October 1843? Sometimes the evidence we uncover leads to even more questions.

All of the adults, excluding Ellen, were buried in elaborate coffins and dressed in clothing from daily life. Was Ellen's burial different because her death occurred before the family was well-to-do? Perhaps there was no money to waste on coffins in the 1850s, while the family shared a home with outsiders. It is also possible that plain coffins were still the standard in the community at the time. Recent studies have found that highly decorated burial receptacles were not common in the mid-nineteenth century, even in the graves of the wealthy. Alternately, her death may have occurred suddenly and may have predated the availability of ready-made coffins in Dubuque. Regarding the clothing, it may have seemed impractical to bury Ellen in an outfit that could be passed on to her four sisters. Additionally, the trend of burial in the clothing of daily life may not have reached the frontier at the time of her death. Eliza's burial in a metal casket is also interesting. Does the choice of coffin indicate that Eliza died away from Dubuque? Or does the selection of an expensive casket reflect favoritism within the family? Perhaps the fact that she and her brother had identical coffins indicates that their deaths occurred around the same time.

When the materials from Blake graves are compared with the findings from the rest of the excavation, the lack of religious grave goods stands out. Of the six adult graves, none contained a rosary, and only one individual, William, was buried with a religious medal. Their religious inclinations were expressed instead in their coffin hardware, which included cross-shaped handle lugs and cross-shaped thumbscrews, as well as engraved lid crosses. Another curious detail is the absence of headstones. With such a large expenditure on many of the coffins, it seems incongruous that the Blake graves would have been marked by nothing but wooden crosses. The infant graves that were moved must have been well marked in order for them to be disinterred almost thirty years later. Local stone was plentiful, and multiple listings for monument carvers appear in the Dubuque city directories during the years the cemetery was active. All grave markers visible on the surface of the cemetery were moved to Mt. Olivet in the 1940s, but no Blake monuments were among them. The Blakes' names do not appear on any of the headstone pieces discovered during the excavation. Where did they go? Tombstone appropriation has been an issue at other historic cemeteries. Sometimes the nice, flat stones are too much temptation for nearby homeowners wanting to expand a patio, pave a sidewalk, or even shore up a foundation. Is this what happened in Dubuque? The absence of headstones is yet another unsolved mystery from Third Street.

While the identifications of these individuals cannot be proven beyond a shadow of a doubt, we gathered enough evidence to strongly suggest that the people in these graves were the Blakes. Sadly, the story ends with the identification. The family left Ireland for a life in the New World and even prospered for a while, only to die out on the western bank of the Mississippi. The widow, Ellen, and the spinster daughters, Mary and Nettie, spent the remainder of their years rambling around the crumbling family home. Unable to join their loved ones in the old cemetery, all three were interred at Mt. Olivet instead. The family graves at Third Street grew derelict because no one remained to remember them, to bring them flowers, and to clear the plot of weeds.

TEN

Conjured from Paper and Stone

WE WERE UNABLE TO CONNECT any other excavated skeletons to people known to be buried at Third Street. A few burial groupings appeared to be family plots, based on unusual skeletal traits, identical grave goods, or, in one case, the prevalence of dental work. However, none of these family groupings could be matched to any historical records without at least a partial name to work with. Documentary evidence of family plots was found in the surnames repeated on the few extant headstones and in newspaper obituaries. Though little information was available concerning any one family, the vignettes cobbled together from census records and newspaper clippings provide another window on life in early Dubuque.

THE HEADSTONE FAMILIES

The Farrells

The Farrell family came to our notice because their stones are among those that have wandered away from the cemetery over the years. The fact that the stones happened to be documented at all is almost miraculous. That one of the stones disappeared from its new home in Mt. Olivet Cemetery sometime in the last twenty years is mysterious.

On August 19, 1937, a photograph of Jeremiah Farrell's headstone was published in a *Telegraph Herald* feature titled "Do You Know Your Dubuque History?" At that time, it stood in the Third Street Cemetery. By 1939, when members of the Daughters of the American Revolution recorded the headstones still present at Third Street, Jeremiah's stone was gone. However, the ladies of the DAR recorded a stone dedicated to Jeremiah's children Margaret and Thomas Farrall [*sic*]. This stone was moved to Mt. Olivet Cemetery in the 1940s and was recorded there by the Key

City Genealogical Society in the late 1980s or early 1990s. When we went looking for it in 2008, though, the stone was no longer present in the Third Street section of Mt. Olivet, and the superintendent had no idea why. Meanwhile, during our archaeological excavations at Third Street, we found an incomplete marble headstone representing another member of the Farrell family. The marker bore the inscription "EDWARD FAR—— / DIED / Oct. 9, 187—— / AGED / 27 years, 6 mo—— / ——16 days."

Who were the Farrells? Jeremiah and Mary Farrell were both born in Ireland. They probably came to America in the 1840s, since their oldest son was born in New York around 1842. They traveled to Iowa shortly after that and settled on a farm about fifteen miles south of Dubuque, east of the town of Zwingle. Between 1842 and 1853 the couple had seven children, six boys and one girl. Jeremiah died in 1855, when his oldest son, Thomas, was only thirteen years old, but Mary apparently prospered in her widowhood. Her assets totaled $2,960 in 1860 and $7,500 in 1870, which was about average for farmers in the vicinity.

Thomas, Margaret, and Edward followed their father to the graveyard over the next seventeen years. Margaret is the only family member for whom an obituary could be located. The brief item in the September 1862 newspaper specifies that her funeral was to be held at the cathedral but does not give the cause of her death at the young age of fifteen. By the time of the 1880 census, no living members of the Farrell family were left in Dubuque County. Mary and two of her remaining children, Richard and William, had settled on a new farm in Fremont County, over 350 miles southwest of Dubuque. We don't know what became of her other two sons, Daniel and Jeremiah Jr.

At the time Jeremiah Farrell Sr. died, Third Street was the Catholic graveyard closest to the family's property in Washington Township. Why did the family choose burial in the consecrated ground of the cathedral cemetery fifteen miles away rather than simply burying their patriarch on their large rural property? Perhaps this choice of burial location reflected the Farrells' strong religious beliefs. After the opening of the more conveniently located Key West (Mt. Olivet) Cemetery, the family continued to use the Third Street Cemetery. They may have wanted to keep all their loved ones together, or they may simply have been making use of an already-purchased family plot. The remaining Farrells moved away from

Dubuque before the Third Street Cemetery fell out of use. With no one to tend them, the family headstones were eventually broken, stolen, and forgotten.

The McCanns

According to the 1870 census, the family of Arthur and Catherine McCann lived on the same block of Bluff Street as the Murphys. Mr. McCann appears to have been heavily involved with the goings-on at the cathedral, or at least with the associated cemetery. He was listed as one of the fence-design committee members and was a signer, along with John Blake, of the articles of incorporation of the St. Raphael's Cemetery Association. He may have simply been a civic-minded parishioner, or perhaps he took a special interest in the graveyard because it held the earthly remains of four of the seven children his wife bore between 1853 and 1869. A headstone found during the archaeological excavations at Third Street was dedicated to Anna M. McCann, who died in 1857 at the age of four, and Edward McCann, who died in 1855 at the age of three months. The inscription states that these were "Children of A & C McCann." An obituary for Julia Malinda McCann, aged eighteen months, appeared in the *Dubuque Herald* in 1860. Almost three years later, an obituary for daughter Frances, who was under two years old, was published.

Like the Farrells, Arthur and Catherine McCann were born in Ireland and came to America in the 1840s. By 1853, the year Anna M. was born, they were living in Iowa. The family was prosperous. Mr. McCann worked as a grain dealer in the 1860s. On the 1870 census he is listed as the county treasurer, with $30,000 in real estate and $12,000 in personal property. This works out to around $750,000 in today's money. Sadly, no amount of wealth could protect the family from the high infant mortality rate suffered by the rich and poor alike in nineteenth-century Dubuque. The McCanns had three daughters who lived to adulthood—Helena, Blanche, and Venice/Bernice. When she was in her late thirties, Helena married John McKinlay, a bookkeeper from the Treasurer's Office, but the couple had no children. Blanche is shown living with them on the 1910 and 1920 censuses, but it is unknown what became of Venice. No one from the McCann family appears on the census records for Dubuque after 1920.

Since the McCanns still lived in town at the turn of the century, they would have been aware of the derelict state of the cemetery. They would have read in the newspaper about the ever-changing plans for the grounds and for the people interred there. For whatever reasons, though, they chose not to move the children's graves to Mt. Olivet Cemetery, where Arthur, Catherine, Helena, and Blanche were all eventually buried.

The Nadeaus

In the Catholic Church, All Souls' Day (November 2) is set aside for remembering the dead, praying for the souls in purgatory, and visiting cemeteries to clean and decorate the graves of loved ones. On November 3, 1871, the following editorial appeared in the *Dubuque Daily Herald*: "On a visit to 3d street cemetery yesterday, we found but one series of graves or lots . . . decorated—that of the departed portion of the family of N. Nadeau. Wreaths of flowers adorned the gravestones of five of his family—but not another stone or lot showed such respect for the memory of the dead. Many of the early citizens of Dubuque were buried near by, but there was no husband, or father, or son, or daughter to pay respect to the memory of the dead." Interestingly, this editorial appeared almost twenty years after the last of the Nadeaus was buried at Third Street and ten years after the patriarch of the family last appeared on any records in Dubuque. Who, then, remained to decorate the graves? Perhaps the author of the unsigned editorial?

Narcisse Nadeau was born in Canada around 1810. He married Marie Louise Philibert (b. ca. 1821) in St. Louis on May 9, 1842. By July 1842 the newlyweds were living in Dubuque, as evidenced by Mr. Nadeau's recorded attendance of the first meeting to organize a Masonic lodge in the city. An enterprising man, Mr. Nadeau opened the first steam-powered flour mill in Dubuque, the Nadeau, Rogers & Company mill, in 1847.

Narcisse and Marie had six children between 1843 and 1852: Joseph Octave, Ernst, Marie Estelle, Amelia, Joseph Jules, and Leon Michel. Marie Estelle and both Josephs died in infancy and were buried in the bluff-top cemetery. Their matching headstones currently stand in the Third Street section at Mt. Olivet. According to cathedral records, Marie Louise died in 1852, just a few days after the birth of her son Leon. Her headstone was not moved to Mt. Olivet with the others in the 1940s, but a footstone with the initials "M.L.P.N." was noted beside the children's stones when the Key City Genealogical Society recorded the markers in that section of Mt. Olivet. This footstone has since disappeared.

Narcisse Nadeau returned to St. Louis shortly after his wife's death and found a new bride. In 1853 he married Julie Virginie Sanguinet, who was twenty years his junior, and the couple had at least five more children. All but one of the children were born in Missouri, and the family is not listed on any census records for Dubuque. It is clear, though, that Mr. Nadeau still had business dealings in the city. He maintained a residence at the corner of Clay and 10th Streets until ca. 1860. The Nadeau, Rogers & Company mill suffered a fire in 1855 but was rebuilt and appears in business directories through 1859. Between 1857 and 1859 Mr. Nadeau was a party to the Central Island proposition, a land deal with the city council of Dubuque that led to a public scandal. He had an interest in private land acquisitions as well. Taking advantage of the peak of the Iowa land speculation boom in the 1850s, he acquired over three thousand acres using military bounty land warrants purchased from veterans who preferred hard currency to acreage on the frontier as a reward for their military service.

The 1870 census shows the Nadeau family living in St. Louis. Mr. Nadeau is listed as owning real estate valued at $60,000 and personal property valued at $100,000. Less than a year after the item about All Souls' Day appeared in the *Dubuque Daily Herald*, Mr. Nadeau was dead. His second wife continued living in St. Louis through 1920. Several Nadeaus who may be descendants or distant relatives appear in current phone listings for St. Louis.

The question remains: Who decorated the graves of the departed Nadeaus? Perhaps Mr. Nadeau returned to Dubuque now and then over the years, even after his retirement. Perhaps the family still had friends living in the area who remembered Marie Louise and her children fondly enough to bring flowers to their graves. Only four members of the Nadeau family are known to have died in Dubuque, but the newspaper editorial mentions five stones. There may have been another child who is not in the records and whose grave marker disappeared along with Marie Louise's headstone. Or perhaps the editorial writer was simply wrong about the number of stones. In any case, it is strange that the writer found the majority of the graves in the cemetery so neglected just a year and a half after the community rallied to save the burial ground from the desecration of mining.

The Reillys

A headstone dedicated to Terence Reilly was found lying on the ground surface during tree-stump removal at the Third Street Cemetery in 2007. Two sets of human remains were found below this headstone, but it is uncertain whether or not one of these was Mr. Reilly. Since the headstone was not standing, we cannot be sure if the marker was found at its original location or if it had been moved.

Mr. Reilly and his wife, Bridget, were both born in Ireland. They must have moved to the United States before 1830, because their daughter Margaret was born in New Jersey around 1829. The other three children who survived to adulthood—Mary, Ann, and Andrew—were also born in New Jersey. Sometime in the 1840s the family started moving west. They were recorded living in Michigan City, Indiana, in 1850. The family had arrived in Dubuque by 1855, when Mr. Reilly began buying land. In that year, he purchased six noncontiguous lots comprising more than 560 acres. How a man who was listed as "laborer" on the census records accrued the cash to invest in land is unknown. The 1856 Iowa state census shows sixteen boarders living in the Reilly home, so renting may have been the family's major source of income. Mr. Reilly obviously intended to increase his wealth with small-scale land speculation, but these plans were cut short. He died on December 5, 1856, at the age of fifty-eight.

According to probate records, his fifty-two-year-old widow was left to collect the debts owed by tenants occupying the purchased lands. After seven years, she asked to be released from these duties, since her children were of age and her own health was failing. The children must have been successful in collecting the debts, because the 1870 census shows the family with $10,000 worth of real estate and a personal estate of $3,000, up from a total of $300 for both in 1860. This is a considerable increase, even when accounting for post–Civil War inflation. Two of the daughters left home, but Margaret and her brother, Andrew, a bookkeeper, continued to live with their mother during the last decades of the nineteenth century. Spinster sister, age sixty-eight, and unmarried brother, age fifty-nine, still lived together in a rented house in 1900. This entry marks the last time the Reilly family appears on any census records.

The Sullivans

A descendant of the Sullivans, Ron Seymour, provided extensive information about his forebears who settled in Dubuque, some of whom were buried at the Third Street Cemetery.[1] The headstone dedicated to Mr. Seymour's great-great-great-grandmother Mary Desmond O'Sullivan was still standing in the graveyard when members of the DAR recorded the extant markers in 1939. Her son Michael D. O'Sullivan's headstone also stood at that time. Neither stone was moved to Mt. Olivet in the 1940s, and neither was found during the archaeological work at the site.

Mary Desmond O'Sullivan was born in Ireland around 1782. Her husband's name is not known, but the family lived in County Cork before immigrating to America. They lived briefly in Troy, New York, and then made their way to Iowa. When they arrived in Dubuque in 1836, Mary's son Michael began working in the lead mines. Later, he worked as a carpenter with his brother John D., a bricklayer. According to her headstone, Mary Desmond Sullivan died on October 27, 1839, at the age of fifty-seven. She has the distinction of being the second death recorded in the surviving volume of the burial register. From her entry in the register and her headstone inscription, it is clear that the family dropped the "O'" from their name sometime after their arrival in Dubuque.

In 1842 Mary's son Michael went to St. Louis and brought back Ellen Casey, also a native of County Cork, to be his bride. The couple lived in a house across the street from the cathedral and had three children, Joseph, Mary Ellen, and Francis. Joseph died in 1848 and was probably buried in the Third Street Cemetery along with his grandmother. Michael Sullivan died in 1855 and was also buried on the bluff top. His death left his widow, Ellen, with an estate of more than $50,000, a considerable amount of wealth for Dubuque at the time. As adults, the children of Michael Sullivan prospered. Both of their weddings were covered in detail by the local newspapers. The widow, Ellen, and both of her children survived until after the Third Street Cemetery fell out of use, and all were buried in Key West (Mt. Olivet) Cemetery.

Michael's brother, John D. Sullivan, a wealthy mason, also remained in Dubuque until his death. John, his wife, Elizabeth, and five of his children—Margaret, Dinnes, Daniel, William John, and Francis—are buried at Mt. Olivet Cemetery. However, at least one of these deaths predated the founding of Key West / Mt. Olivet. Margaret died in 1847 and could not have been buried in Key West originally. Sullivan descendants believe that she was most likely buried at Third Street and that her grave was moved. Dinnes and Daniel died while the Third Street Cemetery was still in use and may also have been buried there initially. For reasons unknown, one branch of the family decided to remove their loved ones from the old cemetery, while the other left their departed relatives behind.

At the time of our research, there were around fifty known descendants of Mary Desmond Sullivan still living and probably many more. According to Ron Seymour, though, not one of the fifty or more Sullivans who currently live in Dubuque is a descendant of Mary.

David Twomey and the Collins Family

From the scant historical records, David Twomey and Cornelius Collins appear to have been the best of friends. The actual nature of their relationship is unknown, but we found no evidence that they were related by blood or marriage. They must have been fairly close, though, since the two men were naturalized on the same day—April 6, 1840—in Dubuque, and Twomey shared a home with Mr. and Mrs. Collins. Having no heirs, Twomey named Cornelius as the sole executor and apparent beneficiary of his estate. The four-sided tombstone erected by Mr. Collins in memory of his wife, Catherine, also has an inscription dedicated to David Twomey. This monument was removed from the Third Street Cemetery in the 1940s and stands in Mt. Olivet today.

Two other individuals are memorialized on the Collins monument, Mary McGrath and Mrs. Esther Dempsey. Both of them are listed in the Collins household on the 1856 Iowa state census, but their association with the family is unknown. Cornelius and his wife, Catherine, had no children of their own, or at least none that survived long enough to be listed in census records. Perhaps that is the reason they opened their home to so many people over the years, including a niece and nephew (who may have been orphaned) and several seemingly unrelated individuals.

According to his 1900 obituary, Cornelius Collins was born in County Cork, Ireland, in 1818. He emigrated in 1837 and lived in New Hampshire before coming to Dubuque with Surveyor General James Wilson in 1840.[2] He married Catherine O'Neal in Dubuque in 1844. Mr. Collins is listed in various census records as a laborer (1850), a teamster (1856, 1870), a farmer (1860), a retired capitalist (1885), and a landlord (1900). The 1870 census shows him owning $20,000 of real estate and having personal property valued at $2,500. He was heavily involved with the church and was one of the founding members of the St. Vincent de Paul Society in Dubuque. He joined the cemetery fence-building committee in 1865 and signed the articles of incorporation of the St. Raphael's Cemetery Association. And the newspaper's biographical sketch of John Blake mentions that his "old friend" Cornelius helped move his children's graves to the new family plot in 1870. When Catherine Collins died in 1877, she was buried at Third Street, presumably in the same plot as the three family friends who preceded her in death. Cornelius remarried almost immediately, and his new bride, Ann, who was more than thirty-five years his junior, bore him four children before his death in 1900. His second wife followed him to Mt. Olivet Cemetery in 1910, while Catherine and her friends remained at Third Street.

A GLOWING OBITUARY:
THE FAMILY OF MARY ANN AARON

Mary Ann Aaron died of heart disease in 1876 at the age of forty-five and was buried in the Third Street Cemetery. Her fourteen-line obituary in the August 26 edition of the *Dubuque Herald* praises her good character and provides more details of her life and death than most death notices of the time. The length of the obituary is all the more exceptional because she and her husband were "colored"—or, at least, her husband was. The language of the article is not clear, and Mary Ann could not be found in the census records. The family she married into, though, was well documented, having arrived in Iowa in 1837 and appearing on census records for Dubuque from 1840 to 1870. Baptiste and Mary Aaron, the parents-in-law of Mary Ann, are sometimes listed as "black" and sometimes "mulatto."

Baptiste was born in Kentucky, and Mary was from Virginia, and the family lived in Missouri before settling in Iowa.

Phillip Aaron, the husband mentioned in Mary Ann's obituary, was probably the son of Baptiste and Mary. He does not appear in their household listing because he was likely already an adult when the family was first recorded on the census in Iowa. Phillip and Mary Ann had five children, four of whom preceded Mary Ann in death and were probably buried at Third Street. Phillip's profession is unknown. His father, patriarch Baptiste Aaron, worked as a general laborer but valued education in his household. Every member of Baptiste's family learned to read and write. His son Baptiste Aaron Jr. became a barber, and sons Felix and Eli were boat firemen. Daughter Mary worked as a stewardess. Her line in the 1870 census reports a personal estate worth $150, an unusual entry, since values were rarely recorded for unmarried women still living at home. The widowed matriarch Mary Aaron declared $1,500 in real estate on the same census. Josiah Conzett recalls the family in his memoirs: "A Two Story Frame where Lived A Negro Familie by Name of Aron. The Man was Very Large allmost A Giant with the Strength of An Ox. He was A Dray Man his Wife Was A Coal Black Negress. They had One Son Bob — he Was one of our Play Mates. we made no distinction of Color in Them days. For many Years he was A Barber and had A Good run of Buisness."[3]

Baptiste Jr. (Bob) eventually moved his barbershop to Sioux City, Iowa. By 1885 he and his Canadian wife, Annie, had six children, with two more arriving before 1900. In 1910, at the age of seventy-five, he was still working as a barber. By 1920 Baptiste Jr. was dead, and his son Charles had taken up the family business. Charles was likely the nephew of Mary Ann Aaron. Unfortunately, since we never learned the name of Mary Ann's only surviving child, we could not find out what happened to him or her. By 1900 no Aarons remained in Dubuque County.

THREE MEN WHO MADE THE PAPERS

Charles H. Mix

The story of Charles Mix is remarkable because his body traveled over fifteen hundred miles after his death in 1870. Though the exact date of his death is unknown, news of his demise reached his hometown of Dubuque on January 26. Burial in the Third Street Cemetery did not take place until February 9, more than two weeks later.

Mr. Mix was born in Bradford County, Pennsylvania, in 1831, and his parents brought him to Dubuque in the 1840s. He met his future wife, Mary Semper, in Dubuque, and the two were wed in 1853. Over the years, Mr. Mix worked as a clerk in the surveyor general's office as well as serving as the city auditor. Like many local men, he dabbled in small-scale land speculation. On the 1863 Iowa draft registration he is listed as a sutler, a civilian who sold provisions to the military.

Several years before his death, Mr. Mix contracted tuberculosis. In October 1869 he left Dubuque for Texas in hopes of improving his health. By the time he reached New Orleans, his health had deteriorated to the point that he sent for his wife, Mary, and their two daughters, Julia and Virginia. While still in New Orleans, he converted to Catholicism. After his wife and daughters arrived, the whole family continued the journey to San Antonio. Mr. Mix died not long after reaching his destination, but his wife decided his remains would be buried in Dubuque. On February 9, the funeral took place at the home of the deceased and at St. Raphael's Cathedral. According to the local newspaper, the body, "enclosed in a handsome casket," was then conveyed to the Third Street Cemetery.[4]

The remains of Charles Mix were not positively identified during the excavations at Third Street. However, some details noted in Burial 897 (see chapter 7) were reminiscent of the story of Charles Mix. The burial held the remains of a man of approximately the right age. Unfortunately, the poor preservation of the ribs and vertebrae prevented us from observing any evidence of pulmonary tuberculosis. The man was buried with a rosary, as well as a large, brand-new Miraculous Medal of unusually fine workmanship. The medal, which was unlike any other recovered from the site, could have been purchased by the recently converted Mr. Mix in New Orleans. The coffin contained a large amount of charcoal, which may have been placed there to absorb odors and fluids from decomposition. Cast-iron coffins were preferred for long journeys, but metal coffins might not have been readily available in San Antonio at the time, since the nearest licensed manufacturer was in New Orleans, and the railroad had not yet reached that part of Texas. A third unusual aspect of this burial was the fact that the coffin handles had mismatched lugs. This haphazard construction is consistent with a hastily procured coffin, which would have been needed for Mr. Mix to begin his final journey as soon as possible. The coffin is *not* consistent, however, with the newspaper's description of a "handsome casket." The individual from Burial 897 may not be Charles Mix but instead a gentleman with a similar story. Or perhaps the journalist just didn't look that closely at Mr. Mix's casket.

After the death of Mr. Mix, his widow, Mary, and daughter Julia entered the convent of the Sisters of Charity of the Blessed Virgin Mary, just south of Dubuque. His daughter Virginia "Jessie" Mix married a freight agent named Brad Smith, but the marriage ended quickly for reasons not clear in the historical record. Jessie Mix Smith reappears in the marriage records of Arapahoe County, Colorado, where she wed William Greenhow in 1899. Their only daughter, Adeline, returned to Iowa as an adult and married a bricklayer named Frank Pocta. By 1940 Adeline and Frank had moved to Minnesota, where many descendants of Charles Mix reside to this day.

Francis Gillick

Francis Gillick is one of two hanged murderers known to have been buried at the Third Street Cemetery. Vivid details of his life, crime, and execution were published in the newspapers of the day. The memoirs of Josiah Conzett include his eyewitness accounts of the murder and the hanging.

Gillick's story was a tragic one. Born in County Cavan, Ireland, in 1820, he enlisted in the British army at the age of fifteen and was immediately sent to war in Spain. In less than two years of service, he participated in fifteen enemy engagements, receiving the Cross of Ferdinand for his bravery. During his last battle, he was severely wounded and sent home. According to Gillick, of the one hundred men with whom he left Dublin, only seventeen remained alive, and not one of these was unwounded. He married his wife, Mary, in 1840 and soon after immigrated to the United States. If the couple had any children, none of them lived to be recorded in any census. In 1847, during the Mexican-American War, he joined the United States Army and was sent to Veracruz. He survived several bloody engagements in Mexico and was honorably discharged at the end of the war. After some wanderings, he took up residence in Dubuque and worked as a tailor.

On March 30, 1858, Mr. Gillick shot his wife through the chest. Since the shooting occurred in the middle of the city and in midafternoon, there were many who heard the shot, rushed to the scene, and saw him standing over his wife's body. Gillick never denied shooting his wife but claimed it was an accidental discharge of the weapon rather than intentional murder. Because he had a history of abusing his wife when he was drunk, and because he had threatened that he would kill her one day, he was convicted of murder and sentenced to death. Shortly before his execution, a local newspaper interviewed him and reported on his state of mind: "He thinks that after facing death on more than 20 battlefields, it is hard that he should be choked like a dog for an event which he declares was unpremeditated."[5]

The execution, a widely attended spectacle, took place at Eagle Point on April 27, 1860. The procession included three military companies and a band, which played music requested by the condemned man himself, the "Dead March" from Handel's *Saul*. The crowd, estimated at five to ten thousand, included men, women, and children. In *My Civil War Before, During and After*, Josiah Conzett gives this account of the execution:

> *The Display-Parade and fuss made over his Execution was really like a 4th of July Parade. . . . When they took him out of the Jail, [the sheriff's wife] Mrs. Cummings was leaning out of A Window. She was Crying as if her Heart would break and Waved him Goodby. . . . The Bluff near and for as far as I could see were Black with People that . . . were there to see this Tragedy—A fright farce as we now see it. . . . Then the Sheriff cut the Rope and in 10 minutes Gillick was in Eternity and He was driven in an Express Wagon the Horse on a Gallop to the Catholic Cemetary on Third St. This was the last Public Execution in Dubuque County.*[6]

The St. Vincent de Paul Society took charge of the body, presumably because Gillick had no living relatives in the area, and paid for his burial. None of the individuals excavated during our project had evidence of perimortem trauma to the vertebrae of the neck, which often occurs in cases of judicial hanging. Then again, relatively few individuals had well-preserved cervical vertebrae, so we could have excavated his grave without recognizing it. Alternately, Gillick may have been buried in one of the portions of the cemetery destroyed by the various construction projects or left unexcavated. According to tradition in some parts of Ireland, the northern boundary of a cemetery is reserved for unbaptized children, strangers, and persons who had committed certain crimes. Most of the northern boundary of the Third Street Cemetery was graded away in the 1970s.

Daniel Clifford

The story of the execution of Daniel Clifford, also covered by the Dubuque newspapers, lies in stark contrast with that of Francis Gillick. Since Clifford was a young man, few details of his life prior to his crime were provided. He was hanged in the jail yard behind closed doors, with little spectacle for the newspapers to report.

Clifford was born in Ireland sometime around 1835. In 1859 he and a man named Edward Mooney crushed the skull of a miner named Wood with a stove leg and stole $27—less than a month's wages for a laborer—from the victim. Clifford did not deny that he had committed the crime he was convicted of but assured reporters that he was not guilty of darker misdeeds, as it was rumored. The papers did not publish the details of these other alleged transgressions.

A crowd of around thirty, including county officials and journalists, witnessed the execution on an October day in 1860. The newspapers reported that the knot slipped during the hanging and that the man died of strangulation rather than a broken neck. It took at least thirteen minutes for Clifford to die. One reporter remarked that though the crowd was solemn and decorous, "there was but little of the sympathy exhibited that was shown in the case of Gillick."[7] Clifford's wealthy relatives in Ohio had turned their backs on him, so the St. Vincent de Paul Society took charge of Clifford's body and made the arrangements for the burial. Perhaps they dug his grave close to Gillick's, since the two men were hanged within six months of each other.

THE FAMILIES AND individuals whose stories came to light during our research are just a few of the thousands of early Dubuquers who were buried at Third Street. The selected few are not representative of the population of Dubuque or of the parish of St. Raphael. Rather, they are some of the people who were wealthy, respected, or infamous enough to warrant large grave markers, obituaries, or newspaper articles. The majority of those who ended up in the Third Street Cemetery died unannounced deaths, and their passing left little mark on the historical record. They are remembered only as the collective dead in the oft-repeated stories of the bluff-top burial ground.

ELEVEN

Forgetting and Remembering the Dead

DURING AND AFTER THE PROJECT, we asked ourselves again and again, How could people not know there were over nine hundred burials here in just part of the cemetery? How can such a large group of people be erased from memory? In reality, they were more misplaced than forgotten—the people who remembered them believed they were somewhere else. Their sudden reappearance in the cemetery was a matter of interest for many but a massive inconvenience for the landowner, who had to deal with all the red tape and pay for our excavation. By the time we finished the job, the landowner had canceled construction of the condominiums. The lot lay vacant, the subject of a lawsuit.

FIGURE 17. Progress vs. preservation. Photo by Patrick Stanton.

Even prior to the last recorded burial at the Third Street Cemetery in 1880, the grounds had fallen into disrepair. Despite the repeated efforts of members of the Catholic community to build or rebuild fences, clean up the weeds, or remove the dead to a different cemetery, all attempts at salvaging the graveyard and its occupants failed due to insufficient financial backing or church member involvement. The property became an eyesore and the subject of newspaper articles bemoaning its decrepit condition for several decades, continuing into the 1930s. What happened next? Did the community just turn a blind eye to the conditions at the cemetery? Two older Dubuque men relayed their memories to us—of playing among the headstones on Kelly's Bluff when they were children in the 1930s and 1940s. What did the dead mean to these boys or to any of Dubuque's citizens by this time?

Several factors probably contributed to the ultimate abandonment of the cemetery and the memory of its occupants. During the period when the dead were interred at Third Street, the population of Dubuque was constantly increasing. The mortality rate was high in the nineteenth century. The rarity of medical intervention and the absence of antibiotics contributed to many untimely deaths. As in most cities, sanitation was poor, and little knowledge existed of how diseases were transmitted. The cemetery filled to overflowing in just a few decades.

Dubuque was also a very mobile community. Many people who migrated from the eastern United States and elsewhere settled in Dubuque for only a few generations. Opportunities in the American West lured many to search for gold, homestead in the plains, or seek employment in big cities like Chicago and St. Louis or in California. Census records reflect this mobility. While trying to trace Third Street Cemetery names, we found that some families moved on after spending only a few years in Dubuque.

By the 1860s, when the cemetery's condition began to deteriorate and the original lot was already used to capacity, where were the families of those interred in the 1830s and 1840s? Many of the early settlers of Dubuque were single men seeking work at the lead mines or men who left their families behind while they worked in Iowa. It is likely these men had no local relatives to mourn at their gravesides or tend to their plots. Disease and accidents could have wiped out whole families, again leaving the dead alone in their graves with no one to care for or about them. This was especially true for immigrant families, who made up a large portion of Dubuque's population. With no extended family in the area, the passing of these foreign settlers was quickly forgotten.

In addition to high mortality and mobility, other factors affecting the condition of the Third Street Cemetery may have been the limited public mourning period in American society and the shift of cemetery management from public to private hands. As David Stannard writes in *A Time to Mourn* by Martha V. Pike and Janice Gray Armstrong, neglect seems to have been the rule for Christian cemeteries across America prior to the rural cemetery movement of the mid-nineteenth century. With the soul safely (presumably) in heaven, the survivors and sextons paid limited attention to the resting place of the corpse. Even when people across the country adopted strict mourning protocols in the late nineteenth century, the prescribed period—a maximum of two years—was relatively short compared to the life of a cemetery. The Victorians who could afford ostentatious grave markers presumably maintained them for longer than the two years of official bereavement, but what about the lower classes? In the early twentieth century, Americans began to regard public displays of grief as vulgar and unseemly, but by then mourning no longer had any connection to grave maintenance. With the rise of the funeral industry and the growing popularity of prepaid "perpetual care," cemetery plot tending became the responsibility of groundskeepers rather than individual families. Once American consumers accepted that the care of new graves was part of the usual funeral package, it was easy to forget that the graves of older forebears were not being tended.

Based on the low number of stone markers unearthed at the cemetery or previously moved to Mt. Olivet, we surmised that many graves at Third Street had been marked by wooden crosses or maybe wooden plaques rather than engraved headstones. Perhaps some burials had no markers at all. Over the years, these wooden reminders would have deteriorated, leaving little or no trace of the persons interred there. Even during the decades of the cemetery's usage, grave shafts were dug into older graves, coffins were stacked on top of each other, and plots were reused and resold. By the twentieth century, there were few aboveground indications of the cemetery's existence.

What was the responsibility of the Catholic Church to the dead? Certainly the church guided its members during their lifetimes and tended to the sick and dying. The clergy performed last rites and funeral services. The deceased received those rites necessary for the ascension to heaven if they had led Christian lives. But from the point of interment onward, the church administration appears to have been uninterested in the "remaindered clay." Prior to the existence of perpetual care cemeteries, the responsibility for maintaining each grave plot usually fell on the individual families. The role of the church was primarily to provide consecrated ground for proper burial. If a map of the plots at Third Street ever existed, it may not have been kept up-to-date. Additionally, community members appear to have been using the cemetery without permission of the clergy. No wonder the situation was confusing and probably out of hand for the priests tending to the cathedral records.

In Europe and elsewhere, the purchase of a plot has not always provided the deceased with a permanent resting place. Historically, and even now in countries like Sweden and Norway, when cemeteries filled up, the skeletal remains were removed to make room for newer burials. These disinterred remains have been treated in many ways, including storage in catacombs (e.g., Italy and France) and placement in the church crypts (England) or charnel houses (Jerusalem, Japan). This kind of treatment of the dead was not considered disrespectful but a necessity due to overcrowding in small "kirkyards." At least three churches in Europe used the human bones of their past parishioners as decoration. Near Prague, the Sedlec Ossuary, or Kostnice v Sedlci, contains the bones of tens of thousands of medieval people arranged inside the church in bell-shaped mounds, a chandelier, garlands, and a coat of arms.

Without a formal order from the archdiocese for the removal of the graves from the derelict Third Street Cemetery, most families of the deceased buried there had little motivation to move their loved ones to another location. First and foremost, living relatives or close family friends still had to be residing in Dubuque to be aware of the abandoned state of the burial ground. Second, they had to be able to find their family graves among the weeds and tumbled-down stones. Third, they had to be able to afford the cost of relocation to another cemetery. A person would need to be hired to do the disinterment if the relatives did not want to do the job themselves. The body would have to be transported to the cemetery chosen for reinterment. The family then had to pay for a new plot, plus the charges for digging a new grave and putting up a headstone or marker. While the costs would have been low compared to the charges for hiring heavy equipment to perform a similar removal and reinterment today, the expense may have been too dear, especially for families living on the edge of poverty.

With each passing generation, fewer and fewer relatives of the Third Street dead remained in Dubuque, or those relatives were too many generations removed to have retained knowledge of their ancestors on the bluff top. After the final news article about the cemetery appeared in 1939, the people of Dubuque (and the rest of the world) were too preoccupied by the war to care about an abandoned graveyard. The cemetery was just another weedy lot awaiting development. Nevertheless, it is surprising that the discovery of graves during the construction of the St. Dominic Villa did not hit the headlines. How the archdiocese and the construction company managed to keep the situation hushed up is baffling. The discovery of burials in the 1970s and 1990s did get some press, but exposure of these "few" graves failed to raise any red flags about the possibility that many more dead still lay in the old graveyard. The belief that the majority of the graves had been moved long ago precluded any real concern.

In 2007, when the cemetery was rediscovered, over fifty-seven thousand people lived in the city of Dubuque. Busy with their own lives and concerned primarily with the here and now, many had no idea what they were driving past as they traveled up and down the Third Street hill every day. The branch of the Dominican Order that had occupied the land just south of the cemetery for over fifty years had returned to Sinsinawa, Wisconsin, and most of the sisters who actually lived on the property had long since passed away. The location of the cemetery had all but disappeared from legal plats of the bluff top. And it was the last thing on most locals' minds.

REMEMBRANCE AND REDISCOVERY

At least one group of citizens showed concern for the Third Street Cemetery, even though they believed it to be long gone. Members of Dubuque's Key City Genealogical Society, particularly local historian

Biays Bowerman, gathered information from old obituaries and newspaper articles about the cemetery, as well as from longtime local families. Using this information, they compiled a list of persons likely to have been buried in the graveyard on the bluff and published this list in the society newsletter. During the massive undertaking of recording all the headstones in Mt. Olivet Cemetery, the society documented the markers standing in the Third Street Cemetery section of Mt. Olivet. This information, as well as a short history of the original graveyard, was published by the society in 2001. In 2005 a new incarnation of the genealogical society, the Phoenix Group, published a transcription of the St. Raphael's burial register. So it is unfair to say that the Third Street Cemetery was forgotten entirely. Rather, it was an object of fascination for those who believed they were researching a place that existed only in the past. After the excavation, we were happy to introduce them to the cemetery of the present day. And they were happy to share with us the fruits of their labor of many years. Without the contributions of Biays Bowerman, Tom and Vicki Schlarman, Kathy Spangler, Ron and Judy Seymour, and others, we would never have gathered as much history about the cemetery and its residents. Our budget could not possibly support the kind of delving they did on evenings and weekends over the course of decades.

Also, as we noted earlier, community memory was not lacking completely. Many people who spoke to us retold the same old stories we had heard before, sometimes with variations. Folklore gathers around many old burial grounds, and the stories of mass graves and hidden treasure connected to the Third Street Cemetery are hardly unique.

Mass Grave Myth, Take 2

A descendant of an old Dubuque family contacted one of the authors with an interesting variation on the usual theme of cholera mass graves. She suggested that the graves we excavated on the bluff were actually interments related to the 1918 flu pandemic. According to the older members of her family, the other cemeteries in Dubuque filled up during the outbreak, so the church allowed the Third Street Cemetery to be used again. She pointed out that because public funerals were outlawed at this time, there would be no record of the interments. Due to the shortage of caskets, she believed multiple people were buried in the same grave without any burial container. Her grandfather recalled watching people carry their dead past the family's house on Third Street all night long on their way to bury them in the cemetery at the top of the bluff.

The story makes little sense, given that Linwood, Mt. Calvary, and Mt. Olivet Cemeteries were all operating at the time and are still not full today. True, the Third Street Cemetery is closer to the center of town and more convenient for quick disposal of the dead, but our excavation turned up no evidence of twentieth-century graves. Such burials, even if hastily per-formed, would have stood out from our mid-nineteenth-century burials in several respects. By the 1910s, most urban Americans purchased rect-angular coffins. Also, the trend of being buried in clothing rather than shrouds or gowns would have resulted in a larger number of buttons, often rubber or plastic, being found in these graves. We probably would have seen a difference in bone preservation between the 1870s graves and people buried more than forty years later. And, of course, we would have noticed if multiple people were buried in the same grave with no coffins.

This adaptation of the standard mass grave story perhaps offers insight into the core of the social memory. Cholera itself is not important to the story. The essential elements—consistent across the variations—are the town's devastation by disease and the accompanying fear. The survivors, who blinked away their tears while toiling up the steep hill, buried the dead quickly to prevent the spread of disease. In this version, however, the dead are established Dubuquers, while in most renditions they are newly arrived outsiders.

Dubuque is not the only community with an incorrect memory of mass graves. In Matagorda, Texas, conscientious citizens maintained a mound in a cemetery for over a hundred years because they believed it marked a mass grave. Local lore attributed the dead to one of three different catastrophes. Some believed the grave held the victims of an 1826 conflict between set-tlers and the Karankawa Indians, while others thought the dead had fallen during a yellow fever outbreak in 1862. Many believed the mound marked the grave of twenty-two Confederate soldiers who died of hypothermia when their boat capsized on December 31, 1863. Archaeological investiga-tions conducted in 2001 found that the mound covered a row of five indi-vidual grave shafts and the corner of a sixth. The deceased were interred circa 1850 to 1885, and none of the evidence suggests they were buried in a single episode. The skeletons bore no trauma to indicate the people had died in an attack. Since the dead included an infant, a toddler, two young men, and a young woman, they were clearly not Confederate soldiers.

For reasons unknown, the area was selected as the focus of community activity at some point in the distant past. Archaeologists found that the site had once been enclosed, though the placement of posts suggests the fence was constructed after the exact locations of the graves had been forgotten. In the early twentieth century, members of the community constructed a brick curb around the spot. Regular scraping of growth from the grave area resulted in the development of a low mound, typical of burial grounds in Texas and other southern states. Additional improvements to the mound continued through the 1980s. Finally, the community that had invested so much in the care of the mass grave asked archaeologists to excavate the mound in hopes of learning the history of the individuals below. What a surprise it must have been to find that there was no mass grave at all!

A similar legend in Crestview, Florida, focuses on two rows of sandstone rocks standing in Old Bethel Cemetery. The stones reportedly mark a mass grave dug for Confederate and Union soldiers who perished in a skirmish along the Yellow River nearby. Another version of the story claims the grave holds Confederate soldiers who died from disease rather than war wounds. Researchers have been unable to identify a specific documented clash that might have resulted in the grave, but the story persists in the community. Archaeologists who conducted remote sensing and limited excavations at the site uncovered no evidence of a mass grave at that location. The mass grave may lie elsewhere on the property, or it may simply be a story that grew out of the grief of a town that suffered heartbreaking losses in a terrible conflict.

Though the mass graves in all three cases were imaginary, the situation in Texas and Florida lies in stark contrast with the Third Street Cemetery. The people of Matagorda and Crestview believed the graves held venerable and heroic ancestors and treated the areas with reverence. In Dubuque, the fabled mass graves of non-Catholic outsiders, made more unclean by their cholera deaths, served as a reason and excuse for having abandoned the cemetery altogether.

Since most marked cemeteries are left undisturbed and unexcavated, the local lore surrounding them can never be corroborated or debunked. Are the pockmarks on the gravestones at Copp's Hill Cemetery (Boston) really the result of British soldiers using the markers for target practice? Is the grave of "Gypsy Queen" Kelly Mitchell in Rose Hill Cemetery (Meridian, Mississippi) really reinforced with steel bars to guard the valuables she was buried with? Is a lovers' triangle memorialized in a group of graves at Oakland Cemetery (Atlanta)? Without fieldwork, archaeologists cannot answer these questions any more than they can address legends of graveyard ghosts and ghouls. In Manhattan, Kansas, though, researchers were able to solve one mystery posed by local stories about Meadowlark Cemetery.

Prior to the archaeological excavation to make way for new residential units, locals in Manhattan could not agree on who was buried in Meadowlark Cemetery, a rural graveyard active during the second half of the nineteenth century. One local tradition held that the cemetery provided the final resting place for children who died in an orphanage on the property. Another variation claimed the dead came from a poor farm, or from a poor farm *and* an orphanage. Historical research and the evaluation of the graves provided clues. The man who claimed the land in 1855, Dr. William Stillman, received money each week from the county commissioners for keeping some of the county's poor on his property. Documents suggest that at least three of the county poor who passed away were buried on Stillman's land. Some graves containing very plain burial containers or coffins that were too small for the deceased likely represent the interments of poor farm residents. Since coffins were priced by size, forcing the destitute into the smallest coffins possible would be a cost-saving measure. Local historical society records and the presence of a few decorated coffins suggest that the Stillman family and members of the larger community also used the cemetery. No evidence of an orphanage or orphan burials was found during the project. That part of the story proved to be nothing more than a sentimental invention.

A team from the Smithsonian busted another cemetery myth in 1987, when planned highway construction led to the discovery of a long-forgotten burial ground in Allegheny, Pennsylvania. Locals believed the graves in Voegtly Cemetery, used by members of the Voegtly Evangelical Lutheran Church as early as 1833, had been moved to a new cemetery shortly after its establishment on Troy Hill in 1861. The absence of headstones at the original cemetery site supported local beliefs. But archaeologists uncovered the burials of 724 of the 823 people listed in the Voegtly Cemetery records, proving that only 12 percent of the graves had actually been moved. This is slightly higher than the 8 percent disinterment rate we observed at the Third Street Cemetery, which was also supposedly moved. The archaeological report from Voegtly suggests that several factors contributed to the community's belief that the graveyard was empty: the establishment of the 1861 cemetery, a century of alterations to the church, and the church's ultimate disbandment.

Myth and Landscape

More than one person who heard about our work suggested we should try "witching" to locate the graves before our excavation. Also called "dowsing," this old-time method of remote sensing can be done with two metal or wooden rods or a spinning pendulum. There are many explanations for how this "accepted" practice allows people with particular acuities to locate not only graves but also water, buried foundations, buried treasure, and oil. Essentially, witching can be used to locate whatever the practitioner wants to find underground.[1] If such methods were truly effective, archaeologists could avoid the high costs of ground-penetrating radar and magnetometry to locate graves and other archaeological features. However, our personal experience on the subject of witching has been negative. Graveyards that have been witched are seldom ground-truthed; that is, archaeologists rarely excavate to find out if there are burials at the identified locations. Controlled scientific experiments have shown time and again that dowsing is completely ineffective at detecting the presence or depth of water. Yet many people faithfully accept the results of witching for burials. Perhaps we could have debunked the whole idea had we employed someone to witch the site before we excavated.

Like the witching experiment, a true investigation of collective memory about the Third Street Cemetery was outside the scope of our project. To properly study local folklore, we would have had to prepare a set of identical questions to ask each interviewee, focusing not just on the stories themselves but also on when and where the tales were first heard. By examining the oral recitations along with the printed versions, we might have been able to identify the core elements and trace the timeline of the appearance of each variation.

Even without a formal study, we can learn something from the mythology of the cemetery. Clearly, the specter of cholera inspired dread in the citizens of Dubuque, a feeling that haunted them long after the danger passed. The number of fatalities in town neither filled the cemeteries nor necessitated the digging of mass graves, though both of these occurrences continue to be transmitted orally to subsequent generations. Meanwhile, the community consensus that all the graves had been moved from the bluff perhaps reflects the wish of the parishioners that all of the dead could reside in garden-like Mt. Olivet instead of the overgrown wilderness on Third Street. Memory is linked to the landscape, and when the landscape changes, memories can change or disappear. In the case of the bluff-top cemetery, it is possible to imagine how easily people came to believe that the cemetery had been moved. The evidence of its existence—the headstones and markers—was all but gone and the lot covered by brush and trees.

Though most locals believed the Third Street Cemetery had been emptied, the community continued to interact with the dead through the retelling of these stories. And when the allegedly moved pioneers slumbering on the bluff were abruptly rediscovered, their presence affected the lives of many people, including the land developer and his employees, the Sinsinawa Dominican sisters, the Archdiocese of Dubuque, the excavation and lab workers, the cemetery neighbors, and the community at large. As one anthropologist noted, "It is at this intersection between landscapes, space, and memory where archaeological excavations can be a factor in reconstructing a public memory and locating 'forgotten' aspects on the landscape that are still present underground."[2]

By the end of the project, though, we were left wondering why people cling to old stories even after being told the facts. Maybe it is easier to remember the exciting fictional version than a recitation of dull history. Or perhaps it is difficult to accept the idea that something "everybody knows" is incorrect. The reinforcement of misinformation repeated time and again in the media also lends strength to the popular version of history. Whatever the reasons, the old rumors of epidemics, the removal of the burials, and Kelly's gold remained fresh in the minds of many Dubuquers in the twenty-first century. Newspaper articles exaggerated and misinformed the public about the archaeological excavation, with the usual need to sensationalize every front-page story. Fortunately, this press coverage seemed to have little effect on our public relations when the excavation was over and historical research efforts began.

We established rapport with members of the genealogical society, personnel at the Center for Dubuque History at Loras College, and direct descendants. Our initial meeting with the archdiocese archivist, though, yielded very selective and limited information, including some misinformation. Multiple requests for access to the St. Raphael's burial register were denied. We were not informed of the existence of the transcribed version until we appealed to the archbishop, explaining the importance of providing an accurate history for the site we were essentially erasing from the bluff. It felt as though the staff at the archdiocese had little interest in helping us determine what had happened to the cemetery and its dead over the last century. Perhaps they were avoiding involvement while the lawsuit of the landowner against the Dominican sisters was still pending.

While the barrier created by concerns over the lawsuit and public relations issues was perhaps understandable, it was unfortunate and largely unnecessary. None of the locals who talked to us expressed any anger over the church's abandonment of the cemetery. Though some who learned the truth were saddened by the actions of the archdiocese in the 1940s, only the land developer seemed concerned with the current administration's responsibility for the dead on the bluff. Open communication—in both directions—would have facilitated research and helped us reach possible descendants in the parish. Though the administration avoided involvement in the project in its early phases, staff members later assisted us by providing vital genealogical information for some of the cemetery families. Also, the archdiocese paid for the reinterment of the human remains from Third Street at Mt. Olivet Cemetery, with a priest overseeing the reburial.

This reburial was especially significant for people like Kathy Spangler, a Dubuque resident with two, possibly three, relatives originally buried in the Third Street Cemetery. Her great-granduncle John O'Hearn's military headstone was moved to Mt. Olivet in the 1940s, and the list from the Ashworth and Bennett Funeral Residence indicates that his bones were moved at the same time. Bernard "Barney" McClosky, who married Kathy's great-grandaunt, does not appear on this list, but his military stone now stands just a few feet away from John's. The grave of her great-grandfather Daniel O'Hearn may never have been marked with a headstone since he died at a young age, leaving behind a pregnant wife and two children. Kathy is not even sure that Daniel was interred at Third Street; though the 1865 newspaper article gives details of his fall through the ice and the recovery of his body two weeks later, his obituary does not specify where he was buried. Her family has no private records and, in fact, was unaware they had ancestors buried at Third Street prior to Kathy's genealogical research.

Asked how she felt about the burial ground being abandoned and later excavated by archaeologists, Kathy opined that the cemetery's fate was inevitable, given its location in the heart of town and its chronic neglect. She wishes, though, that all of the graves on the bluff had been moved together to the same location before the site was ever disturbed. Not knowing where all of the dead ended up is the saddest part. She can visit the headstones of her two veteran forebears at Mt. Olivet, but she has never had a place where she could pay her respects to her great-grandfather. We cannot say whether or not the remains of Barney and Daniel are among those we excavated, but at least everyone we removed from the bluff now rests in the meticulously maintained Third Street section of Mt. Olivet.

The descendants of James Gregory might also have been interested to hear about our project and the subsequent reburial. We know that they cared about the "grave" of their ancestor because they requested a replacement headstone for him from the U.S. Department of Veterans Affairs in 2002. The original marble marker that was moved from Third Street to Mt.

Olivet in the 1940s was damaged and difficult to read; and, based on the funeral home list, it was moved without his remains. We may have excavated his grave during the course of the project. Unfortunately, we could not get in touch with the descendants who applied for the new headstone. The superintendent of Mt. Olivet had no record of the family's request, and Veterans Affairs would not release their names. Nevertheless, Gregory's descendants exemplify why it is important to preserve cemeteries for future visitors.

If archaeologists are going to contribute to keeping community memory alive, then we need to keep neighbors, interested parties, and descendants informed and provide a forum for them to voice their concerns. Although it is the policy of the OSA Burials Program to be discreet in any burial excavations and keep the press and the public at arm's length whenever possible out of respect for the dead, our experience taught us that community outreach is also important. Descendant and community discussions occur when Native American burials are of concern, but they did not happen with the 1994 and 2007–11 excavations of the Third Street Cemetery because of the constraints of time and the policy under which we were operating. While we eventually identified and connected with most of the interested parties, this communication occurred only after the excavation was complete. Ideally, this kind of communion would take place before fieldwork even begins.

TWELVE

Mediating for the Dead

HERE WE RETURN to the question we raised at the start of the book: Who mediates when the living disturb the dead and, as a consequence, the dead disrupt the plans of the living? The Third Street Cemetery archaeological excavation is not the only one of its kind in the United States. Old cemeteries, and even some more recent ones, are often removed for purposes of road improvements, airport expansions, new building construction, and other aspects of urban and rural development. Public reaction varies widely. Federal and state laws protect the dead from desecration but not necessarily from removal. It falls to archaeologists, developers, descendant groups, and the governing authorities to work out compromises so that the needs of living relatives are considered alongside the other issues.

A VERY BRIEF HISTORY OF GRAVE DESECRATION AND THE LAWS

In states such as Illinois, Ohio, Iowa, and Arkansas, farmers plowing their land in the nineteenth century turned up arrowheads (projectile points), copper objects, pottery, and sometimes human bones. These were often found within and near mounds that had been created in the landscape. In a practice we would now, we hope, find appalling, families occasionally held Sunday picnics on these mounds. While the women tended the food and children, the men would use horses and plows to trench through the mounds, seeking treasures. The advent of museums (such as the Smithsonian Institution, founded in 1846) only exacerbated the collecting frenzy. In fact, the Putnam Museum in Davenport, Iowa, was founded in 1867 based on the acquisitions of local armchair archaeologists and collectors. Early anthropologists and museum curators were eager to acquire Indian skulls, even taking entire bodies from graves. Modern anthropologists view this disrespectful collection as "a broader example of European-based treatment of the bodies of vanquished enemies."[1]

It was not until 1990 that a federally mandated law, known as the Native American Graves Protection and Repatriation Act (NAGPRA), made it illegal to disturb Native American burials, although a few states, including Iowa, already had their own laws. NAGPRA is complex and, like many such acts, sorely underfunded. In addition to protecting intact graves, NAGPRA stipulates the inventory of all human remains, grave goods, sacred objects, and objects of cultural patrimony previously removed from Native American sites and their repatriation to Native tribes.[2] An object of cultural patrimony is defined generally as any object that has cultural significance to the tribe as a whole. For example, the American flag is an object of cultural patrimony to U.S. citizens. The entities and institutions required to comply with NAGPRA are all those receiving federal funding, including colleges and universities and many museums. The exact way in which human remains and related objects are repatriated is up to the individual affiliated tribes. Many tribes have asked that the OSA Burials Program arrange for reburial in Iowa.

Iowa was the first state in the nation to pass a law protecting ancient burials. The 1976 state statute assigned the duties in this legislation to the state archaeologist. Maria Pearson, a Lakota Sioux, spearheaded the efforts to create the law. She brought her anger and indignation over the differential treatment of Native American burials to the attention of then Iowa governor Robert D. Ray. In one particularly telling incident, the burials of a Native American and "several whites" were discovered at approximately the same time. The "white" remains were reburied in a nearby cemetery, while the Native American's bones were sent away for "study." The law, chapter 263B of the Iowa Code, resulted from the efforts of many individuals, including Native American representatives, then state archaeologist Duane Anderson, Governor Ray, and state legislators. Primary responsibilities of the state archaeologist include investigating, preserving, and reinterring ancient human remains. The statute also called for the establishment of a cemetery for the reburial of these remains. The state archaeologist also has the authority to grant or deny permission to disinter any remains that are over 150 years old. The OSA maintains records of all known or possible ancient burial sites in Iowa.

The Iowa law was enacted at a time when many Native peoples asserted themselves, some forming the more outspoken activist group AIM, the American Indian Movement. Unfortunate disrespectful incidents in Iowa such as the blatant desecration and display of Native American remains finally brought about protection for *all* burials in Iowa. The OSA Burials Program became the repository for many of both the public and private collections of materials taken from Native American graves across the state and elsewhere. Four cemeteries have been established for the reburial of these remains, or else they are returned to affiliated tribes, depending on the tribe's wishes. Some reburials in the newly established cemeteries have been accompanied by Native Americans and a medicine man. All work performed by the Burials Program is conducted with respect and solemnity. Because the program is responsible for all burials over 150 years old, this moving date now includes early pioneer graves in the state, as well as ancient Native American burials. The ethical treatment of all human remains continues, offered to any and all who may pass through our lab.

Many other states have enacted laws that deal specifically with historic, non–Native American cemeteries. The legal requirements for obtaining a permit to disinter remains from unmarked or abandoned burial grounds vary from state to state. Such permits are generally granted if the property is condemned by the governing authority as a nuisance property or if a party wishing to develop the land demonstrates that the cemetery is neglected. Several states, such as Tennessee and Wisconsin, require the publication of a notice of intent to remove human remains before any disinterment is authorized. These notices must appear in newspapers with general circulation in the county in which the graves are located. Other states, including Oregon and Georgia, have laws that call for public hearings at which all interested parties may be heard. Georgia further requires that each application for a disinterment permit includes a plan prepared by a genealogist for identifying and notifying the descendants of those buried or believed to be buried in the abandoned cemetery.

Illinois burial protection laws do not stipulate that newspaper notices must be published in advance of the removal of an abandoned cemetery, but such announcements have become customary and are considered a "best practice." According to the Iowa Code, the court may issue a disinterment permit without any descendant input, but "due consideration shall be given to the public health, the dead, and the feelings of relatives." In the case of the Third Street Cemetery, the court found that living relatives were not ascertainable. Neither the land developer nor the Burials Program placed a notice of our upcoming excavations in the Dubuque newspaper. Such a notice would have allowed for consideration of descendant opinions before the remains were removed and reburied. When future cemetery excavation projects arise, we strongly suggest that archaeologists in Iowa and other states adopt the policy of publishing announcements, even when they are not legally obligated to do so.

SOMEONE HAS TO PAY

Because of the laws governing the treatment of human remains, the discovery of the forgotten Third Street Cemetery on what had become private property was a serious problem for landowner A. J. Spiegel, a local manufacturer turned developer. What were Spiegel's responsibilities and legal obligations? The Third Street Cemetery was in use from the 1830s to the 1880s, falling under the authority of both of the two agencies responsible for upholding Iowa laws protecting ancient and more recent burials. As a result, the archaeological work involved two permitting institutions, the OSA and the Iowa Department of Public Health. The landowner had to foot the bill for the OSA's excavations, and that sum was not small.

Not surprisingly but to the dismay of the heavily Catholic community, Spiegel filed a lawsuit against the Sinsinawa Dominican sisters who sold him the land. The suit claimed that he had asked about the "Roman Catholic Grave Yard" mentioned in the property's legal description and that the real estate broker representing the sisters had assured him that all of the bodies had been removed in the past. The Dominicans maintain that they were unaware graves remained on the lot and that they provided no false information during the sale. Damages listed in the suit included the cost of the excavation, Spiegel's legal expenses, and loss of the use of the property. His out-of-pocket expense for the excavation alone was probably a little under $1 million for the 939 graves. This surely seemed like an outrageous sum to remove the bodies of people who had long been forgotten.

For comparison, we looked at the expenses for the archaeological excavation of the Alameda-Stone Cemetery in Tucson, Arizona. It was excavated in 2006 by a privately owned, commercial archaeological firm that conducted extensive background research, did descendant outreach, and had detailed research questions in place prior to archaeological work. Their project included extensive postexcavation research involving in-depth osteological analysis, the use of high-tech equipment, and detailed statistical analyses. The total cost of the project (which also included excavation of pits, privies, and structures created after the cemetery's abandonment) ended up being close to $15 million for the 1,083 grave shafts and 1,338 individuals. The firm's highly detailed technical report is available on-line and runs for hundreds of pages in multiple volumes. A more succinct academic book followed the technical report, summarizing the larger volume.

Most development-related archaeological projects are not executed at this scientific level. We compared the Alameda-Stone bill to the cost of a simple cemetery relocation, in which the graves were excavated carefully but none of the material was taken to a lab for analysis. One such project, performed in 2009 by the archaeological branch of an engineering firm in the southeastern United States, cost approximately $1,500 per grave, including the expenses of reburial. This is considerably lower than the $10,000 per grave for the Arizona project but still above our less than $1,000 per grave. Overall, the Dubuque landowner got a deal by hiring a not-for-profit state agency, though it is understandable that he did not see it that way. He was also fortunate that the excavation of the Third Street Cemetery was not controversial.

CONTROVERSY AT THE AFRICAN BURIAL GROUND

Forgotten cemeteries can become legal and public relations nightmares for the developers and contractors who must deal with them. One of the most controversial and publicized cemetery removals took place in part of the New York African Burial Ground. During an archaeological survey conducted prior to the construction of a federal building in Lower Manhattan, the investigators found a cemetery on the proposed building site. It had been established in 1712 as an African or Negro burial ground, and enslaved blacks were buried there until 1794. It is believed that around fifteen thousand people were originally interred in an area covering approximately six acres. The excavation required for construction of the federal building covered less than one city block, a small portion of the cemetery.

The archaeological excavations were conducted from the summer of 1991 to the summer of 1992 in conjunction with construction. That is, the burials were being removed just ahead of the bulldozers. Unfortunately, no archaeological research plan was in place, meaning the excavators had no strategy for what was to be done with the burials once the project was over. The methods laid out in such a strategy would usually be guided by specific research questions, but these were also lacking.

News of the burial ground's excavation was met with massive protests against the cemetery's desecration, and prayer vigils were held by members of New York's African American community and others. New York City's first black mayor, David Dinkins, and other black legislators became involved in attempts to work with the U.S. General Services Administration, which was in charge of the building construction. Most wanted an end to the excavation and the establishment of a memorial on the African Burial Ground. Controversy over the cemetery made its way to the U.S. Congress in 1992, and that body eventually called for work on the site to cease. Community activists and New York's Landmarks Preservation Commission recommended the formation of a group, composed of faculty and researchers from Howard University and other institutions, to analyze and report on the remains of over four hundred graves that had been removed from the burial ground. In the end, approximately two hundred burials remained in place within the city block where the new federal building was constructed. The site is now a New York State and National Historic Landmark, and the Ted Weiss Federal Building includes a memorial to the dead, as well as a visitors' and interpretive center.

The head of the African Burial Ground research team, Michael Blakey of Howard University, summarized the significance of the African Burial Ground.[3] It was a slave cemetery in a state where educated people had been taught that few blacks and no slavery existed in the eighteenth century. It opened up a whole new history of New York's enslaved Africans and their descendants. These myths, perpetuated for centuries, were now debunked.

Cemetery excavations are not always controversial. In one particular case, a small town worked with professionals to save a historic cemetery. The town of Grafton, Illinois, is located near the confluence of the Illinois and Mississippi Rivers. Following the hundred-year flood of 1993, around one-third of the town's population was displaced or moved away, leaving fewer than seven hundred residents. The citizens began rebuilding their town on the uplands, well away from the river, using funds from the Federal Emergency Management Agency (FEMA). An archaeological survey, conducted under FEMA's requirements, resulted in the discovery of the historic Grafton Cemetery, used from around 1834 until about 1873. Professional archaeologists and osteologists were hired to find all the old burials, excavate them, study the material remains, and reinter them in the town's Scenic Hill Cemetery (established ca. 1872). Two hundred and fifty-two grave shafts were identified, and over 97 percent of the dead were still present in the cemetery. Very few disinterments were noted. Grafton Cemetery's occupants and material remains discovered with them were very similar to those found at the Third Street Cemetery, representing an immigrant and first-generation population of Europeans primarily from Germany, Ireland, and England, although mostly of the middle class. As with the Third Street Cemetery, the locals in Grafton believed the graves had been removed from their cemetery sometime near the end of the nineteenth century, and no headstones remained. The story of the Grafton Cemetery project tells how archaeology saved a town's pioneer cemetery through careful excavation followed by reinterment in safer grounds.[4]

The removal of the Alameda-Stone Cemetery in Tucson, Arizona, provides an example of yet another scenario for such projects. In the early twenty-first century, the government of Pima County drew up plans for a courthouse to be built on the location of this large burial ground. The cemetery included a military section that was open from 1862 to 1881 and a civilian section used from the 1850s or early 1860s until 1875. At that time, the cemetery was the only public burial ground, and people from diverse cultural and religious backgrounds were interred there. Pre-excavation research led to the discovery of a notice published in January 1882 in Tucson's English-language and Spanish-language newspapers. The citizens of Tucson were given sixty days to remove any relatives or friends buried in the cemetery and move them to a newly established cemetery.

Apparently this was all it took for the general public to come to believe thereafter that the old cemetery had been moved. However, the archaeological contractors were not fooled, especially since over a hundred graves were disturbed by construction of a building on the site in the 1950s. Prior to excavation, they held consultations with descendant groups, including Hispanics and local affiliated Native American tribes, to ensure that proper protocols were followed in the handling and analysis of the burials. These consultations, which also included the media, local politicians, and the general public, began over two years before the fieldwork started. Different descendants had conflicting ideas about proper procedures, and every aspect of the field and lab work had to be agreed upon. Excavation of the cemetery began in 2006, and over thirteen hundred individuals were recovered. Separate reburial ceremonies were held at several locations for the reinterment of individuals from different cultural backgrounds. In this instance, consultation and cultural sensitivity were the keys to avoiding controversy over the disturbance of a large number of graves.

THE MARGINALIZED

Burial grounds like the Third Street, Alameda-Stone, and Grafton cemeteries, which hold the remains of a cross section of society, are not the type most often excavated in the United States. As one anthropologist has noted, "Many if not most of the larger historic period cemeteries excavated in this country in recent decades . . . have been associated with poorhouses, institutions, and African-American communities, none of which would necessarily reflect the biology or material culture of the middle- or upper-class communities of European origin. In essence, then, it is the well-maintained European cemetery that is lost from study, whereas those of lower socioeconomic status, while perhaps more likely to be completely destroyed, are also more likely to be excavated and studied."[5] Historically, Native American burials were often treated as curiosities, containing treasures and the remains of individuals whom American settlers saw as not wholly human or civilized. Their burial places were for the "Other," people who had been marginalized and dehumanized. Today, abandoned historic cemeteries are often regarded by developers with a similar level of disrespect when they get in the way of "progress." Without living descendants to speak for them, the dead become disenfranchised. Also, because most of us believe that our long-dead relatives are in cemeteries that include perpetual care, people are often surprised to hear that cemeteries come to be abandoned or destroyed. New York City's African Burial Ground presented a case of cemetery excavation that could have had a very different outcome. Had the pressures of progress, the completion of the new federal building, won out over the voices of protest and descent, this burial ground would just be another example of marginalizing a segment of our population. And the contributions to our understanding of slavery in the North would have been lost.

In the past twenty-five years, archaeological excavations have included at least two cemeteries of freed African slaves, Freedmen's Cemetery in Alexandria, Virginia, which dates to the time of the Civil War, and Freedman's Cemetery in Dallas, Texas, in use from around 1869 to 1907. In the case of the Alexandria cemetery, members of the community voiced strong opposition to any impact on the "newly discovered" cemetery. Minimal archaeological excavations identified the locations of graves, but the remains were not removed. In this way, construction plans for the area were modified to avoid disturbance to the burial ground. A memorial park is now located on the site. In Dallas, over eleven hundred individuals were excavated from Freedman's Cemetery, which was unfortunately in the way of a new expressway. However, local activists made sure the site was not forgotten. It is now a historic landmark that includes bronze statues dedicated to Dallas's early African American citizens. Many of the artifacts recovered from the cemetery are in the collections of the African American Museum in Dallas. The remains were reburied shortly after exhumation.

Our category of the marginalized also includes the poor. In 1984 the Monroe County Poor Farm cemetery (used from 1826 to 1863) of Rochester, New York, was excavated, with the removal of 296 individuals. In 1990 120 individuals were excavated from the Cook County Poor Farm (the Dunning Poorhouse) in Chicago, in use from 1851 to 1869. Over 1,600 burials were excavated from the Milwaukee County Institution Grounds (MCIG) in 1991–92, and several hundred more burials were removed in the summer of 2013. The MCIG was a public burial ground used to inter individuals who died in Milwaukee County institutions, including the poor farm, the isolation hospital, the Asylum for the Chronically Insane, and the Home for Dependent Children, as well as unidentified individuals from the coroner's office and Milwaukee County residents unable to afford burial fees.

These unmarked, abandoned burial grounds are particularly vulnerable to disturbance in two ways. First, their lack of conventional grave markers greatly increases the potential for accidental discovery after a major development project has already begun. Then, without inscribed headstones, there is no way to track down direct descendants for consultation.

Even well-marked cemeteries with known descendants are sometimes moved in the name of progress, occasionally against the wishes of some of the families. One highly publicized example is the St. Johannes Cemetery (1849–2006), which was condemned and purchased by the city of Chicago through eminent domain. After years of court battles, the city finally removed 1,494 graves to make way for a new runway at O'Hare Airport. The seventeen-million-dollar project included extensive genealogical research and reburial of remains based on the preferences of the individual families. Many descendants were pleased in the end, while others still harbor hard feelings.

However, it is simply not possible for every spot where a human being was ever buried to be held sacred for all eternity; highways, airports, and courthouses have to be built somewhere. We advocate that it is the joint responsibility of the developers, archaeologists, and governing agencies to assure that the removal process is completed as respectfully as possible and that community and descendant voices are heard.

THIRTEEN

Continuity of Care

FEDERAL LAWS, as well as many state laws, outline the legal obligations of any person who disturbs the dead. But what are our ethical obligations? What do archaeologists and human osteologists owe the dead beyond compliance with various statutes? As we noted in the first chapter, it is essential that we provide continuity of care. Our actions must be an extension of the respectful handling provided by loved ones in preparation for funeral rites. No matter how ancient the remains, every individual has a right to be treated with dignity.

Such projects as the African Burial Ground in New York City and the Alameda-Stone Cemetery in Tucson demonstrate that working with descendant communities should be part and parcel of all burial removals. When archaeologists reach out to the interested parties, their efforts can lead to cooperative agreements among many disparate voices. This helps prevent archaeology from being performed in a vacuum, a secret academic world that only some are privy to.

At the same time, treating the dead with respect is essential to maintaining professionalism. That is why most burial excavations in America are not performed in the public eye. We are carrying out an act of remembrance. Unlike the artifact collectors and museum curators of the late nineteenth and early twentieth centuries, we do not pose skeletal remains for photos or display them gratuitously to people who view them with morbid curiosity. Though descendants are usually unknown, we behave as though our actions might be scrutinized by the relatives of the deceased. A good rule of thumb taught in embalming schools (and relayed to us by cemetery superintendent Pat Leonard) is to treat the dead as if you're going to meet them again.

Since our project started off as the salvage excavation of "a few burials," we did not have any specific research objectives in place prior to fieldwork.

We did, however, have an arrangement for the reburial of the remains. A complete research plan should include not just questions to guide the investigation but a provision for the ultimate disposition of the dead, whether it includes lengthy analysis, immediate reburial, or long-term storage. Storage should only be considered when the particular population offers unique research opportunities for the future and direct descendants do not object or are no longer known. During several recent cemetery removal projects, archaeologists and osteologists have worked with descendant communities and come to mutual agreements regarding the fate of the disinterred remains. We can avoid controversy by empowering the living through participation in decisions concerning their ancestors.

Some projects in the past have been conducted without the level of consideration most people would like to see in regard to their ancestors. This situation can arise sometimes from a simple lack of funding. Some projects have no research plan, no budget for analysis, and no provisions for proper storage. If reburial is not part of the project proposal, remains can end up languishing in substandard conditions indefinitely. Such was the case with the individuals excavated from the MCIG in 1991–92. During a road construction project, a portion of one of these unmarked cemeteries, dating from 1882 until 1925, was excavated, yielding 1,649 burials. The bones sat in limbo, largely unanalyzed, and shuttled back and forth between two institutions for more than fifteen years. Fortunately, in 2008 the University of Wisconsin–Milwaukee Archaeological Research Laboratory was granted final disposition of all the human remains and artifacts from the excavation. The collection, now stored in a secure, environmentally controlled space, is the subject of ongoing research projects. The transfer to UW-Milwaukee opened up new avenues of investigation and research potential about a marginalized population.

Nevertheless, in 2012, when further excavations were proposed at the MCIG to make way for a hospital expansion, some locals objected to the plan. Initially, it seemed the most vocal opponent was concerned that no real research had been conducted on the remains from the first excavation in the 1990s. In fact, he opposed the remains being studied at all and insisted that such treatment robbed the dead of their dignity. He advocated that all of the remains, from both the new excavation and the original project, be reburied. Interestingly, though, he made a distinction between the Milwaukee dead and those who *could* be considered scientific collections: "These are not prehistoric people. These are not remnants of some ancient civilization. These are our own near relatives."[1] Should the more recent dead be treated differently from our ancient predecessors? In this case, his argument seemed to focus on relatedness rather than antiquity. The idea that it is acceptable to study skeletons of "Others" but that it is disrespectful to examine one's own ancestors is considered antiquated and unenlightened in modern America, a perfect example of ethnocentrism.

In the absence of identified blood relatives, descendant communities usually make the decisions about what constitutes proper care for the dead. For Native American graves, affiliated tribes or NAGPRA protocols have the final say. In the case of the Milwaukee poor, Wisconsin state laws gave the Wisconsin Historical Society and the Burial Sites Preservation Office the authority to determine the fate of the remains. The project went forward, and the people excavated from the MCIG joined the others at the University of Wisconsin–Milwaukee lab.

The court order for the Third Street Cemetery disinterment permit included a provision for analysis to be conducted prior to reburial of the remains, the results of which we presented in the preceding chapters. As we conducted this research, we continued to treat the human remains respectfully following their removal from the cemetery. All the materials, not just the skeletal remains, were meticulously cleaned, measured, and documented. Having removed these items from their original resting place, we had an obligation to gather as much information as possible. The contribution of this analysis to the body of knowledge about the early history of Dubuque and life in nineteenth-century America counterbalances the unfortunate loss of a large portion of the cemetery itself. All items found with or near the body of an individual, as well as any coffin hardware with religious iconography, were reburied with the respective remains.

All the cemeteries we have mentioned in this book were archaeologically excavated. The findings from these excavations and analyses have been reported in academic papers (theses and dissertations), publications in academic journals, or contract and proprietary reports not easily accessible to the general public. Fortunately, some projects have funding to make their findings available. A website provides the history and burial records of Freedmen's Cemetery in Virginia. Motivated and patient readers can download the massive scientific reports from the Alameda-Stone Cemetery and the New York African Burial Ground from the Pima County and National Park Service websites, respectively. Members of our own team have attempted to make information about the Third Street Cemetery available to a wide audience by disseminating our report and by doing a variety of community talks in addition to our professional presentations—and, of course, by publishing this book. As a consequence of our efforts, the Third Street Cemetery has been put back "on the map." The cemetery appears (albeit at the incorrect location) on the 2010 and 2013 topographic maps of Dubuque produced by the U.S. Geological Survey.

Perhaps it is easy to think of "continuity of care" in the same sense as perpetual care. However, we have given over *perpetual* care to the cemeteries created during and after the beautification of death movement. We count on others to mow the lawns, repair broken headstones, and not accidentally dig into existing graves. Of course, some cemeteries are better at these tasks than others. We are relieved to know that Mt. Olivet is well maintained and that the Third Street Cemetery section is included in that upkeep. By coincidence, during the first year of our excavation, Pat Leonard, the superintendent of Mt. Olivet, worked with Eagle Scout Jesse Jaeger and a group of volunteers who helped clean up the Third Street Cemetery section, gluing together some broken pieces of headstones and setting the markers in new concrete bases. We transferred the many headstone fragments we recovered during excavation to Mt. Olivet, and one member of the staff works on refitting these pieces, if possible, during the winter months. Perhaps more headstones will be added to the Third Street section someday.

Our people of Third Street, for that is how we have come to think of them, are now in their new resting place at Mt. Olivet Cemetery. The first reburial occurred in 1994, followed by a service in 2010 for the remains excavated in 2007 and 2008. On September 6, 2013, we attended the reburial of the 2010 and 2011 remains (figure 18).

On that sunny, breezy, late summer morning, we gathered at Mt. Olivet and stood surrounded by lush grass and silent white monuments as Father Brian Dellaert consigned the mortal remains back to consecrated ground. It was an intimate affair, as most people involved in the project over the

FIGURE 18. Father Brian Dellaert performing graveside services at Mt. Olivet Cemetery, Dubuque, Iowa, September 6, 2013.

years had moved on to other states. The only member of our field crew who could attend was Jesse Begle, the backhoe operator who had invested much time and interest in our project. Cemetery superintendent Pat Leonard and his son William, the groundskeeper, paid their last respects as well. Biays Bowerman, whose years of research kept the memory of the Third Street Cemetery alive, came to the service, along with Joan Tallman, another local genealogist. Sister Carol Hoverman, from the Archdiocese of Dubuque, looked on as "our brothers and sisters" were returned to their own community, laid in a vault beside the remains previously reburied from our Third Street excavations, arranged in two neat rows.

After the service, we chatted with those in attendance and found that several had noted the same deficiency, a final touch still wanting. At Mt. Olivet, the Third Street Cemetery section is well known to locals interested in the cemetery's history but is not marked in any way. There is nothing on the bluff top overlooking downtown Dubuque that designates this place as the Old Cemetery, Old Catholic Cemetery, the Third Street Cemetery, or a cemetery by any of its many names. Maybe someday the archdiocese or the parishioners of St. Raphael's will be able to provide a fitting memorial at Mt. Olivet and a historical marker on the bluff, a reminder of those who have gone before and of the burials still there.

FOURTEEN

The Tender Mercies of Our Successors

DUE TO UNFORESEEN CIRCUMSTANCES, we became involved in the archaeological excavation and study of the skeletal remains of more than 900 people who had been buried at the Third Street Cemetery. This forgotten graveyard on the bluff kept its secrets for almost 130 years until backhoes and "progress" interrupted the residents' slumber. Years of lab analysis and historical probing revealed much about these early people of Dubuque and their battles to survive the many obstacles that life presented in the nineteenth century. When thinking over all that has taken place since 2007, we cannot help but wonder about the fate of cemeteries, about what death might bring for us, and if all our efforts to tell the stories of the dead will be forgotten.

WHY CEMETERIES?

How do we, or even *do* we, define a sacred place? For many people, it is a place somehow connected to a deity or having a religious purpose, and for those people, it is deserving of veneration. To many Native Americans, sacred places or spaces are more broadly defined than those of most Euroamericans. Native Americans point to hills, valleys, rivers, canyons, mountains, and burial grounds as just some of their sacred landscapes. What landscapes do those of us who are not Native American define as sacred in our country? Do some of us consider our cemeteries sacred? Perhaps not.

What good is a cemetery if those buried in its grounds are not guaranteed eternal rest? Ever since the beautification of death movement transformed cemeteries from overcrowded, ill-kept properties into scenic, garden-like destinations, burial grounds have served as more than just repositories for corpses. People visit their departed loved ones at the cemetery perhaps because they believe that spirits are present or because the quiet place, separated from the outside world, allows contemplation and remembrance uninterrupted by the hubbub of daily life. Additionally, these peaceful spots provide paths for dog walking, jogging, and biking; monumental art for the appreciation of tourists, painters, and photographers; and a goldmine of information for genealogists and historians. The period in which these appealing rural burial grounds were created was, however, relatively short. The twentieth century saw the rise of the easily maintained lawn cemeteries. With their identical horizontal grave markers and restricted decorations, they offer little of interest to anyone besides mourners.

Now, in the twenty-first century, as the corporeal dead are increasingly removed from the modern funeral service, and as cremation overtakes inhumation as the most popular form of body disposal, the fate of the American cemetery is uncertain. While it is true that many columbaria (buildings that house ashes) are built within existing cemeteries, some city zoning ordinances permit them on other properties, such as church lawns. Some families choose to retain the ashes of loved ones at home, while others scatter them in symbolic locations. With trendy "celebration of life" parties replacing the graveside services of yesteryear, will there still be a need for traditional cemeteries in the future? The cynical among us might suggest that the fortune to be made off cemetery "real estate" will motivate those involved in the business to keep the tradition alive. Perhaps. Or perhaps, despite current trends, Americans will continue to need a landscape where memory and sentiment can persist. As Marilyn Yalom, in her book *The American Resting Place: Four Hundred Years of History through Our Cemeteries and Burial Grounds*, says, "We like to think that visitors rescue the dead from oblivion."[1]

THE PERSISTENCE OF MYTH

And what about the Third Street Cemetery? How long will it be before the current residents of Dubuque are gone and no one remembers there are still people buried on the bluff? The land, which lay undeveloped at the time of writing, may not be built on for many years. If houses or condominiums are constructed, will the residents be told that there are still graves beneath the lawn? Perhaps locals will remember our excavation and say, "Oh, all those burials were moved back in the early twenty-first century," a new version of an old myth. In fact, with the completion of our project, the community is probably certain (again) that all the graves have been removed from the Third Street Cemetery, though this is not the case. There is little doubt that this prime real estate will be disturbed again and that more graves will be encountered. The story behind the new mass reburials in Mt. Olivet Cemetery may be forgotten or misremembered. In a couple of different unknown locations, there are probably caches of bone-filled soil from the graves bulldozed in the 1940s just waiting to be discovered. The story of the Third Street Cemetery is not finished yet.

WHAT'S NEXT?

Our society has gone from grave robbery to grave protection. And when burials cannot be left in place, we have established protocols by which to conduct the proper removal of burials and sometimes reburial in a place where we hope they may rest forever, undisturbed. With each new project we learn better ways for construction companies, archaeologists, and the public to cooperate and interact with one another so that misinformation and acrimony do not arise. There are people who care about the early pioneers, the poor, the freed slaves, and other forgotten dead, but often their voices are drowned out by the drone of heavy construction equipment. We must listen to the voices of the living if we hope to speak for those long past.

And now we leave the people still buried on the bluff top and those in Mt. Olivet Cemetery to the tender mercies of *our* successors. May they treat them with kindness.

Acknowledgments

A PROJECT OF THIS SCOPE involved dozens of individuals. Without their contributions, we would not have been able to complete our task of unraveling the story of the Third Street Cemetery.

Professionals at the University of Iowa Office of the State Archaeologist (OSA) freely offered their expertise in a variety of areas: Mark Anderson, John Cordell, John Doershuk (state archaeologist), Colleen Eck, Dan Horgen, Kurtis Kettler, Michael Perry, Cindy Peterson, Melody Pope, Shirley J. Schermer (Burials Program director), and William Whittaker. Some of these individuals and numerous others served as OSA field volunteers in 2007. Thanks to Linda Langenberg for making sure the paperwork all went properly and keeping us in line.

The excavations could not have proceeded smoothly without the amazing field crew. Our thanks to all of the archaeological field technicians: Andrew Creasey, Matthew Cretzmeyer, Joseph DeAngelis, Reed Dilley, Kourtney Donohue, Heather Drought, Nicole Geske, Sarah Harrah, Tom Kearns, Kurtis Kettler, Lindsay Lamont, Kate Lamzik, Jim Lindsay, Elizabeth Macken, Dan McCullough, Kayla Resnick, Jennifer Roberts, Brian Ross, Patrick Stanton, Aniela Travers, and Kevin Verhulst; and to Luke Wiederholt and Jesse Begle, backhoe operators.

Laboratory analysis, detailed inventories, data collection, cleaning of the burial materials, and any mundane tasks assigned were cheerfully and meticulously performed by a number of University of Iowa student workers. They are the best: Brooke Colbert, Katherine Hove, Katelyn Ingersoll, Elizabeth Macken, Sarah Moore, Jessica Peel-Austin, and Tyler Perkins. And the analysis of the skeletal remains could not have been accomplished in such a short period of time without the expertise of assistant osteologists Kourtney Donohue and Nicole Geske.

The illustrations were produced by two talented individuals: Tyler

Perkins (OSA student worker) and Deanne Wortman (Iowa City artist and University of Iowa faculty in the Department of Art).

Numerous individuals freely, and often very enthusiastically, contributed their knowledge, experience, and expertise to our historical research and various laboratory analyses: Susan Black, Archdiocese of Dubuque archives secretary; Biays Bowerman, Dubuque resident and author; Sister Deanna Marie Carr, Sisters of Charity of the Blessed Virgin Mary, Dubuque; Dubuque County Courthouse personnel; Dubuque Public Library archivists; Gary Frost, Conservation Library, University of Iowa, for identification and assistance with the ambrotype; Muriel Ghys, Les Amis du Musée Funéraire National; Michael Gibson, Loras College Center for Dubuque History; Kelly Gillikin, National Folklore Collection, University College Dublin; Christian Haunton, University of Iowa, Department of Anthropology; Guy Hemenway, Dubuque Planning Services Department; Sister Carol Hoverman, Archdiocese of Dubuque, newspaper editor; Pat Leonard, superintendent, Mt. Olivet Cemetery, Dubuque; Patricia Lysaght, professor of Irish folklore, University College Dublin; Diane Mack, translator of French correspondence; Ronald Mack, Irish famine research; Sister Maureen McPartland, Archdiocese of Dubuque archivist; Linda Mathewson, Office of the Dubuque *Telegraph Herald*; Cindy Nagel, Tallgrass Historians, L.C., Iowa City, coffin hardware analysis; Father Loras Otting, Archdiocese of Dubuque archivist, retired; Dr. Patricia Richards, University of Wisconsin–Milwaukee, Department of Anthropology; Tom and Vicki Schlarman, Phoenix Group Genealogical Society members; Ron and Judy Seymour, retired, Dubuque residents, members of the Key City Genealogical Society; Mary Simon, Illinois State Archaeological Survey, Prairie Research Institute, coffin wood analysis; Kathy Spangler, genealogist; Bill and Arden Thomas, contributors to Murphy family genealogy; Jim Wall-Wild, River Museum, Dubuque County Historical Society archives; Dr. Steven Vincent, head of the Department of Oral Pathology, University of Iowa College of Dentistry; Father Matthew Worthen, Sacred Heart Cathedral, Pensacola, Florida.

A special thanks to those who participated in the reburials on November 18, 2010, and September 6, 2013: Pat Leonard and his son William, who made the arrangements, and Father Loras Otting and Father Brian Dellaert, who performed the graveside services.

This book would not have been possible without the continued enthusiastic support and insightful comments of acquisitions editor Catherine Cocks, managing editors Charlotte Wright and Susan Hill Newton, and copyeditor Mary M. Hill at the University of Iowa Press. We also thank reviewer Robert Powers for his helpful suggestions and Jack Isleib for help on early drafts.

If we have left anyone out of our acknowledgments, please forgive us and know that you have our gratitude for helping us complete this monumental project.

People Buried at the Third Street Cemetery

Surname	Name	Age	Death date
Aaron	Mary Ann	45	8/25/1876
Aaron	?		
Aaron	?		
Aaron	?		
Aaron	?		
Adam	Eva	30	5/7/1850 funeral
Alli	Louis	37	9/7/1846
Bacon	Moses	1	7/24/1842
Bass	John	50	4/16/1846
Bassien	Victoire		7/13/1846 funeral
Beams	Mary		1/24/1845 funeral
Beaubien	Ansilla/Aurelia	35	4/3/1860
Beaubien	Edward Lewis		2/31/1851 [sic]
Beaubien	Elizabeth	19	11/13/1854
Beaubien	Mark	41	11/1/1860
Beimbehest	Richard	4	5/24/1854
Bellehumeur	?		6/7/1852
Belliman	Joseph	11 months	7/1/1847 funeral
Bensam	Mary	20	7/8/1851 funeral
Benson	John Henry	2 months	8/18/1845 funeral
Beregan	Briget	32	10/15/1846
Bern	Helen		4/22/1851 funeral
Beste	Henricus	68	7/22/1851
Beutzen	Christine Louise	3	6/8/1842
Bigle	Michael	19	9/7/1846 funeral
Bird	Mary	45	7/24/1850
Bladher	John	ca. 30	5/1/1846
Blake	Charles	10 days	2/5/1845
Blake	Ellen		1850–56
Blake	Elizabeth		after 1870
Blake	John	61	8/11/1870
Blake	John	3	10/20/1843

Surname	Name	Age	Death date
Blake	John Joseph	19	10/24/1870
Blake	Julia	3 weeks	3/13/1846
Blake	Susan	38	3/4/1876
Blake	William	37	1/19/1868
Blechlangar	Francisca	1	4/22/1851
Blechlangar	Ursula		4/25/1851 funeral
Bohomme	Marie Louise	104	3/6/1846 funeral
Boubien	?		8/12/1845 funeral
Bouclar	Francis	27	8/19/1851 funeral
Bouhen	John		2/19/1844
Bourgeois	Maria Acine	82	9/19/1841
Bower	Agatha	2	8/27/1850 funeral
Boyden	James		7/11/1848 funeral
Brauckman	Mary	30	10/5/1847
Braukman	Joan	33	9/27/1847 funeral
Braun	Catherina	26	6/29/1849
Brebender	Eve	65	1/4/1850
Bredy	Salé	45	2/10/1842
Bremott	Stephanus		11/3/1853 funeral
Bren	James	6	3/10/1853 funeral
Brewer	?	27	6/10/1852 funeral
Briand	George	55	11/25/1848
Brisson	Mary		6/24/1851
Brodie	Daniel John	48	10/18/1848
Brodie	David	ca. 26	11/28/1848
Broun	Catherine	26	7/1/1849 funeral
Brown	James	57	1854
Brown	Mary	75	11/19/1847
Brown	Thomas	50	10/16/1852
Brulet	Joseph		6/20/1851
Brula	Edmond	11 months	9/28/1840
Buckley	Ed S.		
Burke	Mrs.	[76]	7/7/1873
Burke	Michael	ca. 38	7/?/1873
Burke	Walter	2	6/12/1854
Burns	John	26	10/3/1849
Burns	Patrick	21	10/10/1849
Butterworth	Alexander	54	6/12/1852
Butterworth	Catherine	120	8/1/1847 funeral
Butterworth	Mary		12/24/1841
Byrnes	Patrick		7/19/1858 funeral
Byrnes	Patrick	70	2/9/1869

Surname	Name	Age	Death date
Cain	Anne		4/8/1856 funeral
Caliceur	Fabella	ca. 60	11/9/1854
Callanan	?		1/15/1855
Camick	James C.	60	8/18/1840
Camody	Catherine		8/3/1840
Canchelor	Michael		12/15/1843
Canavan	Ellen		1/22/1853
Canivan	Elizabeth		8/22/1845 funeral
Carlan	Emily	8	5/28/1852 funeral
Carney	Catherine		8/3/1854
Carney	Teresa	7	4/18/1868
Carr	Catherine	60	10/3/1841
Carr	Maggie	21	10/31/1871
Carr	Patrick	45	5/1/1855
Carrol	Mary	24	12/26/1847
Caseley	Jean Baptiste	2	11/3/1845
Casey	John		3/23/1843
Cegalig	Casper		6/23/1854 funeral
Chorington	?		7/14/1847
Choupe	Joseph		8/19/1850
Chresente	Antonia		4/20/1852 funeral
Christman	Margaret	12	4/26/1840
Christman	Peter		
Christmann	Mary		1/20/1851 funeral
Cibaut	Jean Baptiste		12/10/1841
Clark	Terrence	63	11/28/1865
Clarke	Julia	2	6/4/1850
Clement	Joseph	24	10/25/1854 funeral
Clifford	Daniel	22	10/24/1860
Clins	Patrick	3 months	11/17/1850 funeral
Coby	Thomas	32	6/19/1849
Cochran	M——ha——	3	1/11/1860
Code	Henry	3 1/2	1/28/1842
Coffee	?		1/25/1847
Coffee	Mary	9	4/2/1846
Colegan	Mary	9	7/25/1844
Collier	Louis	4	8/10/1844
Colligan	John	45	9/15/1842 funeral
Collins	Catherine	58	3/25/1877
Collins	James		9/22/1844
Collins	Margaret	53	11/18/1865
Collins	Margarit	ca. 11	5/6/1846

Surname	Name	Age	Death date
Collins	Mary	4	8/14/1847 funeral
Collins	Maryann	6	1/29/1847 funeral
Collins	Patrick	ca. 50	1/8/1847 funeral
Collins	Timothy	29	6/6/1852
Columbe	Francis	37	5/15/1855 funeral
Comday	Michael	13 months	10/3/1840
Compfeen	Mary		9/21/1840
Conden	James	3	7/30/1848 funeral
Conly	Mary	3	3/27/1849
Connell	Patrick	10	6/17/1847 funeral
Connivan	Timothy	6 months	11/23/1846 funeral
Connor	Patrick		12/22/1853 funeral
Conrad	Johanna	59	8/23/1848
Considine	Patrick	27	7/29/1870
Conway	Anna	47	3/12/1861
Conway	Catherine	7	6/6/1852 funeral
Conway	Ellen		3/17/1851
Conway	Ignatius Alphonsus		7/22/1851
Conway	Margaret	3 months	1/3/1846
Conway	Martin		1/14/1851 funeral
Conway	Michael		7/25/1851 funeral
Cooney	Mary Ann	3	10/3/1856
Cooney	Thomas	38	5/19/1855
Corbet	Joseph		5/21/1855 funeral
Corbett	Patrick		7/8/1847
Corbstein	Maria (Mrs.)		7/25/1847
Corcoran	Mary	42	10/29/1865
Corcoran	Mary Anne		
Corkery	Ellen	78	2/19/1878
Corkery	Patrick	50	3/2/1846
Corson	Mary	25	2/4/1849 funeral
Cosgrove	Catherine	35	4/5/1870
Cosgrove	Mary		7/24/1851 funeral
Cotar	Edward	18 months	11/15/1850 funeral
Cote	Jeane		9/27/1850
Cote	Mary	8	8/14/1846
Cottes	Thomas	2 weeks	2/28/1843
Coupfield	Mary	30	7/10/1849
Covinghton	Patrick	60	9/28/1849
Crepin	Andre	63	4/9/1866
Crevier	Joseph	30	11/5/1846 funeral
Cu——	James		

Surname	Name	Age	Death date
Cunighan	Michael	3 1/2	3/18/1842
Cuningham	Martin	4 days	11/18/1852 funeral
Curran	?		
Curran	James		1/2/1854
Curran	Patrick	14 months	9/8/1841
Curtis	Catherine	67	1/16/1853
Cutter	Joseph	18 months	6/12/1848
Daily	Patrick		1855
Daley	W.		9/15/1845 funeral
Dauen	Andrew		10/16/1843
Dawson	Catherine		11/15/1853 funeral
Delany	Ellen	17	6/21/1851
Delay	Cornelius		
Delay	Johana	1 1/2	8/17/1845 funeral
Deley	Anna Clara	11 months	8/10/1846
Delisle	Joseph	ca. 28	6/30/1848
Dely	Mary	36	7/10/1850
Dempsey	Esther	55	12/26/1871
Dentinger	Frank	33	8/23/1852 funeral
Depre	Mathias	8 months	9/14/1848
Derbers	Honora Jane	3	10/19/1852 funeral
Desevres	Lucy	30	6/22/1852 funeral
Desnoyers	Etienne	3 months	7/2/1842 funeral
Desnoyers	Merance	20	5/30/1842
Desselle	Aime	17 months	2/27/1852 funeral
Detrot	Louis	6 weeks	9/9/1849
Deyber	John	55	8/31/1847 funeral
Dietrey	Margaret	49	9/28/1854
Dillon	Charles		7/16/1854 funeral
Doggin	Mary Brigitte	4 months	7/8/1850
Dohany	Clarence Jerome	3 months	1/18/1852
Dohanny	Jeremie	3 months	1/19/1850
Doherghty	Michael	21	7/15/1849
Dolaheti	Thomas	4	1/13/1842
Dolan	?		8/11/1848 funeral
Dolan	Catherine		4/3/1845 funeral
Dolan	Catherine		4/27/1845 funeral
Dolan	Catherine		7/18/1845 funeral
Dolan	William	11 months	9/17/1848
Dolenty	Richard	60	8/19/1840
Dolohanty	John	52	10/14/1849
Dolohonty	John	1 1/2	11/4/1849

Surname	Name	Age	Death date
Donlap	Alexander	21	4/26/1852 funeral
Doster	Margarita	4	6/14/1848
Dougherty	Thomas		10/5/1842
Doughroty	Anna	16	1/26/1847 funeral
Dowlan	John	few months	9/28/1849
Downs	Joseph		9/4/1866
Downy	Marguerite	14 months	12/3/1849
Downy	Mary	35	1/6/1852 funeral
Dowson	William	3 1/2	10/22/1854
Doyle	Ann		Prior to 11/2/1866
Doyle	John	16	8/18/1866
Doyle	John	27	6/2/1876
Droher	John		12/30/1854 funeral
Dubois	Etienne		8/14/1842
Dubois	Etienne	4 months	12/5/1842
Duffet	Emilie	5	2/24/1853
Duffit	Claude Francis		4/9/1851 funeral
Duffy	Francois Alexandre	3 months	8/11/1848
Duffy	Owen	34	9/7/1864
Duffy	Thomas	8	6/18/1864
Dugan	Mrs.		
Dugan	Martin	2 1/2	8/30/1845 funeral
Dugan	Michael		6/15/1840
Dugan	Thomas	16	7/31/1848
Dugan	William		5/15/1842
Duggan	Honora		9/22/1845 funeral
Duggan	John	50	5/28/1853
Duggan	M.	6	8/13/1845 funeral
Duggan	Michael	48	4/25/1838
Duggan	Thomas	40	5/21/1855
Dumphey	Catharine	83	5/27/1878
Dunn	?		8/11/1848 funeral
Dunn	?		8/11/1848 funeral
Dunn	Peter	ca. 45	9/23/1848
Dunn	Thomas	1 month	8/23/1848
Durbin	John E.	25	1/23/1847 funeral
Durbin	Rachel	49	10/17/1846
Durgan	Catherine		8/24/1840
Duvie	Ellen	48	10/26/1852
Eltia	Mary	ca. 3	8/9/1846
Emerson	Mary	1	5/24/1846
Emerson	Mary	ca. 24	4/5/1848

Surname	Name	Age	Death date
Even	John	5 months	2/21/1853
Fagan	Josephine	3	6/19/1847 funeral
Fagan	Mary	17 months	9/22/1851
Fahrey	Timothy		8/25/1845 funeral
Fainjen	Henry	42	10/22/1847
Falvey	Edward	10 months	8/27/1845 funeral
Fanning	James	54	5/3/1857
Fanning	Lucy	1	10/[1]4/1842
Fanning	Michael	6	8/22/1847 funeral
Fanning	Timothy	53	2/17/1863
Fanning	Valentine	3 months	5/30/1846
Farley	?		7/9/1846
Farley	Michael	8 months	8/11/1846
Farley	Thomas		10/27/1853 funeral
Far[rell]	Edward	27	10/9/187[2]
Farrell	Jeremiah	41	2/4/1855
Farrell	Margaret	15	9/6/1862
Farrell	Thomas	20	9/6/1862?
Feely	Catherine	2 months	3/15/1847 funeral
Feely	Hellen	40	12/3/1851
Feltes	Michael	24	12/3/1850
Fies	James	ca. 45	8/21/1850
Filts	Sibilla	55	1/10/1846
Finn	Anthony	2 weeks	9/8/1846 funeral
Finn	Catherine	58	7/16/1870
Finn	John	3	9/19/1846 funeral
Finn	Margret	32	8/20/1852 funeral
Finn	Mary		7/13/1851
Finn	Patrick		7/12/1851
Finy	Bernard		10/9/1845
Fisher	Elizabeth	6 weeks	12/7/1847
Fisher	Mariann	10 months	9/16/1848
Fitzgibbon	Denis		9/22/1845
Fitzpatrick	?		6/28/1849 funeral
Fitzpatrick	Ann ——ayward		7/31/1846
Fitzpatrick	Anna Parson		5/31/1846
Fitzpatrick	Catherine Gribbin	82	10/8/1857
Fitzpatrick	Ellen	33	7/4/1861
Fitzpatrick	Mary	10	6/22/1849
Fitzpatrick	Mary		6/28/1849
Fitzpatrick	Mary Cowan	24	10/28/1842
Fitzpatrick	Michael	12	6/22/1849

Surname	Name	Age	Death date
Fitzpatrick	Owen	83	9/22/1854
Fitzsimmons	John	60	11/3/1854
Flanagan	Maria		8/16/1854
Flanagan	Thomas		4/30/1840
Flanegan	Peter	5	7/2/1851 funeral
Flannagan	Ann	40	4/15/1871
Flannagan	Michael	60	5/25/1872
Fleen	William	41	
Fleener(?)	William	40	9/18/1840
Fleury	Marguerite Piete	45	10/12/1846 funeral
Flinn	Hellen	30	8/23/1851
Flyn	Margaret	2	1/22/1853
Flynn	John	15 months	2/15/1843
Foght	John	10 months	7/11/1850
Foley	?		3/29/1851 funeral
Folly	Richard	15 days	12/17/1845
Fontaine	Pauline		4/16/1854
Frick	Lewis	3 months	9/9/1851
Fromalt	Anton	3 weeks	11/22/1852 funeral
Galarnau	John	1 day	12/26/1841
Gallispi	Margaret	1 week	9/1/1842 funeral
Gallaspy	Hellen	16	1/30/1847 funeral
Gallaspy	Mary	22 months	8/18/1849
Garin	John		
Garrels	Joe (IS?)	51	6/4/1857
Garrigan	Ellen Frances	21 months	7/30/1866
Garvin	?		
Gaspard	Elizabeth	1 month	8/14/1847 funeral
Gawnie	Victoriae Celina	2	5/26/1852 funeral
Gehnen	Peter	4	11/1/1849
Gehrig	Joseph Lucius	13	9/8/1846
Gellen	Barbara	7 months	8/5/1848
Georges	Louis	55	7/21/1849
Geren	?	0	12/17/1851 funeral
Gerich	Anton	48	8/25/1846
Gering(?)	J. C.		
Germain	Frederic	24	12/14/1842
Gillen	Eliza	4	6/26/1851 funeral
Gillen	William	7	6/29/1851 funeral
Gillick	Francis	40	4/27/1860
Gilmartin	Martin		12/3/1852
Glenot	Adelaide (Mrs.)	29	7/16/1847

Surname	Name	Age	Death date
Gollar	Maria Anna	36	1/31/1847 funeral
Gorius	Augustine Siegfried	40	7/17/1850
Gorius	Mary		7/18/1850
Goudere	Felix		11/15/1839
Goyette	Elizabeth		3/?/1853
Grace	Francis	25	10/17/1845 funeral
Grace	Patrick		8/3/1839
Gradey	Patrick		
Graves	Charles	54	6/28/1851 funeral
Grebens	Neal	30	11/10/1849
Green	Michael	50	8/5/1848 funeral
Gregory	James	45	7/25/1869
Grevier	Louisa	6 months	10/16/1849
Greyham	William	42	9/27/1840
Gribbon	Brigitt	14	10/18/1854
Grogan	Michael	70	11/4/1854
Grus	Catherine	13	4/26/1849
Gubfuge	Adrianna	18 months	10/15/1849
Guellen	Peter	3 months	2/28/1847 funeral
Guerety	Michael	6 months	10/26/1849
Guerick	?	14	9/23/1846 funeral
Guerick	Antony	48	8/26/1846
Guerick	Catherine	ca. 40	9/23/1846 funeral
Gulvenbagh	Maria		9/6/1854
Ha ??			
Hagney	William	21	7/26/1850
Haley	Patrick		2/14/1863
Hall	William		2/28/1854
Halloran	William		2/28/1854
Hambert	Peter	2 days	12/6/1847
Hammel	Margaret Joseph	32	10/4/1854
Hanen	Angelique	3	10/9/1847
Hares	Margaret	7	12/25/1843 funeral
Harigar	Maria	1 month	10/30/1846 funeral
Harman	?		8/2/1845 funeral
Harmen	Edward	15 months	8/7/1844
Harpman	Louisa		7/4/1852
Harrington	Ellen	3	10/19/1854
Harstock	Rosanna Maria	18 months	8/6/1849
Hartsock			2/19/1851
Hayden	Mortimer M.		7/24/1876
Hayden	Mary Aurelia	1 month	4/19/1846 funeral

Surname	Name	Age	Death date
Heaky	Elen	2	6/3/1848
Hellrigel	George	1	9/8/1852 funeral
Helthian	Mary	9	8/17/1846
Hemon Schetrig	Fridrich		7/10/1851
Hennesy	Jeremiah	39	7/26/1851
Henry	Mrs.		2/2/1866
Herne	John	14	10/31/1847
Hiden	Henry	8 months	12/19/1847
Hile	Michel	19	10/7/1847
Hille	Louis		7/21/1854
Hiller	Catherine Elizabeth	3	9/15/1853 funeral
Hiller	Helena	59	7/20/1846
Hiller	Isabella	37	5/3/1864
Hinley	John	58	8/3/1852 funeral
Hippen	Susana	51	9/11/1843 funeral
Hirtz	Mary	80	8/12/1851 funeral
Hoare	James	43(?)	12/24/1868
Hoffman	Bernard	2	8/26/1850 funeral
Hoffmann	Louisa	6	9/12/1853 funeral
Hoffsteter	Mary	1 month	2/21/1850
Hofman	John	ca. 38	10/29/1847
Hogan	Anthony		6/15/1852
Hogan	Michael	45	7/13/1852 funeral
Hogan	Patrick		5/27/1864
Holds	Michael	50	8/7/1846
Hook	Mary	10 days	12/15/1851 funeral
Horton	Edmund	47	5/16/1840
Hotel	?		12/31/1851
Hoteli	Susanna	2 months	12/9/1846 funeral
Howard	Clarence Edward	2	3/4/1868
Hughes	Michael	45	11/12/1849
Hurley	Edward	21	2/25/1843 funeral
Hurley	Mary	15 months	9/20/1849
Hurley	Patrick	15	6/26/1870
Hurley	Thomas	35	1851
Hyland	Ann	9	10/10/1843
Iven	Juran	24	9/14/1847
Iven	Michael	26	9/14/1847
Ivers	Charles		7/22/1846
Jack	John	72	11/12/1849
Jaegly	Christian Hylary	3	7/25/1850
Jolivet	Josephitte	73	8/17/1850

Surname	Name	Age	Death date
Jones	Carolus Dunn	2	4/5/1847
Joy	Bernard	35	12/11/1847
Jungen	Johan	ca. 36	9/27/1850
Kallen	Patrick	50	1/27/1847 funeral
Kanavan	?		8/20/1878 funeral
Kearnen	James	30	6/20/1852 funeral
Keas	Anna		7/28/1851 funeral
Keenan	Michael	25	3/16/1848
Keesecker	Frances Louisa		1/19/1840 funeral
Kelly	?	1	8/22/1851 funeral
Kelly	Brigett	1	7/11/1842 funeral
Kelly	Catherine	18 months	7/30/1848
Kelly	Elisabeth		7/25/1851 funeral
Kelly	Elizabeth		
Kelly	George		
Kelly	Margaret	1	7/28/1851 funeral
Kelly	Mary Ellis	80	3/2/1856
Kelly	Michael	2	12/10/1841
Kelly	Michael	55	7/27/1849
Kelly	Patrick		
Kelly	Robert	1	7/28/1851 funeral
Kelly	Thomas	1	9/25/1841
Kelly	Thomas	3 months	6/26/1846
Kelly	Thomas	30	7/5/1877
Kelpher	Catherine	9 months	12/5/1845
Kenny	M.		9/23/1843 funeral
Kerby	James	40	11/30/1848 funeral
Khorig	Joseph Anton	42	9/5/1852 funeral
Kinchlow	Martha	68	8/24/1846
Kine	Elisabeth		7/12/1851
King	Louis	2	6/4/1850
Kinsela	Denis	20	6/6/1852
Kinsila	Susana	4 months	8/20/1851 funeral
Kinslow	William	33	8/31/1846
Kirby	Maurice	58	2/3/1859
Kleffner	Matilda	11 months	7/7/1856 funeral
Knight	William		6/1/1853
Knight	Louisa	10 months	7/19/1866
Kranoker	Cresentia	16 months	1/27/1848
Krebs	Sophia	15 months	7/10/1846
Lacy	Martha	3 weeks	3/3/1880
LaFoye	Jean Baptiste	6 days	5/16/1840

Surname	Name	Age	Death date
Lagan	Anthony	9 months	5/1/1852 funeral
Lagan	Patrick	3	7/27/1852 funeral
Lalor	Mary	68	4/12/1855
Lambert	Elizabeth	63	7/8/1863
Lambert	Patrick	4	9/11/1852
LaNeuville	N. Couturier	46	8/22/1840
Lang	Anna [L]eggarty	34	2/22/1842
Lang	John	65	5/5/1865
Langton	?		12/30/1888 funeral
Laporte	Christopher	13 months	9/22/1852
Laporte	Sophie	9	3/8/1842
Lasey	Margaret	18 months	9/7/1853 funeral
Latourelle	Archange	18	5/27/1850
Latourelle	J. Baptiste		9/27/1843
Latourelle	Jean Baptiste		1/18/1840
Latourelle	Louis	4 days	4/27/1842 funeral
Latourelle	M.	1 1/2	8/11/1851 funeral
Latourelle	Marie	4 months	10/4/1846 funeral
Latourelle	Ursule	19	11/8/1844
LeClair	Xavier		5/27/1852
Le Clerc	Baptiste	2	1/13/1848
Le Clerc	Cleophas	2	8/25/1849
Ledoux	Baptiste	72	6/11/1850
Ledoux	Marie		7/25/1850
Lee	Jane	68	1/7/1851
Leidy	Mary	33	6/18/1850
Leite	Elbert	5 months	8/6/1852 funeral
LePage	Baptiste	ca. 50	4/2/1841
LePage	Baptiste		4/4/1841
Levett	?		3/27/1863 obituary
Leyden	James	38	8/21/1858
Leye	Patrick	16	4/25/1851 funeral
Linehan	Thomas	14	4/1/1868
Linerd	James	50	9/18/1848
Lockston	Rosana	12	8/30/1848
Logndon	Joseph	9	9/29/1846
Logston	Joseph	11	10/18/1846 funeral
Logston	Maryann	60	12/2/1849
Logston	William	40	10/28/1847
Long	Richard J.		2/3/1864
Longuemarre	Mary Alphonsine		8/1/1840
Longueville	Paul	ca. 45	9/23/1846 funeral

Surname	Name	Age	Death date
Lorimer	Louis	ca. 2	6/2/1848
Lucies	Louis	18 months	9/28/1853
Ludvic	John	25	6/8/1852 funeral
Lullmess	John	3	9/18/1846
Lyerthy	Peter		9/13/1845
Lynch	James	9 months	11/28/1849
Lynch	James	7	7/7/1852 funeral
Lynch	John	1 month	2/7/1864
Lynch	Jerry		10/13/1864
Lynch	Mary		6/28/1851 funeral
Lynch	Owen	ca. 70	10/18/1854
MacKensey	Elizabeth	37	1/30/1847 funeral
MacKeon	Anna		10/27/1853 funeral
MacNamara	Margaret	10	5/9/1843 funeral
Magher	John		12/16/1854 fun
Maginnis	Mary	14	4/5/1847 funeral
Magrove	William	66	7/16/1850 funeral
Maguigen	Henery		7/29/1854 funeral
Mahar	Patrick	3 weeks	12/20/1845
Maher	Mary		7/16/1854
Mahoney	?		5/16/1850 funeral
Mahoney	Daniel		
Mahoney	Timothy		2/6/1871?
Mahony	Ann	13	2/6/1871
Malany	Michael		6/25/1852
Mallet	M. M.	1	8/18/1846 funeral
Mallet	Margaret	ca. 70	12/28/1840
Mangold	Henrietta	5 months	9/5/1848
Mangold	Mary	2	11/22/1847
Mangolrick	Anthony	30	5/16/1846
Marechol	Jacques	44	9/16/1846
Martin	Charles	7	6/21/1847 funeral
Martin	Peter		12/11/1865
Mathew	Patrick	ca. 40	9/19/1854 funeral
Mauerer	Euphemia	29	7/3/1851
Mayer	Joseph Peter	6 days	10/15/1850
Maynard	Catharine	51	7/18/1871
McBride	Hellen Coligan	22	10/23/1845
McCann	Anna M.	4	7/8/1857
McCann	Edward	3 months	7/16/1855
McCann	Frances	1 yr 9 m	7/13/1863
McCann	H.	5	3/12/1852 funeral

Surname	Name	Age	Death date
McCann	John	7	8/21/1851
McCann	Julia Malinda	18 months	12/21/1860
McCann	Mary Ann	3	8/22/1851 funeral
McCann	Rosa		3/4/1852
McCarteney	Bernard		
McClosky	Bernard	40	12/19/1872
McCollen	Edward Pious	2	6/4/1850
McConnell	Rosan	8	3/1/1846
McCoy	Bernard		5/13/1851
McCreason	James	25	6/6/1852 funeral
McCullins	Ann	3	6/19/1848
McDonald	Bernard	infant	1862
McDonald	Catherine	6	1862
McDonald	John	75	1/1/1867
McDonald	Mary Ann	70	1/8/1867
McDonald	Thomas	9	1862
McDuggan	Mary Ann	9	11/5/1844
McEvoy	Brigitte	1	8/26/1850 funeral
McEvoy	Patrick	15 months	7/25/1853 funeral
McGehan	William Henry	ca. 2	8/5/1846 funeral
McGennis	Elena	35	9/1/1849
McGevin	William	14 months	5/31/1849
McGloughlin	Mary Ann		2/3/1842
McGoldrick	Thomas	2 weeks	8/17/1846
McGorden	Patrick	15 months	6/12/1848
McGoulric	Mac	18 months	12/7/1842
McGoulric	Patrick Henry	10 days	1/22/1843
McGovern	Mary Ann	7	7/3/1851
McGowan	Peter	3	6/27/1851 funeral
McGown	Catherine	2	12/11/1851
McGrath	Mary	65	12/24/1860
McGrath	Patrick	30	11/20/1843
McGrath	Theresa A.	17	9/2/1873
McGuire	James		5/25/1844
McHagan	Michael		12/7/1847
McLain	Daniel		3/7/1864
McLaughlin	David	1	1/15/1853 funeral
McLean	James	68	10/12/1860
McLoskey	John	24	9/2/1851
McMahan	Honora	ca. 38	8/30/1852
McMahan	Mary		4/24/1840
McMahan	Mary	16	9/15/1841

Surname	Name	Age	Death date
McMahan	Patrick	30	10/24/1845 funeral
McMahan	Simon		6/29/1853 funeral
McMahon	John		10/26/1866
McManus	James	34?	11/15/1861
McNamara	Margaret		9/21/1840
McNamara	Mary Josephine	3 months	3/15/1848
McQuillan	John	38	8/24/1846
Mehigan	Honnora	17	10/19/1869
Mehigan	James Edward	21	10/20/1871
Mehigan	Michael	58	10/7/1867
Menol	Anthony	3 weeks	9/7/1849
Miller	?	78	10/16/1844
Mix	Charles H.	39	1/27/1870 obituary
Mohan	Mary J.J.	28	4/30/1855
Molan	John	6	12/9/1852
Mollet	Marie	6 months	8/17/1846
Moloney	John		9/21/1845 funeral
Monet	David	26	6/8/1852
Mooney	Sara	22	8/9/1848
Moran	James	23	11/25/1854
Moran	Michael	47	6/6/1852 funeral
Moreau	John	45	9/12/1846
Morgan	Catherine	19	9/14/1852
Morgan	John	ca. 25	11/7/1847
Morheiser	Phillip	17	8/18/1849
Morhiser	Jacob	28	10/18/1846
Mornin	James	3 1/2	11/29/1850 funeral
Moeser	Christian		5/25/1852
Mulcahey	Morris	35	11/1/1862
Mulcahy	Mary	28	2/8/1852
Mulhall	Jane A.	23	9/6/1863
Mulkueany	Michael	4	10/26/1852
Mulligan	Patrick	28	1/24/1858
Mullin	Grace	24	7/10/1849
Mullin	Thomas	37	7/3/1849
Mulqueeny	James	50	6/20/1852 funeral
Murphy	Anna Elizabeth	8 months	7/17/1847
Murphy	Cecelia	78	2/27/1870 obituary
Murphy	Francis	25	6/26/1851 funeral
Murphy	James	26	6/8/1852 funeral
Murphy	John	2	9/8/1843 funeral
Murphy	John	56	5/23/1854

Surname	Name	Age	Death date
Murphy	John		
Murphy	T.	73	5/14/1854
Murphy	William P.	76	7/25/1871
Murray	Patrick	42	11/3/1841
Myer	Pamelia H.	45	1854
Myers	Catherine	80	2/13/1854 funeral
Myers	Wilhelm	3	12/14/1842
Myres	William	3 1/2	12/13/1842
N——	Maria	2 months	2/27/1852 funeral
N——	Moses	48	8/19/1843 funeral
Nada	Emile	20 months	12/12/1847
Nadeau	?		
Nadeau	Joseph Jules	1	1/30/1851
Nadeau	Joseph Octave	6 months	10/15/1843
Nadeau	Marie Estelle	1	12/12/1847
Nadeau	Marie Louise Philibert	36	5/4/1852
Nagle	Ellen	40	1854
Nagle	Hellen	3	1/3/1847 funeral
Nagle	John	49	12/13/1838
Nagle	Margaret	59	11/10/1855
Nagle	Mary	28	6/6/1866
Nagle	Mary	18	4/2/1856 funeral
Nagli	Francisca		9/14/1853 funeral
Nailan	Patrick		6/2/1849
Naugle	Mary	6 weeks	7/31/1880
Neep	Anthony	1	8/27/1850 funeral
Negler	Francisca	30	11/11/1854 funeral
Neiglen	Helena	3 months	11/21/1840
Newman	James	53	10/2/1840
Neyglet	Gueret		5/24/1840
Neylan	Michael	24	10/12/1866
Nicoll	Maria	28	11/1/1875
Nihill	Michael	73	5/22/1869
Nillus	Peter	1	9/19/1850
Noble	Mary	18 months	7/8/1849
Noble	Mary	ca. 45	7/13/1850
Noel	Francis	2 months	9/13/1846
Noon	?	6	9/21/1852
Noon	John	8	10/1/1852
Noon	Michael		
Noonan	Patrick		
Noone	James	1	4/19/1854

Surname	Name	Age	Death date
Norman	J. J. E.	57	12/12/1872
Northon	Honora	9 months	12/15/1849
Northon	Mary	5	12/19/1849
Norton	Ann	20	4/22/1849
O'?	Rac[hel]		
O'Brien	Bridget	46	8/14/1849
O'Brien	Catherine	18 months	5/18/1841
O'Brien	Josephine	3	5/16/1841
O'Brien	Mary	50	5/15/1841
O'Brien	Mary	40	11/24/1845
O'Brien	Nicholas		
O'Connell	Marguerita		1/18/1851
O'Connell	Catherine	ca. 45	1/4/1850
O'Conner	Mary Catherine	1	2/26/1852 funeral
O'Connor	Dennis		11/20/1850 funeral
O'Connor	Eloner	40	7/1/1851 funeral
O'Connor	Margaret	42	2/1/1870
O'Connor	Mary Ellis	28	8/1/1877
O'Donnel	John	65	11/19/1849
O'Donnel	Sandy	32	5/31/1864
O'Donnell	Mary Catherine	4	11/15/1852
O'Donnell	Matilda	2	11/16/1852
O'Flaharty	J.	62	2/20/1844 funeral
O'Hair	James	2	1/9/1845
O'Hair	Patrick	40	9/11/1846
O'Halloran	James Patrick	18 months	7/21/1846
O'Halloran	Matthew	27	8/3/1861
O'Hara	Mary	ca. 35	11/29/1845 funeral
O'Hare	Edward	55	7/30/1854
O'Hare	Ned		7/31/1854?
O'Hare	Patrick	38	4/28/1868
O'Hearn	John		
O'Hern	Ellen	56	5/16/1852 funeral
O'Mara	Catherine	3 1/2	2/8/1848
O'Mara	John	ca. 35	10/18/1848
O'Meara	Honora	20 months	7/25/1860
O'Meara	Patrick	2 months	4/16/1863
O'Neil	Ann	25	9/18/1842 funeral
O'Regan	Rachel	13	10/20/1852 funeral
O'Reilly	Catherine		12/16/1863
O'Reilly	Mary Frances	22	12/14/1845
O'Rourke	Emily A.	5	8/11/1866

Surname	Name	Age	Death date
O'Shea	Dennis	2	8/20/1852 funeral
O'Shea	Hellen	22 months	10/9/1845
O'Shea	John	6 months	1/6/1850
O'Shea	Josephine	3	5/25/1855 funeral
O'Shea	Mary	32	8/16/1847 funeral
Oehler	Joseph	14 days	4/13/1849
Olinger	Peter	32	5/25/1860
Orbinger	Mary	49	11/6/1849
Oster	Joseph	30	5/7/1852
Oswald	Francisca		3/28/1851
Oswol	Richard Louis	few months	9/28/1849
Ottentat	Anton	2	9/7/1846
Ottli	Bernard		12/23/1850
Pasquare	Margaret	92	12/14/1862
Patterson	Adam	25	10/7/1841
Pelligord	George	22	9/24/1840
Pelligord	Joseph George	8 months	9/24/1840
Penny	Ellen	13	6/3/1852 funeral
Pentecost	Ruth	68	3/4/1846 funeral
Periot	Marie	60	2/15/1842
Petit	Felix		7/8/1851
Pfiffner	Jacob Martin	3 weeks	8/3/1850
Phelan	John	60	7/30/1878
Pickley	Anna Marguerita	5	4/1/1847 funeral
Piete	Marguerite	45	10/11/1846 funeral
Pifner	Martin	ca. 50	8/10/1846
Plant	John	42	10/29/1852
Plefin	Peter	12 months	10/12/1849
Port	John	3	8/16/1850
Potts	Catherine	5	7/19/1852 funeral
Potts	Patrick	6 months	8/?/1852
Potts	Thomas	12	1850
Power	Catharine	11 months	9/23/1854 funeral
Power	Margaret	1 month	11/21/1840
Power	Martha	18 months	5/3/1846
Power	Mary Francis	3	10/24/1853
Power	Michael W.	51	9/15/1856
Powers	Philip		7/11/1851
Powers	Johanna	36	5/1/1863
Preston	?		
Preston	?	1 day	2/18/1872
Preston	Augusta C.	28	2/20/1872

Surname	Name	Age	Death date
Proctor	William	2	3/15/1842
Prudent	Louis		4/8/1842
Quarter	John	42	9/2/1846
Quigley	?		
Quigley	?		
Quigley	Catherine	80	8/8/1878
Quigley	Daniel O'Connell	42	11/12/1871
Quigley	Katie R.	11	3/15/1870
Quigley	Margaret	17	3/31/1852 obituary
Quigley	Michael	8	7/21/1840
Quigley	Patrick	66	8/10/1865
Quinn	James	30	2/24/1852 funeral
Rayden	Joseph	3	7/11/1848
Reed	Emma		2/11/1851
Reid	Francis	2	7/5/1856 funeral
Reid	James A.		5/1/1856
Reid	Mary Ann	41	8/5/1867
Reilly	Charles	16 months	11/4/1852
Reilly	Terence	58	10/5/1856
Reinfried	Elizabeth	85	4/25/1850
Reingfreid	Christina	2	3/11/1842
Remlein	Lawrence	58	10/3/1843
Reuter	Catherine	5 months	4/15/1850
Reynold	John	1	11/5/1843 funeral
Reynold	Mary	ca. 35	11/5/1843 funeral
Ritter	John Conrad	50	8/11/1848
Robert	Paul	17	7/7/1848
Robert	Thomas	4	7/21/1851
Robillard	Josephine	10	11/6/1853 funeral
Robillerd	Catherine	3	9/11/1852 funeral
Robin	Thomas	3	8/30/1848
Roche	Catherine Canavan	26	5/4/1868
Roche	Lawrence	28	10/28/1846
Roche	Mary	4 months	3/16/1862 obituary
Roche	Michael	41	9/28/1869
Roche	Patrick	2 months	6/3/1852 funeral
Rolofs	Peter		12/21/1853 funeral
Roony	John Louis	10 days	1/19/1845
Roony	Marguerit	11 months	8/31/1849
Roony	Michael	14 months	12/19/1847
Root	John	11 months	9/28/1840
Rosui	Mary Catherine	1	7/26/1847 funeral

Surname	Name	Age	Death date
Roth	Jacob	13	5/24/1850
Rowan	Emerson	1	1855
Ruden	Mary	6 1/2	9/27/1844
Ryan	Mary		4/17/1842
Sandwich	Elizabeth	2 weeks	10/9/1846 funeral
Sauce	Ann		2/1/1851
Schaffner	?	15	7/27/1856
Schaus	Maria	9	10/19/1846 funeral
Schmid	Phillip	4 months	9/13/1850
Schmid	Christina	58	1/20/1854
Schmitt	Catherine	16	11/4/1845 funeral
Schmulieger	Johannes	51	8/22/1851 funeral
Schons	Dorothea	6 weeks	12/13/1850
Schons	Margaret	4 months	12/12/1850
Short	Michael	75	7/6/1872
Schrep	Catherine	8 days	2/23/1850
Schwan	Maria	1	7/21/1851
Schwan	Susana	28	7/23/1851
Scot	Philip	6 days	8/31/1841
Serres	Mary Delano	10 months	10/22/1850 funeral
Scully	Edward	54	4/1/1852 funeral
Seegar	Mary Louisa	15 months	9/23/1852
Sculey	Johanna	ca. 36	2/12/1849
Setack	Anthony	59	9/8/1840
Sexton	Mary	[74?]	2/2/1864
Sexton	Patrick	74	8/[2]8/1856
Shadrick	Mary	75	9/13/1842 funeral
Shaffner	?		10/8/1845
Shaffner	Marguerit	2	9/23/1848
Shaffus	?	10	9/12/1845 funeral
Shannon	Elizabeth	40	7/26/1846
Shannon	Mary Honora	20	3/5/1845
Shannon	Tadeus	3	11/28/1852 funeral
Shannon	Thomas		4/18/1840
Shay	John		
Shields	?	30	10/19/1844
Short	?		4/24/1851 funeral
Short	Michael	75	7/6/1872
Short	Peter	8	8/25/1852 funeral
Shuister	William	5 months	8/8/1849
Sierry	Margaret Burhle	26	9/16/1847 funeral
Sievi	Rose	2 months	1/21/1847 funeral

Surname	Name	Age	Death date
Simon	Elizabeth	ca. 28	11/14/1848
Simons	Louis	1	10/29/1849
Simplot	Charles	26	12/3/1841
Simplot	Francis Henry	15 months	3/6/1845
Simplot	Henri	48	12/27/1846 funeral
Simplot	Jean Francois	9 months	9/27/1840
Simplot	Josephine	19 months	6/16/1847 funeral
Simplot	Napoleon	14	5/23/1841
Sions	Nicholas	2 days	5/18/1850
Sirsers	Catharian Margerita	6 months	10/30/1842
Slattery	Bridget		7/28/1851 funeral
Smith	?		7/11/1842 funeral
Smith	Andrew	18 months	8/25/1849
Smith	Catherine Stolz		10/14/1845
Smith	Eliza	22	2/18/1843
Smith	Francis		7/14/1851
Smith	James		
Smith	James X.	26	6/18/1866
Smith	John E.		1/30/1862
Smith	Margaret	2	7/25/1851
Smith	Mary	8 months	4/18/1846
Smith	Mary	3	7/16/1850
Smith	Mary Catherine	13 months	10/24/1847 funeral
Smith	Owen	65	12/23/1852
Smyth	Michael	98	12/11/1866
Spalding	Mary		4/30/1852
Stewart	Robert	57	8/18/1871
Stewart	Rosa	42	7/13/1861
Sullivan	Cornellius		
Sullivan	Dinnes	3	8/15/1858
Sullivan	Jeremias	ca. 35	4/18/1848
Sullivan	John	12	2/27/1847 funeral
Sullivan	Joseph	5	12/30/1848
Sullivan	Margaret	3	9/6/1847
Sullivan	Mary Desmond	57	10/27/1839
Sullivan	Michael D.	35	9/5/1855
Supple	Maria	4	12/16/1852
Tabbin	Patrick	3	5/31/1849
Tagler	Louisa	3 1/2	4/18/1849
Tebeau	Sarah	47	6/16/1860
Teiser	Helena	8	9/19/1847 funeral
Teiser	Helena Cless	42	9/5/1847 funeral

Surname	Name	Age	Death date
Teiser	Maria	6	9/2/1847 funeral
Thibeau	Oliviere		9/26/1850
Tibeause	Louis	18 months	5/22/1843 funeral
Tobin	Catherine	3	6/13/1852 funeral
Tollis	Patrick	2	1/11/1847 funeral
Tool	Joseph	13 months	10/3/1840
Toole	John	2 days	1/16/1852
Troy	?	2	9/1/1852 funeral
Troy	John	55	9/16/1849
Toss	Thomas	6	9/30/1847
Trudell	Frank	27	3/4/1869
Trudell	Olipher	3	10/15/1852
Truesdall	S.	37	10/14/1841 funeral
Twomey	David	55	3/15/1852
Vallet	Joseph	60	5/5/1844
Vaughan			
Victoire	Louisa	1	7/16/1856 funeral
Vogler	Aloysia	44	9/9/1846 funeral
Wachter	Anna Mary	38	8/1/1851 funeral
Wachter	Christian	40	8/1/1851 funeral
Wagner	Anton	13 months	12/26/1850
Wagner	Pierre	40	10/12/1846
Wallis	William		4/29/1847 funeral
Walsh	Catherine	16	1/23/1854 funeral
Walsh/Welsh	Mary	56	7/23/1852
Walsh	Robert	7	6/13/1870

Surname	Name	Age	Death date
Welch	Edward "Ned"	62	12/24/1866
Welsh	Ann	28	1/8/1860 obituary
Wheeler	Rev.	50	3/11/1861
Wildhaber	John	27	7/16/1847
Wilging	?	2	8/28/1852 funeral
Williams	Mary Margaret	21	6/6/1852
Willming	Hilere	30	11/30/1847
Yager	Francis	ca. 38	11/22/1852 funeral
Zimmer	Martha	30	8/29/1850 funeral
——rit	Friedert	10 months	8/7/1854
?	Charles		
?	Fran——		
?	Johanna		?/6/1859
?	Mary	6	10/17/1848
?	Sabina		7/12/1851
?	Thomas D.		

This table includes the names of people who are known or believed to have been buried in the Third Street Cemetery. The majority of the entries were taken from the St. Raphael's burial register, but names were also gathered from sources such as local newspaper obituaries, family histories, and accounts from the later years of the cemetery. We found other names on headstones currently standing in the Third Street section of Mt. Olivet Cemetery and on headstones and coffin-lid crosses found during the excavation. This list includes all the names we discovered during the course of our research, but it is by no means a complete record of everyone who was ever buried in the cemetery.

Notes

CHAPTER ONE

1. Robin M. Lillie and Jennifer E. Mack, "Bioarchaeology and History of Dubuque's Third Street Cemetery, 13DB476, Dubuque County, Iowa," *Research Papers* 37, no. 1, Office of the State Archaeologist, University of Iowa, Iowa City, 2013. An electronic copy is available online at https://www.academia .edu/6118271/Bioarchaeology_and_History_of_Dubuques_Third_Street_Ceme tery_13DB476_Dubuque_County_Iowa.

CHAPTER TWO

1. Josiah Conzett, "My Recollections of Dubuque 1846–1890," 274–75, manuscript on file, Captain Bowell River Library, Mississippi River Museum and Aquarium, Dubuque, Iowa. A transcribed version may be viewed at http:// conzett.org/josiah.htm.

2. Oldt, *History of Dubuque*, 49.

3. *The History of Dubuque County, Iowa, Containing a History of the County, Its Cities, Towns, etc., Biographical Sketches of Citizens, War Records of Its Volunteers in the Late Rebellion, General and Local Statistics, Portraits of Early Settlers and Prominent Men, History of the Northwest, History of Iowa, Map of Dubuque County, Constitution of the United States, Miscellaneous Matters, etc.* (Chicago: Western Historical Company, 1880), 361.

4. Langworthy quoted in Elsie Datisman, Joseph Flynn, and Rev. M. M. Hoffmann, *Dubuque: Its History and Background* (Dubuque: Dubuque County Historical Society, 1950), 10.

5. Today it may seem strange that Bishop Hennessy himself rather than the diocese purchased the bluff-top lots (and many additional properties). However, by Catholic canon law, a bishop owns property as a "corporation sole," a legal entity consisting of a single office. The property then passes from one officeholder to the next rather than to the heirs of the individual holding the office. During Hennessy's time, state laws did not accommodate this interpretation of ownership. Iowa did not officially recognize the office of bishop as a corporation sole until a court case in 1917. This issue proved problematic later on, when the archdiocese wanted to liquidate properties acquired by

Hennessy. Because Hennessy died prior to the 1917 court ruling, his lateral heirs may have had a valid legal claim to his estate. Before the land could be sold, the archdiocese had to locate these heirs and ensure that they did not plan to make any claims.

6. *Dubuque Daily Times*, February 4, 1870, 4.

7. *Dubuque Daily Times*, December 17, 1876, 8.

8. James Mooney, "The Funeral Customs of Ireland," *Proceedings of the American Philosophical Society* 25, no. 128 (1888): 243–96.

CHAPTER 4

1. "Death of Thomas Kelly. His Eccentricities and History. Incidents of His Life," *Dubuque Daily Herald*, May 16, 1867, 4.

2. "Old City of the Dead," *Dubuque Daily Times*, August 5, 1906, 15.

3. "Kelly's Bluff, Its Ancient Cemetery and Foundations of Proposed but Abandoned Seminary; History Recalled," *Dubuque Telegraph-Herald*, October 25, 1914.

4. "The Story of Kelly's Bluff," *Dubuque Telegraph-Herald and Times-Journal*, January 25, 1931, 12.

CHAPTER 5

1. The analysis of the skeletal remains followed the professional guidelines developed by the Paleopathology Association. See Jane E. Buikstra and Douglas H. Ubelaker, *Standards for Data Collection from Human Skeletal Remains*, Arkansas Archeological Survey Research Series No. 44, Fayetteville, 1994.

2. Primary, secondary, and tertiary syphilis refer to the early, middle, and late stages of the disease, respectively. It is during the late, tertiary stage that the body's organs and skeleton are affected, and the bony changes can be used to diagnose the disease during osteological studies.

CHAPTER 6

1. Margaret Coffin, *Death in Early America: The History and Folklore of Customs and Superstitions of Early Medicine, Funerals, Burials, and Mourning* (Nashville: Nelson Publishing, 1976), 102–3.

2. Robin M. Lillie, Jennifer E. Mack, and Cindy L. Nagel, "Coffin Construction and Hardware," in Lillie and Mack, "Bioarchaeology and History," 176–211.

3. James Mooney, "The Funeral Customs of Ireland," *Proceedings of the American Philosophical Society* 25, no. 128 (1888): 243–96.

4. Juliane Lippok and Sylvia Mueller-Pfeifruck, "'Die Krone habt ihr mir bereit': Totenkronen als Gegenstand interdisziplinärer Forschung" ["The wreath you prepared for me": Funeral wreaths as objects of interdisciplinary

research], *Ethnographisch-Archäologische Zeitschrift* 50 (2009): 69–93.

5. Hermann Kindt, "Myrtle Wreaths and Orange Blossoms," in *Notes and Queries: A Medium of Inter-communication for Literary Men, General Readers, etc.*, 4th series, vol. 1, no. 19 (January–June 1868): 429–31 (London: Oxford University Press).

CHAPTER 7

1. Stephen P. Nawrocki, "Taphonomic Processes in Historic Cemeteries," in *Bodies of Evidence: Reconstructing History through Skeletal Analysis*, ed. Anne L. Grauer (New York: John Wiley & Sons, 1995).

CHAPTER 8

1. *Dubuque Daily Herald*, July 26, 1871, 4.
2. Benjamin Hibbard, *A History of the Public Land Policies* (Madison: University of Wisconsin Press, 1965).
3. "Mourning and Funeral Usages," *Harper's Bazaar*, April 17, 1886, http://www.victoriana.com/library/harpers/funeral.html.

CHAPTER 9

1. *Dubuque Daily Times*, August 23, 1870, 4.
2. Ibid.
3. Conzett, "My Recollections," 194.

CHAPTER 10

1. The complete history of the Michael Sullivan family compiled by Ron Seymour was used as the primary reference for the brief history presented in this book. The full history can be viewed at http://iagenweb.org/dubuque/family/Sullivan_M.htm.
2. *Dubuque Daily Herald*, August 7, 1900, 8.
3. Conzett, "My Recollections," 212.
4. *Dubuque Daily Herald*, February 10, 1870, 4.
5. *Dubuque Herald*, April 27, 1860, 3.
6. Josiah Conzett, "My Civil War Before, During and After (a.k.a. Recollections of People and Events of Dubuque, Iowa: Complete Memoirs to 1913)," 7–8, manuscript on file, Captain Bowell River Library, Mississippi River Museum and Aquarium, Dubuque, Iowa. A transcribed version may be viewed at http://conzett.org/josiah.htm.
7. *Dubuque Herald*, October 20, 1860, 3.

CHAPTER 11

1. The Office of the State Archaeologist publishes a pamphlet, *Grave Dowsing Reconsidered*, by William E. Whittaker, that may be downloaded for free from http://archaeology.uiowa.edu/file/726/download.

2.. Tara Maria Giuliano, "Legend of the Field Stones in Old Bethel Cemetery: Using Archaeology to Explore Social Memory" (master's thesis, Department of Anthropology and Archaeology, University of West Florida, Pensacola, 2013).

CHAPTER 12

1. Linea Sundstrom, "The Meaning of Scalping in Native North America," in *Transforming the Dead: Culturally Modified Bone in the Prehistoric Midwest*, ed. Eve Hargrave, Shirley Schermer, Kristin Hedman, and Robin Lillie (Tuscaloosa: University of Alabama Press, 2015).

2. For further details about NAGPRA, see http://www.nps.gov/nagpra/.

3. Michael L. Blakey, "Introduction: Background of the New York African Burial Ground Project," in *The New York African Burial Ground: Final Skeletal Biology Report*, vol. 1, ed. Michael L. Blakey and Lesley M. Rankin Hill (New York: United States General Services Administration Northeastern and Caribbean Region, 2004), 2–37.

4. A book produced about the Grafton Cemetery contains highly detailed and technical information about the excavations and analysis of the burial goods and human remains. See Jane E. Buikstra, Jodie A. O'Gorman, and Cynthia Sutton, eds., *Never Anything So Solemn: An Archeological, Biological, and Historical Investigation of the Nineteenth-Century Grafton Cemetery*, Kampsville Studies in Archeology and History No. 3, Center for American Archeology, Kampsville, IL, 2000.

5. Nawrocki, "Taphonomic Processes."

CHAPTER 13

1. "Human Remains at Froedtert Have Living Advocate," *Wauwatosa Patch* (online newsletter), October 9, 2012, http://wauwatosa.patch.com/.

CHAPTER 14

1. Marilyn Yalom, *The American Resting Place: Four Hundred Years of History through Our Cemeteries and Burial Grounds* (New York: Houghton Mifflin Harcourt, 2008), xv.

Recommended Reading

Alex, Lynn M. *Iowa's Archaeological Past.* Iowa City: University of Iowa Press, 2000.

Cox, Margaret. *Life and Death in Spitalfields 1700 to 1850.* York, UK: Council for British Archaeology, 1996.

Farrell, James J. *Inventing the American Way of Death, 1830–1920.* Philadelphia: Temple University Press, 1980.

Heilen, Michael P., ed. *Uncovering Identity in Mortuary Analysis: Community-Sensitive Methods for Identifying Group Affiliation in Historical Cemeteries.* Walnut Creek, CA: Left Coast Press, 2012.

Mitford, Jessica. *The American Way of Death Revisited.* New York: Vintage Books, 1998.

Oldt, Franklin T. *History of Dubuque: Being a General Survey of Dubuque County History, Including a History of the City of Dubuque and Special Account of Districts throughout the County from the Earliest Settlement to the Present Time.* Vol. 1. Stockbridge, MA: Hard Press Editions, 2012. Originally published 1911 by Goodspeed Historical Association, Chicago.

Pike, Martha V., and Janice Gray Armstrong. *A Time to Mourn: Expressions of Grief in Nineteenth Century America.* Stony Brook, NY: Museums at Stony Brook, 1980.

Index

Aaron family, 41, 150–1
African. *See* ethnicity
African Burial Ground, 175–6, 179, 181
Alameda-Stone Cemetery, 66, 97, 175, 177–8, 181, 184
antemortem tooth loss. *See* dental disease
Archdiocese of Dubuque, 4, 18, 20, 24, 26, 29, 41, 53, 55, 57, 61, 160, 161, 168–9, 185
arthritis. *See* disease
Ashworth and Bennett Funeral Residence, 56, 169

beautification of death, 13, 22–3, 54, 65, 80, 184, 187
Black. *See* ethnicity
Black Hawk War, 17, 52
Blake family, 119, 127–41; Charles (brother of John Sr.), 130, 131; Charles (son of John Sr.), 128, 129, 130, 137; Eliza, 128, 129, 130, 132, 134, 137–8, 139, 140; Ellen (daughter), 128, 129, 131, 138–9, 140; Ellen (mother), 129–30, 132–3, 141; Helene (Nancy, Anna, Nellie, Nettie), 130, 132, 133, 134, 141; John Joseph, 128, 129, 131, 132, 133, 138, 140; John, Jr., 128, 129, 130, 136, 140; John, Sr., 127, 128–9, 130, 131, 132, 134, 136, 140, 144, 150; Julia, 128, 129, 130, 137; Mary, 129, 132, 133, 134, 141;

Susan, 68, 127, 128, 129, 130, 132, 134, 135, 137, 139, 140; William, 128, 129, 131–2, 133, 134, 135–6, 139, 140, 141
bone fractures, 69, 74, 75, 76, 77, 110, 120, 121, 136
bounty-land warrant, 115, 146
Bowerman, Biays, 162, 185
burial protection law(s), 3, 59, 172–4, 183
burial register of St. Raphael's Cathedral, 23–6, 40, 41, 42, 43, 46, 76, 128, 148, 162

caplifters. *See* coffins
Center for Dubuque History, Loras College, 168
chaplets, 86, 87, 88, 103
cholera. *See* disease
City Cemetery (Dubuque), 17, 38, 43–7, 49–50, 62
city council (Dubuque), 29, 31, 43, 62, 128–9, 146
Civil War, 22, 36
Clifford, Daniel, 155
clothing, 94–6, 100
coffins, 81–5; caplifter, 83, 85, 105, 107; construction, 81–3; escutcheon, 85, 101, 105, 117; furnishings, 84, 107; hardware, 84–5; handles, 85, 101, 105, 107, 108, 117, 135, 141; lining, 84; metal, 82–3, 135, 137–8, 152; price, 84; viewing pane, 57, 83, 101, 105, 107, 118, 135

coins, 98
Collins family, 149–50
colored. *See* ethnicity
Congress, U. S., 18, 19, 20, 23, 32, 55, 176
consumption. *See* disease: tuberculosis
Conzett, Josiah, 16, 35, 39, 41, 42, 47, 92, 130, 133, 151, 154
Cook County Poor Farm (Dunning Poorhouse), Chicago, Illinois, 179–80
County Cavan, 153
County Cork, 129, 148, 150
cribra orbitalia, 72, 103, 121, 136
crosses (pendants), 88–91
crucifixes, 85–8, 91–2, 107, 117

degenerative joint disease. *See* disease: arthritis
dental appliances, 68–9, 78
dental disease, 67–9; antemortem tooth loss, 67; calculus/tartar, 67; cavities, 67, 68, 78; crowding, 69; enamel hypoplastic defects, 68, 103, 106, 109, 110, 119, 135, 137, 138, 140; fillings, 68, 78, 107, 135, 139
dentists, 21, 68, 69, 78
dentures. *See* dental appliances
diarrhea. *See* disease
Diocese of Dubuque, 19, 20, 30, 52
disease, 43–8, 69–74; arthritis, 70, 71, 77, 78, 119, 120; cholera, 18, 25, 43, 45–50, 61, 64, 164; diarrhea, 44, 45, 72; dysentery, 44, 70; gout, 71–2; influenza, 45, 73; malaria, 45, 116, 120; meningitis, 44, 73, 106; osteomyelitis, 74; osteoporosis, 69, 71, 77, 120, 136; periostitis, 70–1, 103, 106, 121; pneumonia, 44, 70, 73, 77; syphilis, 44, 72–3; tapeworm, 72; tuberculosis, 44, 45, 50, 70, 71, 73, 77, 103, 106, 131, 136, 152

disinterment, 13, 32, 57, 137, 166
disinterment permit, 56, 57, 59, 125, 126, 173, 183
Dominican Order. *See* Sinsinawa Dominican sisters
dowsing, 166
drowning, 43, 49
Dubuque Daily Herald, 76, 113, 129, 131, 132, 145, 146
Dubuque Daily Times, 113, 116, 128, 130, 132
Dubuque Democrat Herald, 26
Dubuque Herald, 22, 132, 144, 150
Dubuque, Julien, 16
Dubuque population, ethnicity, 21, 24, 39–42, 92; male/female ratio, 20, 39; religion, 39–40; size, 19, 20, 22, 161
dysentery. *See* disease

Elmbank Catholic Cemetery, 63
embalming, 102
enamel hypoplastic defects. *See* dental disease
endocranial lesions, 73–4, 103
escutcheons. *See* coffins
ethnicity, African, 41, 110, 179; Black, 25, 41, 150, 151, 176; colored, 24, 41, 150; French, 21, 24, 25, 40–1; German, 21, 24, 25, 26, 40; Irish, 21, 24, 25, 26, 40, 66–7, 114; mulatto, 25, 150; Native American, 17, 25, 41–2, 115, 172, 173, 178, 183, 187

Farrell family, 142–4
flu pandemic (1918), 162
Foley, D. V., 56, 63
Freedman's Cemetery (Alexandria, Virginia), 179
Freedman's Cemetery (Dallas, Texas), 179
French. *See* ethnicity
funeral business/industry, 22, 80, 159, 188

funeral customs, 22, 36, 92–3, 96, 102, 104
funeral home, 23, 84, 170
funeral procession, 27, 34, 132, 154

German. *See* ethnicity
Gillick, Francis, 153–5
gout. *See* disease
Grafton Cemetery, 177
grave marker, 22, 42, 47, 51, 57, 62, 63, 111, 112, 141, 146, 159, 180, 188; gravestone, 145, 165; headstone, 4, 9, 12, 36, 39, 56, 61, 62, 63, 141, 142–50, 158, 162, 169, 177; monument, 12, 26, 36, 55, 63, 141, 149
Great Famine, 40, 66
Gregory, James, 169–70

Hartney, Dennis, 27, 32, 33
headstone. *See* grave marker
Hennessy, John, 24, 27, 29–32, 42, 48, 53, 55, 56, 61
Hennessy, Richard "D. J.", 27, 33
Hoffmann Mortuary, 23, 57, 58, 59, 84

influenza. *See* disease
Irish. *See* ethnicity

Jackson Square, 62
jewelry, 97

Keane, James J., 55
Keane, John Joseph, 54
Kelly, Elizabeth, 29
Kelly, Thomas, 26, 27, 29, 41, 52–3
Kelly's Bluff, 26, 29, 52, 53, 63, 158
Kelly's gold, 51–3, 168
Key City Genealogical Society, 146, 161
Key West Cemetery. *See* Mt. Olivet Cemetery
Knight, William, 29–31, 62

land speculation, 146, 147, 152
lawsuit, 6, 49, 56, 58, 157, 168, 174
Leonard, Pat, 181, 184, 185
Linwood Cemetery, 62, 163
Loras, Mathias, 19, 20, 24, 25, 40, 41, 42, 128

malaria. *See* disease
mass graves, 14, 18, 46–8, 58, 162–4, 167
Matagorda, Texas, 163–4
Mazzuchelli, Samuel, 19, 24, 42
McCann family, 144–5
Meadowlark Cemetery, 165
meningitis. *See* disease
Mexican–American War, 115, 153
Milwaukee County Institution Grounds (MCIG), 66, 78, 180, 182–3
mining, 16, 17, 20, 21, 30–2, 33, 41, 52, 62, 74, 130, 147
Miraculous Medals. *See* religious medals
Mix, Charles H., 109, 151–3
Monroe County Poor Farm Cemetery (Rochester, New York), 179
monument. *See* grave marker
mortality schedule, 42, 44, 46, 116
Mt. Olivet Cemetery (Key West Cemetery), 12, 26, 32, 33, 36, 39, 42, 54, 56, 57–8, 59, 61, 83, 112, 131–2, 140, 141, 142, 143, 145–6, 148–9, 150, 162, 169–70, 184, 185–6
Mt. Olivet Cemetery Association, 54, 55, 61
mulatto. *See* ethnicity
murder, 39, 45, 153–4, 155
Murphy family, 112–26; Cecelia (Mrs.), 116, 117, 118, 119–20; William P. (Mr.), 113–7, 119

Nadeau family, 145–51
NAGPRA, 172, 183

Native American Grave Protection and Repatriation Act. *See* NAGPRA

Native American. *See* ethnicity

New York African Burial Ground (NYABG). *See* African Burial Ground

O'Reilly, Mary Francis, 42, 57, 63

Old Bethel Cemetery (Florida), 164

Old Irish Cemetery, 63

Oldt, Franklin, 46

osteomyelitis. *See* disease

osteoporosis. *See* disease

Outlot, 23, 26, 27, 29, 36, 52, 60, 129

periostitis. *See* disease

perpetual care, 126, 159, 160, 179, 184

personal adornments, 97–8

Phoenix Group, 162

pins, 69, 95

pipe smoking, 69, 120

pneumonia. *See* disease

political controversy, 13, 29–32, 175–6

preemption, 18–9

Prosser buttons, 94, 102, 103, 105, 108, 117

Quigley, Patrick, 18, 19

race. *See* ethnicity

reburial, 2, 14, 33, 56, 57, 58, 126, 169, 172, 173, 175, 182, 183, 184, 189

Reilly family, 147–8

religious medals, 88–91, 102, 141; Miraculous Medals, 88–9, 108, 136, 152

rings (finger), 97

Rohlman, Henry, 56

rosary, 86–8, 92, 108, 109, 117, 141, 152

rural cemetery movement, 13, 159

St. Dominic Villa, 1, 56, 57, 58, 60, 63, 161

St. Johannes Cemetery (Chicago, Illinois), 180

St. Raphael's Cathedral, 1, 19, 24, 26, 31, 35, 40, 42, 152, 156

St. Raphael's Cemetery Association, 31, 32, 40, 144, 150

St. Vincent de Paul Society, 116, 150, 154, 155

seminary, 9, 53–4, 55, 56, 61

sexton, 11, 32, 35, 43, 44, 55, 57, 62, 159

shoes, 96–7

Sinsinawa Dominican Sisters, 1, 6, 49, 55, 58, 60, 161, 174

Sisters of Charity of the Blessed Virgin Mary, 42, 57, 153

suicide, 49, 76

Sullivan family, 148–9

syphilis. *See* disease

tapeworm. *See* disease

Toomey, David. *See* Twomey, David

trauma, 43, 69–70, 74

trepanation, 76, 77

tuberculosis. *See* disease

Twomey, David, 149–50

undertakers, 23, 82

vandalism, 13, 51

veterans, 22, 36, 43, 115, 146, 169

viewing pane. *See* coffins

Villa. *See* St. Dominic Villa

Voegtly Cemetery, 165–6

wake, 92, 104

witching. *See* dowsing

wreaths, 92–3

IOWA AND THE MIDWEST EXPERIENCE

———————

The Drake Relays: America's Athletic Classic
BY DAVID PETERSON

Dubuque's Forgotten Cemetery: Excavating a Nineteenth-Century Burial Ground in a Twenty-First Century City
BY ROBIN M. LILLIE AND JENNIFER E. MACK

Iowa Past to Present: The People and the Prairie, Revised Third Edition
BY DOROTHY SCHWIEDER, THOMAS MORAIN, AND LYNN NIELSEN

The Iowa State Fair
BY KURT ULLRICH

The Lost Region: Toward a Revival of Midwestern History
BY JON K. LAUCK

Main Street Public Library: Community Places and Reading Spaces in the Rural Heartland, 1876–1956
BY WAYNE A. WIEGAND

Necessary Courage: Iowa's Underground Railroad in the Struggle against Slavery
BY LOWELL SOIKE

On Behalf of the Family Farm: Iowa Farm Women's Activism since 1945
BY JENNY BARKER DEVINE

A Store Almost in Sight: The Economic Transformation of Missouri from the Louisiana Purchase to the Civil War
BY JEFF BREMER

Transcendental Meditation in America: How a New Age Movement Remade a Small Town in Iowa
BY JOSEPH WEBER

What Happens Next? Essays on Matters of Life and Death
BY DOUGLAS BAUER